About the author

Alix Kirsta is a freelance journalist, broadcaster and writer. Previously a professional dancer and actress, she moved into journalism, becoming Health Editor of *Woman's Journal* and *Options* magazine, developing a particular interest in psychology and stress. Though London-based she regularly visits America to conduct research for books and articles and is a firm believer in the interaction between physical well-being and the unconscious mind, and the effects of the environment upon both.

Alix Kirsta's previous books are *Skin Deep*, *The Book of Stress Survival*, and *The Good Slimming Guide*.

VICTIMS

Surviving the aftermath of violent crime

Alix Kirsta

CENTURY

LONDON   MELBOURNE   AUCKLAND   JOHANNESBURG

First published in 1988 by Century Hutchinson Ltd
Brookmount House, 62–65 Chandos Place,
London WC2N 4NW

Century Hutchinson Australia (Pty) Ltd
PO Box 496, 16–22 Church Street, Hawthorn,
Victoria 3122, Australia

Century Hutchinson New Zealand Ltd
PO Box 40–086, 32–34 View Road, Glenfield,
Auckland 10, New Zealand

Century Hutchinson South Africa (Pty) Ltd
PO Box 337, Bergvlei, 2012 South Africa

Photoset by Deltatype Ltd, Ellesmere Port
Printed and bound in Great Britain by
Anchor Brendon Ltd, Tiptree, Essex

British Library Cataloguing in Publication Data

Kirsta, Alix
    Victims: surviving the aftermath of violent crime.
    1. Victims of crime   2. Violent crimes
    I. Title
    362.8'8   HV 6190
    ISBN 0–7126–1852–X

The extracts on page 170 are reproduced by permission of Haworth Press
Inc., 75 Griswold St.,Binghampton, New York 13904 and are from
Invisible Wounds by Shelley Neiderbach.

Contents

Acknowledgements

I would like to express my sincere appreciation for the help and information given to me by those involved in working with crime victims in Britain, all of whom made me more aware of changing attitudes and new priorities regarding victim trauma. Warm thanks therefore to Captain Thelma Wagstaff, chair of the Metropolitan Police working party on rape, Inspector Sue Best of the Metropolitan Police Crime Prevention Unit, Lady Enid Ralphs, chair of the NAVSS working party on the victim and victims' support in court, Martin Wright, Information Officer of the NAVSS, Sandra Horley, director of Chiswick Family Rescue, Andy McDermott, training director at Ashford Borough Council, Dr Margaret Rich and Janet Cobhill of Victims Aid Scheme, Dr Gillian Mezey, Dr Roderick Orner, Professor Noel Walsh, Dr James Thompson, Surgeon Commander Morgan O'connell of H.M. Royal Navy, Jeremy Wetherall, Paul Slaughter and Sandy Hemingway. I am particularly grateful to Mike Maguire of the Oxford University Centre for Criminological Research whose generous help enabled me to gain access to important research material. In America I wish to thank in particular Professor Dean Kilpatrick, Dr Martin Symonds, Shelley Neiderbach, Jill Stultz, and Martha Burt, without whose pioneer work and kind assistance there would have been little material for this book. Last, but certainly not least, I am grateful to all those indomitable men and women who generously agreed to share with me their experiences of victimization. Their comments and testimonies will surely go a long way towards reassuring other victims that they are not alone in their predicament.

Introduction

In an ideal world there would be no need for a book such as this. As things stand, however, its advent is probably well overdue. As crime escalates so victims' needs become more pressing, but in Britain those needs remain to be fully recognized, let alone adequately met. It was sheer chance, an unexpected introduction to the work of those active within the vanguard of the American victims' rights movement, that led to the inspiration for this book, which is aimed as much at helping victims understand and overcome the effects of violence as at promoting greater understanding amongst non-victims of the complexities and the hidden subtext of victim trauma.

The majority of victims get a raw deal all round; first from the criminal, then from the rest of society which fails to address their needs and rights. What this amounts to in effect is a double injury. Someone who is attacked by a criminal is a victim of crime. However, when society then fails to respond to that person's needs or worse, perhaps blames them for provoking the incident, they then become a victim of society. It is this secondary victimization that constitutes the central theme of this book. The issue of secondary injury, whether perpetrated by state institutions such as the police, judiciary, social and health services or by individual members of the community, is absolutely crucial to our understanding of the distress suffered by so many victims, male and female, young and old. That is why this book is written both for victims and for 'co-victims' – the families, friends and colleagues of victims – whose lives are inevitably touched to some degree by the crisis and who play an integral role in helping or hindering the victim's recovery.

Crime is a subject much beset by myth and lore, and the following chapters should help to dispel the numerous misconceptions surrounding victimization, for instance that it is mainly women, and specifically rape survivors, who have a monopoly on trauma, that men take violence in their stride or that burglary represents a relatively minor crisis bringing with it inconvenience and material losses rather than emotional anguish. The supreme fallacy, bar none, is that those with physical injuries incur the greatest suffering and the most untenable theory of all is that victims are often the unwitting architects of their own misfortune, projecting what criminologists term a 'victim personality'. The flawed logic that supports this particular proposition will become evident to both victims and non-victims alike.

Lastly, an attitude I encountered frequently from outsiders while writing this book was the presumption that the subject must be depressing; long on woe and short on hope. Nothing could be further from the truth. Certainly victimization brings with it the potential for both a negative and a positive outcome. The object of this book is to clarify that potential.

PART ONE
Perspectives of Violence

I
Crime and Fear

It has been estimated that every seven seconds somewhere in Britain a crime is being committed. Violent crime, now a major obsession of our society, has become a burning issue as emotionally charged as nuclear arms and unemployment. Burgeoning crime rates and the escalation of violence within families regularly make front page headlines. Popular newspapers outbid one another to present ever more sensationally lurid coverage of muggings, murders and rapes. In Britain, as in other European countries and the United States, the fight against crime is now enshrined within the manifesto of every political party. As politicians and pundits argue about optimum forms of punishment and debate whether stiffer sentences do or do not deter criminals, statistics soar and the shock and fear of it all is on everyone's lips. But do we in fact live in a society more violent and crime-ridden than, say, sixty or a hundred years ago? History, as well as literature depicting everyday city life in Victorian England and indeed right up to the 1920s, suggests otherwise. We delude ourselves in thinking these are unusually violent and dangerous times. One need only read the works of Mayhew, Boswell, Johnson and Dickens to find very vivid, often horrific documentation of the widespread dangers faced by Londoners of earlier centuries going their way along pitch dark or ill-lit streets amid areas of the most abject and widespread poverty – then the overriding urban norm – where pickpockets, robbers and murderers presented a major and ever present hazard to life and property. Difficult as it is to believe, compared to earlier centuries these are times of unusual civic peace and harmony. Some historians see this, however, as a brief lacuna which will be followed by an increase in violent crimes spawned by new socio-economic problems such as racial tension, mass unemployment, the widespread use of drugs, and the decline of traditional family values.

Crime Soars – Or Does It?

So what are we to make of the dizzily spiralling crime figures? In spite of the statistics, trotted out with increasing and alarming regularity, it is not in fact possible to deduce the full extent of crime in the 1980s, nor to calculate whether more crimes are being committed now than, say, a decade ago, and if so how many more. Crime figures released by Scotland Yard in October 1987 indicated that there was a significant increase in crimes of violence in London in the first nine months of 1987, with physical assaults up 5 per cent to over 16,000, muggings reported up by 16 per cent to over 8,000, and sexual offences including rape totalling 2739. Home Office figures earlier in 1987 reflected a similar nationwide rise in crime of 7 per cent with sex attacks including rape up a staggering 24 per cent. But what do these figures actually tell us? They tell us the number of crimes reported to the police – no more and no less. If you are worried about the real risk you run daily of being burgled or assaulted these statistics actually provide very spurious evidence of the true dangers surrounding you. This is because, as the police are the first to admit, official crime figures represent not the number of crimes committed, but only the number of offences reported by the public and subsequently registered as crimes by the police. Not all reported crime ends up 'on the books'. Research on police forces in Salford and Oxford, for instance, shows that only half of all crimes reported are officially recorded. In cases of domestic violence the figure is as low as 2 per cent. Bearing in mind that it is estimated only about 50 per cent of crimes are ever reported in the first place one may get a picture of how inaccurately these figures reflect the true extent of crime.

The problem facing the police is that very often if there is insufficient evidence either to back up someone's report of an offence or provide a lead in tracking down the offender the incident will be classified as 'no crime'. Impressive as they appear, crime statistics are therefore riddled with imponderables. Until very recently there was a particularly sharp disparity between official police statistics for crimes involving sexual assault and information from other sources. The Islington Crime Survey, published in 1986, found that out of 1,200 cases of sexual assault within one year only 9 per cent were recorded by the police, while the London Rape Crisis Centre estimate that about 70 to 75 per cent of women who call for help have not reported the attack to the police. Even if a woman did report to the police, the standard procedure until very recently was to record the crime officially only if she agreed at the time to press charges and if necessary appear as a witness in court. Since the overwhelming majority of women refuse to do so, only a small minority of rapes were recorded. However, since 1986, all reported rapes and sexual assaults have been recorded in the hope that this will encourage more women to come forward to volunteer information which may help investigators identify the criminal. It is self-evident, therefore, that the recent steep 'rise' in rape is largely a reflection of more flexible attitudes and tolerance on the part of the police, which has led to more crimes being reported, and not necessarily an indication that more rapes are being committed.

Fear Wave

What we do know for sure is that fear of crime, undoubtedly in part generated or heightened by sensationalist media coverage, is becoming endemic. More than the purported 'crime wave', a rising fear wave seems now to be flooding public consciousness. This free floating fear represents as much if not more of a problem than crime itself. There are few people today who would claim to be impervious to this fear which permeates the very fabric of our everyday existence. Fear imposes grave restrictions on our freedom of movement. According to the Islington Crime Survey over 50 per cent of women avoid going out after dark because of fear of attack. Those who stay at home a lot are caught up in a double bind, haunted by obsessive anxieties about being burgled while they are out, fearful of being attacked by an intruder if they stay in. In a sense this is understandable since burglary is by far the most widely reported of all crimes and reported burglaries have risen steadily over the past years. Some police experts believe that official statistics reveal only the tip of the iceberg; that the true crime rate could be as much as five times higher than the reported rate. But these are mere speculations, and it is easy to see why each time such a statement is released by the press, a collective frisson ripples through the nation. While statistics therefore shed little light on the true scale of the crime problem they do illuminate our attitudes towards that problem.

Improving the relationship between victims and police is

fundamental to stepping up the fight against crime, since study after study both in Britain and in America has shown that the overwhelming reasons people give for not reporting crimes is the belief that the police would not treat the matter seriously or pursue investigations vigorously. In the case of sexual offences, people fear that the police would be unsympathetic, hostile, blame the victim for provoking the incident or not believe their story in the first place. In many cases of assault, sexual or otherwise, victims may fail to report the incident because of the erroneous assumption that the offence did not constitute a crime, especially if the attacker is someone they know.

Low Risk, High Fear

How justified are anxieties about public safety? The police now believe that in some cases fear may be rising out of all proportion to the actual risks of becoming a victim. For this they believe the media are largely to blame. There is little doubt that crime, like sex, sells newspapers. While journalists do not fabricate criminal acts they nevertheless, by focusing on the ghoulish *grand guignol* aspect of a handful of uncommon crimes, often generate unnecessary fear among certain more vulnerable sections of the community, mainly women and the elderly. For example, compared to the very high incidence of burglary and car theft the rate of sexual and violent assault in fact appears to be relatively low, even taking into account the disparity between reported and unreported crime. On the other hand there appears to be a vast murky area of hitherto unacknowledged acts of violence such as child abuse, domestic violence, racial assault, sexual harassment and obscene telephone calls which are only now beginning to filter through into public consciousness.

There are more burglaries nowadays than ever before, but these are not on the increase because modern burglars are more sophisticated in their thinking or professional in their break-in methods than in previous decades, but because people in general have more to steal nowadays and opportunities to rob abound. Sadly, many people fail to take sufficient precautions to protect their home and their possessions. Most burglaries are conducted by amateurs, sometimes children of school age, who often live within a mile of the home they burgle. They often break into the same places repeatedly because they know, through experience or a tip-off, that a particular household is an easy target; a persuasive case, surely, for adopting a more vigilant approach to home security. The police point out that although crime overall is higher in deprived inner-city areas where there are high levels of unemployment and racial tension, when it comes to burglary it is hard to find a low risk area in any major city, as the escalating cost of insurance premiums paid by those living in affluent, predominantly white middle-class neighbourhoods testifies.

Stereotypes

The classic image and favourite media stereotype of the victim of violent crime is a frail little old lady, yet in fact it is young men under twenty-five not young or elderly women who make up the largest percentage of victims of burglary and serious physical assault. Men are twice as likely as women to be violently assaulted in the street, at work, in pub brawls, or in disco fights. On the other hand more women now experience street robbery, for example pick-pocketing, handbag and purse snatching, especially in the streets and in shops. Presumably carrying shopping and easily accessible handbags makes women a more obvious target and impedes their ability to register the danger or react to the thief. Very few old people of either sex do get attacked, but when they do it invariably makes front page news. Accounts of vicious and senseless attacks on defenceless and highly vulnerable elderly men and women repulse and enrage us, rightly. Yet, inevitably, these reports add to the fear and dread already rife amongst the elderly, causing them anxiously to anticipate disasters that probably will never occur.

Over-reporting of such incidents not only feeds the public's fears but tends to distract attention from those in reality most at risk; young men and women and, as surveys increasingly show, black and coloured people. Although racial harassment does not as yet figure as a separate category in police statistics on crime, there is mounting evidence of increased racial violence and harassment in poorer multi-racial communities. Although harassment is regarded as a relatively minor offence which does not directly involve violence, victims are liable to come under fire repeatedly, in a war of attrition in which the offender's aim is to wear down the victim's resistance and confidence. In the long run, being on the receiving end of personally directed menacing remarks, graffiti, vandalism, offensive phone calls and letters which are an invasion of privacy, may prove more traumatic than suffering one short sharp physical blow from a mugger who grabs your money and disappears into the night. The true extent of racial assault, however, along with domestic violence and attacks on homosexual men, remains a blur since the great majority of victims fail to report these offences.

In cases of rape and indecent assault, young women between the ages of sixteen and twenty-four make up by far the largest proportion of victims and their attackers are very often men known to them, including work colleagues, neighbours, ex-husbands or boyfriends and other relatives or members of the community in which they live. In many cases of rape and sexual assault there may be a seemingly innocent lead-up to an attack which unfortunately is where some of the classic preconceptions about these incidents – that the victim did in fact encourage, provoke or comply with the attacker – spring from. This fairly and squarely dispels the myth of the average rapist as a crazed weirdo who stalks his prey behind bushes or down dark alleyways, leaping out to attack without warning. It also ties in with reports showing that well over half of all rapes and indecent assaults occur indoors, usually in somebody's home.

Clearly what this suggests is that the majority of rapes and assaults are not reported by women because they suspect the police will not take the matter seriously because their attacker is someone they know and they might be blamed for acting heedlessly, provocatively or even making up an accusation of rape as a form of blackmail against the man. Another very understandable reason for non-reporting where the attacker is known to the victim is fear of future reprisal. Such damning views of police bias are not founded solely on paranoia or hardline feminist doctrine – they have their base often in bitter first-hand experience, as numerous studies and surveys have shown. The police can be seen as a male dominated institution which is intrinsically sexist and racist both in its attitudes and behaviour.

However, one of the most significant developments that has resulted from more women coming forward to give statements to the police is that they themselves are gaining a vital new perspective on the true nature and extent of sexual offences. Additional insight into the diverse circumstances surrounding rape and the wide spectrum of victims and offenders involved is beginning to explode the old cultural belief about which type of woman is likely to be a rape victim and which type of man is likely to be her assailant. Yet large numbers of men and women continue to subscribe to the old adage that 'nice' girls don't get raped or worse, that no woman need suffer rape if she is determined enough to avoid it. According to rape mythology, women are prone to fantasize about violent sexual encounters and will therefore seek out the real thing or simply sometimes fabricate stories about being raped. Police, perhaps for the first time in the history of law enforcement, are now beginning to recognize that the majority of rape victims do not lie about being raped, and certainly do not enjoy the experience.

Further proof of police enlightenment is that rape victims are no longer summarily dismissed if they bear no visible signs of physical injury. That shame, fear and humiliation are as serious side-effects of rape as physical injury, indeed far more so, is something only now beginning to dawn on police investigators as they hear more and more women's experiences as well as the testimonies of counsellors and volunteers working with victims of sexual assault. That the victim's home, her family, social or working environment so often provides a back-drop to sexual offences constitutes another relatively new discovery. This understandi᠎g should do much to strengthen the resolve of very nervous and young victims to come forward and report an assault. After all, the courage and determination needed to report an assault are qualities that develop with age and experience and which consequently may be lacking in those at greatest risk: adolescent and pre-adolescent girls.

It is a horrifying fact that girls aged between ten and fifteen are most likely to become victims of indecent assault – a crime far more common than rape, but one which may often prove infinitely more traumatic and terrifying. In cases of sexual assault on males, while far less prevalent than those committed against females, nearly all victims are under twenty-five, while one out of five boys is under sixteen, a salutary reminder to any parent about the great importance of instilling the principles of personal safety into both boys and girls at an early age.

Violence in the Home

For most of us home and family life are synonymous with safety and well-being. If we cannot count on escaping the spectre of crime within our own four walls then where can we ever hope to feel secure and protected? The realization that for numerous women and children the home is a setting for fear and terror where husbands, fathers and other relatives may be the perpetrators of gross acts of violence is a notion so deeply disturbing that it is hard to comprehend. While the following chapters address the plight of all survivors of crimes ranging from rape to burglary it is almost certain that those people who have experienced domestic violence may find insufficient focus and emphasis on the particular problems associated with these highly complex situations. For one thing victims of domestic violence usually have had to face numerous such incidents often over very long periods. Domestic violence, when it comes to light as it does alas only in the minority of cases reported to the police, rarely if ever represents an isolated one-off incident. On the contrary the tragedy of all domestic crime, whether it involves incest, child abuse, wife- or, less commonly, husband-battering, is that in the main it reflects an ongoing climate of aggression, a domestic status quo based on dominance and exploitation. Wives are rarely battered or beaten just once by their husbands or partners. A father does not usually stop violating his daughter after the initial encounter. A parent who is impelled to direct his or her fury and aggression towards a small child is usually driven repeatedly to carry out acts of outrage which they are quite unable to control, even though they may be filled with bitter remorse perhaps moments later and periods of shame, guilt, recrimination and good conduct may intervene. When domestic violence is exacerbated, as is common, by problems such as alcoholism or addiction to hard drugs, the pattern of abuse is likely to be more predictable and self-perpetuating still.

Child abuse in particular is a crime shrouded from the outside world and often from other family members by an impenetrably complex web of secrecy and complicity. It is only now that such organizations as the NSPCC are beginning to gather evidence of the prevalence of child abuse in Great Britain. It is suggested that as many as one child in ten has been sexually abused at some stage in childhood. Evidence to sustain this claim is based on the growing reports not only by children themselves but also by adults who feel more confident about discussing these past incidents in the new open climate relating to incest and sexual assault. Although cases of child sexual abuse in Britain rose by a horrifying 150 per cent in 1986, as with rape what this figure doubtlessly reflects is that more incidents are now being reported, not that more assaults are in fact taking place. So it seems the cover has finally been blown on what has for decades, even centuries, been a routine covert activity, the ultimate taboo hidden away in the darkest recess of family life.

It is not hard to understand how or why child abuse has for so long been kept firmly under wraps. The child's fear and shame, often reinforced by open or veiled threats of punishment and other blackmail tactics meted out by the offender, usually a father, step-father, uncle or other male relative, are complicated further by that child's overwhelming need and desire for the continued protection and love of the very person abusing them. If the molester is a parent or there is collusion, whether implicit or explicit by the other parent, usually the mother, then the child is inevitably caught up in the cruellest and most irreconcilable of conflicts. The ability of children to adapt to hardship, including violence and molestation, is infinite, and therefore terrifying in its ramifications. Locked into a primary relationship founded on trust, dependent for his or her continued daily survival on the goodwill of the parent, the child who is abused by that parent will, especially if very young, put up with violence or molestation, and struggle with feelings of shame, fear and guilt rather than risk being punished or jeopardizing their own well-being. They have no other choice. Those children who are brave enough to overcome their terror and guilt at the prospect of betraying a parent – who they often continue to love – and report these offences to the police or to other agencies, seem until now to have been very much in the minority.

Battered Wives

Tacit consent, often a key feature in the overwhelming majority of cases of domestic violence, not only confuses outsiders including the police, health and welfare workers but also causes them to underestimate the grave seriousness and extent of such crimes. Overwhelming regard for other people's privacy and our respect for their right to do as they wish at home as long as it doesn't harm us makes it well nigh impossible for us to gain a true perspective on domestic offences. In addition, the prevailing instinct is always not to meddle in affairs that do not concern us. Yet if a stranger beats up a woman the incident will immediately be taken up as a serious offence by the police, but if a husband beats up his wife it may well be dismissed as a marital brawl. Worse, the exclusion of husbands from the ambit of rape law is just one of the iniquities of the judicial system. If such incidents have gone on for a long time unreported there will be even less likelihood of the police assessing the offence within the context of ordinary non-domestic crime, and they may shrug it off as the accepted mode of that particular relationship. Therefore the continuum of violence experienced by children and women can span many years.

Police policy in general until now has been to tread gently

when specific domestic offences are reported, doing very little if anything at all to caution, apprehend or arrest the offender. Domestic disputes, so the reasoning goes, are compounded of a multiplicity of variables, not least of which is the fact that a woman who initially agrees to press charges against her partner or spouse may eventually for any number of reasons change her mind and refuse to give evidence against him in court. Fear of future violence may indeed prevent many women from pressing charges against husbands who physically abuse them. One police estimate puts reports of domestic violence at over 28,000 a year in Britain. But other researchers estimate that the true figure of actual crimes may run at four times that level.

Women who are deeply distressed and frightened are usually advised by the police to seek an injunction in the civil courts to restrain a man from threatening or attacking his partner. Unfortunately, taking out an injunction is usually a time-consuming and complicated procedure and may ultimately afford little in the way of real protection. The fact that in 1984 only 300 cases out of many thousands reported were followed up by the London police testifies to their reluctance to get involved in what they regard as private issues. There are encouraging signs, however, that police are beginning to adopt a more hard-line approach towards arrest and prosecution of men who physically attack their wives or partners.

A recent Metropolitan Police report recommends that the police should adopt a more sensitive approach to victims and cooperate more closely with workers from other agencies, including welfare officers, health visitors, and victim support scheme volunteers. Also, provided there is sufficient evidence, all domestic incidents reported may then be recorded as crimes like any others. Even in cases where a non-chargeable offence has been committed police officers have been instructed that they may still make an arrest to protect the victim or others at risk. Officers can also take an attacker before a magistrate to be bound over to keep the peace. The improved training for new police recruits emphasizes the necessity of following up on assaults that are committed within the home and officers are urged to make sure that women are taken to hospital or to special refuge centres for their own safety and well-being. There are now around 200 women's aid centres throughout Britain where victims of domestic violence may obtain help and temporary accommodation.

The puzzling element of most domestic crimes is that so many women put up with violent behaviour from their partners often for years on end. It is this fortitude, bordering some might say on outright masochism, which is undoubtedly responsible for the hands-off attitude of many police officers and health workers to the problem. Any woman who continues living with a man who regularly beats her up or, having left him, later returns to face more violence, is in a sense responsible for perpetuating her own domestic hell, so the reasoning goes. But can it really be that simple?

For anyone with an abhorrence of violent relationships women's propensity to endure or re-enter a domestic set-up rendered nightmarish by physical abuse and emotional cruelty remains a mystery. Counsellors have propounded numerous theories to explain women's capacity to tolerate even the most consistently and viciously cruel of domestic partners. Are some women, as Erin Pizzey suggests, 'hooked' on violence, due perhaps to a biochemical imbalance? This seems a highly contentious and unlikely proposition and one as yet entirely scientifically unsubstantiated. Or do some with a childhood history of abuse and violence unconsciously seek out violent relationships through a compulsion to repeat those early patterns of dominance and submission? Psychiatrist Dr Gillian Mezey has observed that women who have experienced violence as children repeat the pattern by being attracted to violent men. Abuse, usually from a father or father figure, forms the model for all future relationships. Such women, for whom violence was inextricably linked to love and dependency in their early years may become trapped in a state known as 'learned helplessness' in which violent relationships are familiar and reassuring.

Taken to its most extreme, this sort of conditioning may lead some women to stick by and protect men who they know are guilty of crimes as horrifying as rape, child murder, and terrorism. Taken hostage, they can even fall in love with their captor, sometimes espousing his terrorist philosophy and activities. The case of the kidnapped heiress Patti Hearst, say psychiatrists, offers a classic example of such extreme transference of the victim's affections onto her persecutor. Those counsellors offering aid to battered wives stress, however, that women's acquiescence to violence cannot be reduced to a neat psychological equation. Even women who enjoyed a happy childhood may become trapped in a violent domestic relationship later in life. A multiplicity of factors can influence the decision to stay or continue suffering. Some women may stay within a relationship because of factors such as lack of money, unwillingness to leave their children or to disrupt their home environment, fear and a sense of insecurity at being alone and homeless, shame at what the rest of the family and the neighbours might say if they leave, or terror of even more violent retribution from their partner.

Hard-line feminists contend that all male-female relationships are potentially violent, representing a power game based on men's dominance and women's subordination. So the argument goes, women are likely to continue being conditioned by tradition to be subservient in order to survive in what is still an essentially patriarchal society that exploits and discriminates against women. Yet this surely denies the element of free will and personal choice increasingly available to the majority of women. Such reasoning is also based on the somewhat untenable proposition that women find it easier to react than to act or initiate and that they lack sufficient resources of drive and determination to take responsibility for their own well-being. What they *do* lack, however, is sufficient help and back-up from law enforcement agencies to make their escape from domestic violence less fraught with hardship and hopelessness. The majority of women do not become willing victims either consciously or by default, as is testified by the growing numbers of women caught up in violent relationships who are now reporting to the police and victim support schemes and seeking help from women's aid centres.

Colour Blind

All violence sickens but none more so than that motivated by hatred of another person's race or colour. The issue of so-called racial 'terrorism' in Britain is finally beginning to imprint itself upon public consciousness. And not before time. If there is one thing more odious than the spectre of racial violence itself it is the still widespread public indifference – verging on tacit acceptance – to these crimes. While other offences are calculated to incite public outrage those that are racially motivated impinge rather less on our collective consciousness. This is despite the fact that with the expansion of Britain into a multi-racial society, racial violence is permeating many urban environments and is no longer confined to certain isolated trouble spots.

There is of course nothing new about the phenomenon of racial attacks, only their scale and number. Yet until very recently the problem was deemed to merit little more than a passing nod from police and local authorities whose principal excuse for not addressing the issue was that this is a politically sensitive area requiring specialist skills. While few would argue this point, it cannot surely be used to justify an attitude of non-involvement, still less one of apathy. Thankfully however, due to new, tougher police policies on dealing with racial offences, the direct result of recent government reports highlighting the growing problem of racial violence, a previously forgotten category of victims is fast becoming public knowledge. That knowledge is profoundly disturbing. For example a study carried out in Newham in 1986 found that one in four local black residents had been victims of some form of harassment in the previous year. Two out of three had been victims more than once and 116 victims reported 1550 incidents ranging from insulting behaviour to assault on property or person. The Islington Crime Survey in 1985 estimated that 7 per cent of all assaults aimed at residents were racist in nature and on average black people, especially young men, are twice as likely to be assaulted as whites, with black women aged 25–44 more at risk than white women. The picture is consistent with surveys conducted in other urban and suburban areas of Britain. The 1986 Runnymede Trust Report Racial Violence and Harassment concludes that few areas in Britain can now be regarded as completely safe for black residents.

Getting the Message

As with sexual and domestic violence the main problem remains one of under-reporting. Language barriers – a large percentage of victims are Bengali-speaking Asians – poor community-police relations, fear of reprisals, the mistaken belief that certain incidents such as obscene calls and letters do not constitute a criminal offence are contributory factors in the under-reporting of racial attacks. Much depends on victims' attitudes towards the police. It has been suggested that Asian women and older people tend to cooperate least with the police, an attitude shared with young males in the black community. It should not be overlooked either that many cases of harassment reported by members of the ethnic minorities cover alledged racially targeted execution of the stop and search laws.

To exacerbate matters further those attacks that are reported have tended to be dismissed by police as domestic neighbourhood disputes. In the absence of any laws relating specifically to racial harassment police will often either treat such incidents as just another case of criminal damage or try to persuade victims to take up a private prosecution. In spite of the fact that housing estates provide the backdrop for a large percentage of racially motivated crimes local housing departments have also been extremely slow to recognise the seriousness of these offences and take direct action to ensure tenants' welfare. Estate managers, often the first to be told about an incident can be unsympathetic, inspiring little confidence in victims that their complaints will be treated as a priority. Clearly, alienation is central to the issue of racially motivated crime.

There are other factors which distinguish racial violence from other crimes, especially from the victim's standpoint. Manifested in numerous ways from abusive behaviour (name calling, object throwing, spitting, gesticulating) obscene or threatening graffiti, letters and phone calls, damage to property, physical assault, even attempted murder, whatever its form the racist message is as unambiguous as it is obscene – unlike other crimes there is no absence of motive, no element of chance or accident. Repeated victimisation is a key feature, causing what might otherwise be regarded as an innocuous if distressing incident to generate severe trauma amongst victims. Many, as for example those in the Asian community, are essentially pacifist by nature, thus disinclined to retaliate whilst justifiably fearful of reprisals if they go to the police. What complicates the picture even further is that the crimes usually fit into a framework of deeper, complex socio-economic and political problems in which racial discrimination, high unemployment, poor housing conditions, poverty and drug abuse are crucial elements.

Given the controversy, ignorance and volatile emotions that bedevil all race issues there can obviously be no easy solution to racial violence. The problem can only be alleviated through the concerted cooperation of police, housing and other local authorities as well as community groups such as the VSS. Although many myopic local authorities still refuse to admit that racial harassment is an issue in their area others are starting to implement explicit policies to deal with the problem. In some areas the police, recently invested with wider powers to take action against all types of racial harassment, have already begun to place a higher priority on dealing with offences while liaising more closely with VSS volunteers to ensure victims receive adequate support. Individual landlords and estates have started to initiate security schemes such as anti-vandalism patrols, TV security and alarm systems and the employment of more staff to monitor disturbances. Such initiatives are the direct result of close consultation between local authorities, housing associations and residents to identify the problems of vandalism and harassment.

Certain housing departments are now taking prompt, tougher action against the perpetrators of racial crime, including eviction proceedings, and offers of suitable alternative accommodation for victims. There is new emphasis on special training for local and housing authority employees in the skills needed to establish closer rapport with community members generally and victims of crime in particular. Meanwhile, officially at least, the message from the police is clear – victims should come forward and report incidents of racial harassment. This in itself is encouraging, but only if victims who trust and cooperate with the police can be assured adequate support and the protection necessary to safeguard their right to live safely within a multi racial community.

No Boundaries

Racist elements apart, the average criminal, be he murderer, mugger, rapist or thief, is no respecter of rank, class or creed. Although crime cuts across socio-economic barriers there do remain certain individuals who may be more prone to violent assault through a combination of predisposing circumstances. For example, certain professions, by their very nature, attract a far higher incidence of crime than others.

It is obvious that policemen and policewomen, for example, are persistently exposed to a very much greater risk of violence than, say, office workers. Recent reports of the murders of a number of social workers who had been in contact with violent clients have emphasized the grave and growing problem of violence faced by all members of the caring professions from nurses and ambulancemen to welfare officers and victim support volunteers, the majority of whom are women. Crimes against public transport personnel – in particular bus conductors and railway guards – whose work brings them into contact with a wide cross-section of the general public also appears to be on the increase. The much publicized disappearance of estate agent Suzy Lamplugh, whose mother subsequently set up the Suzy Lamplugh Trust to promote greater awareness of hazards in working environments, highlights the dangers faced by women whose job involves going out alone and meeting strangers outside their place of work. Even the hours of work, in particular night-time employment and shift-work, the need to use public transport late at night or walk through deserted streets or high crime areas after dark significantly increases the risk of violent attack.

Environment and lifestyle may also greatly determine the way we react to violence. It would be surprising if those with a background of domestic violence did not perceive other forms of crime in a significantly different way to those whose relationships with their partners and families are based on mutual trust and an overwhelming sense of moral probity. What so often distinguishes the attitude of someone with no experience of crime is an intrinsic belief in other people's kindness and consideration and, as a direct corollary, confidence in their own safety. For those whom violence strikes out of the blue the immediate impact tends therefore to be one of utter disbelief and a shattering sense of betrayal by society coupled with the terrifying realization of their own vulnerability. But where violence is, or has been in the past, a familiar menace, previous experience will inevitably take the edge off the surprise and outrage which would otherwise accompany the shock of an unexpected attack. Those men, women and children to whom violence is familiar have, sadly, had more opportunity to inure themselves to the psychic pain.

While the sense of degradation and shock of being indecently assaulted or mugged are no less traumatic, those with first hand experience of criminal offences do often develop an infinite and rather appalling capacity to accept the existence of the dangers that surround them and accommodate the trauma of victimization at the cost of often truly dreadful consequences for their emotional well-being and lifestyle. To the person whose value system is tidily laid out with clear distinctions between right and wrong, good and bad, tolerable and intolerable, peace and violence, the prospect of successfully resolving the aftermath of crime with little permanent cost to their mental well-being is often better than for the person for whom the risk of victimization is an inevitable feature of daily life. However, the effects of victimization on both the newly initiated victim and those who have experienced perhaps repeated violent incidents are equally damaging and all-pervasive. The potential effects on mental and physical health and on behaviour are just as pernicious. Thankfully, in the majority of cases, given due care and understanding, none of these effects need be irreversible.

2
Invisible Wounds

For the majority of individuals becoming a crime victim represents a crisis of confidence – both in themselves and in the world around them. Recognition of this 'crisis theory' is crucial to our understanding of the whole phenomenon of victim trauma syndrome. The reaction is both inevitable and understandable and, in more severe cases, one that has been compared to living through natural catastrophes such as earthquakes, floods and fires, or surviving major accidents or active combat. Much of the current research into victim trauma syndrome was originally initiated by parallel studies into the aftereffects suffered by Vietnam war veterans. The traumas of crime, natural disaster and war, it seems, are all in many ways remarkably similar. For many people the crisis of violent crime is every bit as unpredictable and arbitrary as the crisis of natural disaster, except that in most cases it is not a group experience and the victim perceives him or herself as the lone target of a fellow human being's entirely base malevolence. The acceptance we accord to so called acts of God is not something we easily extend to violent acts of crime. Why me? Why should this happen to me, to me of all people? is the inevitable and predictable response of virtually every victim of all types of crime. The need that drives every victim to search for an explanation for something which is ultimately inexplicable forms the seedbed from which all symptoms of victim trauma grow.

On the Line

As babies and young children, we depend on a sense of continuity and order within our environment which allows us to feel secure in the knowledge that the world, in the shape of those nearest to us, will cater for our needs. As we grow up, our confidence and trust in the environment extends from our immediate surroundings to embrace the outside world as we are increasingly involved in the society in which we live. The happier and more well-adjusted our formative years, the greater seems the harmony between ourselves and the outside world. This secure background, based on a predictable rhythm of cause and effect, encourages us to develop confidence in ourselves as independent responsible individuals, able to initiate actions and take decisions. We perceive ourselves as invulnerable and in control of our lives. So, when crime strikes, the incident may amount to a psychic catastrophe, effectively demolishing in the victim two essential beliefs: their sense of control over their lives and their trust in society as benevolent, predictable and protective. Being on the receiving end of crime causes most victims to challenge certain basic assumptions both about the world and themselves. Deeply held beliefs once regarded as universal truths now seem like so much sham. Victims' personal safety as well as their self-worth is now on the line. 'How could the world do this to me?' and 'What did I do to deserve this?' are typical comments illustrating that sense of desolation. The more benevolent our impression of the world, or of the specific environment in which the disaster took place, the more overwhelming the sense of betrayal.

People who are attacked in an environment they have always assumed to be safe, for example their own home, inevitably suffer a far greater shock. The same goes for those who are attacked either by someone they know and thought they could trust or someone they didn't know but about whom they had no prior suspicions. The worse the crime the more likely it is to undermine the survivor's belief in his or her own autonomy. In the wake of a crisis, ego and self-confidence take the biggest knocking. Previously unquestioned feelings of invulnerability give way to states of helplessness, fear and immense self-doubt. As a result not only does the victim's external world appear to fall apart but their inner equilibrium, having received a rude battering, may be thrown dramatically off centre. 'My world fell apart', 'I don't know if I am coming or going', 'nothing makes sense any longer', 'I feel totally screwed up as if I am going to go mad', are typical reactions of the victim who is in shock.

A Safe Distance

Not surprisingly, feelings of vulnerability and helplessness and of being disconnected from the rest of the world are generally at the root of all forms of victim trauma. The biggest mistake any of us can make – victim and non-victim alike – is to believe we should be strong or clued up enough to anticipate and so avoid the impact of that crime on the psyche. After all, would you expect to be able to control your reaction in a shipwreck or earthquake? Obviously not, so why make any exception in the case of such a life-shattering piece of evil as an assault by another human being?

Of course we all know about the evils which exist in the world. Safe in our familiar and predictable surroundings we read the harrowing reports daily in the newspapers and are force-fed the grim facts nightly on television. But these are things, we reassure ourselves, perhaps even complacently, that happen to other people; they will surely never happen to us. Intellectually we attempt to identify with the nightmare world inhabited by others, intent on empathy no matter how far removed from the situation. Yet the received knowledge cannot possibly prepare us since it rarely if ever matches up to subject's experience. BBC newscaster Jan Leeming, interviewed hours after being attacked by intruders at BBC TV Centre, sobbed, 'I can't understand how we can live in such a cruel world.' The next day a columnist in one of the tabloid newspapers derided her for her naivety, suggesting this must be a redundant quality in one who reports regularly on world atrocities. Yet this is surely to overlook the point that knowing a thing intellectually cannot prepare you for experiencing it emotionally at first hand. Ask anyone who has experienced bereavement or divorce – the trauma, the crisis of self are not at all dissimilar.

Losing Control

Each and every crime by one human being against another amounts to a conscious act of violation, whether it is against person or property. The deep vein of malignity which, by implication, runs through all acts of violence may therefore cause, say, the victim of a burglary to experience deep psychological distress less severe but no less real and valid than the survivor of a rape or an attempted murder. Whether the offence was premeditated or random and spontaneous, successfully completed or merely an abortive attempt, the intent of the criminal is to harm his victim in one way or another. The vernacular of violence says it all. 'Do her in', 'rip him off', 'get him', 'show her a lesson', 'finish him off', and 'let her have it', obscenely sum up the criminal's intended aims. To be victimized is, de facto, to surrender control and to become helpless. It is the criminal who is 'in charge' and assumes a position of power, and the victim who must surrender.

An attack by one person upon another is based on one common denominator: violence. The violence may be real and explicit, as when the victim is physically assaulted, or couched within a direct threat: 'if you don't hand over the money I'll shoot'. Furthermore the implied threat of violence may prove just as deeply shocking as the direct experience of it. This is fundamental to the understanding of the causes and effects of victim trauma syndrome. To suffer victim trauma you do not have to sustain physical wounds or be subjected to direct physical assault. The depth and severity of a man's or woman's emotional reaction to victimization is by no means always related to their physical injuries or even to the seriousness of the crime, rather it may be dependent on how serious the perceived threat to their life was. During the course of any violent attack, whether for fleeting seconds or a protracted period, nearly all victims expect that they might die or become seriously injured.

The Threat of the Unknown

Professor Dean Kilpatrick who has conducted extensive and detailed studies into the effects of all violent crimes concludes that you don't even necessarily have to be caught up in a dangerous situation to suffer traumatic aftereffects. Our subjective appraisal of what is dangerous and of the possible harm which could befall us may generate a sense of fear as great as if we were actually being confronted by very concrete dangers. It is not necessary for the criminal to carry a weapon or inflict injuries for the victim to perceive that they are in a potentially dangerous, life-threatening situation.

Even those physical injuries sustained by rape victims tend to be relatively minor and often do not require hospitalization or medical care. Significantly, in one of Professor Kilpatrick's most recent studies, a quarter of all burglary victims at home when the break-in occurred reported that they thought they might have been killed or seriously injured.

At 4 a.m. theatre director Terence Keeley woke up to hear intruders breaking into the ground floor of his house. When he tried to call the police he discovered they had disconnected the downstairs telephone.

My bedroom door was locked and I was trapped, waiting to hear what they would do next. They came upstairs and began rattling the door, shouting for me to come out. 'We're here to get you,' they yelled. I contemplated going on to the balcony and perhaps escaping that way, but reckoned they might catch up with me. It was a nightmare. I really thought this might be the end for me. The only thing I could do was pray. I waited until 8 a.m. and then I opened the door to find my kitchen knives lying on the stairs. They were obviously ready to attack. I didn't get another night's sleep until I sold that house half a year later. I became a prisoner in the house. I never went out in case the place might be burgled but staying at home made me feel terribly uneasy. I became irritable and depressed. I couldn't speak to anybody about it and my doctor warned me I might be on the verge of a nervous breakdown. It's the worst experience I've ever suffered.

After rape and aggravated assault – where the risk of physical harm is greatest – burglary follows close behind as the crime most likely to produce both acute and chronic post-traumatic stress disorders. Although the consequences of completed rape are acknowledged as potentially the most serious, negative and long lasting in the annals of victim trauma, one of Professor Kilpatrick's studies indicates that those women who have experienced attempted molestation and attempted robbery suffered more symptoms of distress than those who experienced completed molestation or robbery. The finding seems paradoxical – but is it?

One of the conclusions drawn by Professor Kilpatrick is that when a criminal tries to attack someone but fails to carry it off as planned, there remains tremendous room for ambiguity in the victim's mind as to what the assailant intended to do and the extent of the danger they were in. Not knowing what you escaped from provides ample room for speculation especially for anyone with an already fertile imagination and a susceptibility to nervous strain and stress. Not only is there a residual fear of what catastrophe might have occurred but also an anticipatory anxiety about what might yet occur.

What Terence Keeley feared most in the months following the break-in was that the same men would return to get hold of what they had left behind.

They were well aware there were other valuables in the house, probably in my bedroom. I was sure they'd be back to do a more complete job.

Harassment can persist for some time after an attack or a break-in, in the guise of verbal threats, vandalism, threatening letters or obscene, menacing or silent phone calls. Unpleasant enough for anyone who has not experienced a violent crime, for the survivor of an assault or burglary such calls, while very often quite unconnected with the previous crime, by preying on the imagination can instil a great sense of fear and unease in the recipient, precisely because the perpetrator is usually unseen and anonymous.

Moira, an advertising executive, had been mugged at knife-point in New York City by a man police suspected had a record of rape and attempted murder.

> A few days after the incident I began getting a number of terrifying messages on my machine saying next time he'd come and really get me and this was how he'd do it. Then there was the sound of machine gun fire. I immediately changed my telephone number but that didn't do much to alleviate my anxiety because I knew that the man who had attacked me in the street knew my identity because my ID papers had been in my handbag.

According to a British crime survey published in 1983 there appears to be no discernible link between receiving obscene calls and becoming a victim of crime. Nevertheless such fears are totally understandable.

Witnesses to the Crime

Distance does not necessarily lessen the impact of a violent episode: simply witnessing a crime where others are threatened with violence or are injured or killed may prove deeply traumatic. For example, carrying out rescue work after an accident or natural disaster may be distressing enough to induce anxiety, hallucin-ations, depression, sadness and sleeplessness for a very long period afterwards. Those who survived a crisis in which others died, for example a serious accident, a terrorist attack, even a war, may continue to be racked by guilt at the fact that they survived. There may be continuous recriminations about their own behaviour during the crisis prompted by the belief that if they had only acted differently others might have been spared. The most recent and tragic example of post-survival guilt is only now coming to light after the capsizing of the ferry the *Herald of Free Enterprise* off Zeebrugge: many survivors, passengers and crew, were forced to watch colleagues, friends and relatives perish, or later to identify their bodies and give evidence at the inquiry and inquest. Many are now suffering serious long-term mental problems significantly different from those normally associated with bereavement. Even when we ourselves are not directly involved, such catastrophic events offer a clear demonstration of our potential vulnerability and compromise our belief in the 'goodness' of society. Bystanders often avoid getting involved when they observe someone else being threatened or attacked. The idea that they themselves might become victimized can act as a powerful brake on the instinct to help out.

Losses

Whatever the nature of the crime and the circumstances surrounding it it is impossible to predict the nature or the duration of the ensuing aftermath. However, personal loss is an experience that is common to virtually all victims of violent crime, whether it is financial loss, loss of health, loss of one's home or job, or destruction of one's trust in others and one's belief and confidence in oneself.

Losing one's material possessions is something most of us can come to terms with. But this depends very much on the emotional value we may have invested in those possessions. It is therefore not difficult to comprehend the trauma of burglary or street theft, especially where the loss involves objects of so called sentimental value, tokens long cherished because of their association with people we loved or significant events in our life. For Juliet Holzmann, being burgled almost a year after her mother's death brought back the grief of that recent bereavement.

> I felt as if a very recent wound was ripped wide open again. The pain was unbelievable. They took the wedding ring my mother had on when she died and other pieces of jewellery she wore constantly which I then often wore after her death to comfort me and ease the pain. They had rifled through her handbag which I had stored away and rummaged through love letters between her and my father. I felt a mixture of indescribable fury at the thought of their filthy hands on these precious things and a sense of utter despair and sadness at being reminded of her death.

Violation of property can for many victims amount to a defilement of self – a self they respect and hold as private and inviolable. So when a pickpocket steals a handbag or a burglar breaks into the house the experience may be tantamount to a bodily assault. Burglary is interpreted by many victims as an act of penetration and trespassing into a private part of themselves, and they frequently report feeling soiled or defiled for weeks or even months after the event. The net cost to victims who have either been burgled or physically attacked is often impossible to calculate until long after the crime.

Financial expenses incurred through moving home or installing an elaborate security system may prove hefty but at least usually ensure a return in terms of a renewed sense of personal safety. Says Terence Keeley:

> The inability to relax cost me both money and sleep. I'd figure out hypothetical future attacks and plan possible escape routes to fit every eventuality. The only way I felt safe enough to get a proper night's sleep was to hire a minder which cost me over £100 a week plus extra food and booze. In the end I sold my house at a loss and moved into an expensive flat with 24-hour porterage. Although I am much poorer I can at least sleep again. I feel totally safe and have regained my health.

Other less lucky burglary victims, usually the poor, the housebound or the elderly, tend to adopt a siege mentality, and become fearful of opening their doors to strangers, living with windows boarded, doors bolted and barred against what they've come to regard as the near certainty of another attack.

Victims of mugging, if severely injured, may find their entire livelihood in jeopardy. Fred Shortcross, who was brutally beaten up outside his home with a lead pipe and had to undergo four operations including a bone marrow transplant followed by rehabilitation therapy before he could walk again, is just such a victim.

> I lost my health, my job, my apartment, I lost all my savings to pay for medical treatment. For months I was totally crippled and had to lie in bed because my legs had been fitted with a special bone healing device. Far more sinister and hard to cope with, I lost my self-respect and confidence and spent many weeks during the recuperation period just sitting in the dark, not wanting to go out or speak to anyone even when I was able to walk again. I felt I was no longer a member of the human race.

What criteria can we as non victims, possibly apply in judging the gravity of a crisis and its potential for causing emotional devastation? The greatest injustice still meted out to crime victims by society, in particular by certain members of the police and legal profession, is the assumption that because they did not suffer undue or indeed any physical injury, or got away before a crime such as rape could be completed, someone who was attacked escaped the worst of the crime and does not strictly speaking qualify as a card carrying 'victim'. The ramifications of this bias and the lack of understanding of the real nature of victim trauma, coupled with society's unrealistic expectations of how fast victims should recover are such that they amount to a form of secondary victimization which helps both to initiate and perpetuate many of the classic features of victim trauma syndrome. One of the most disturbing of these features is the striking analogy between victim trauma syndrome and bereavement and the whole concomitant process of grieving.

According to psychologist Shelley Neiderbach, victims whose lives have been either directly or indirectly threatened or who merely perceived their lives to be in danger, psychologically experience this threat as if it were their actual death. Therefore they need not only to grieve over this symbolic death but to overcome it in order to begin a psychologically new life. Young people especially, hitherto secure in the untested belief that they could live forever are now forced to come to terms with their own mortality. This can come as a crushing blow to victims, especially if death – and any issues related to it such as terminal illness – has always been a taboo subject which they have never confronted. Ex-policewoman Pam White, who suffered severe psychological trauma as a result of being present during the Harrods' bombing, now finds the topic of death an omnipresent obsession.

> I developed a terrible phobia about going near dead bodies and had to keep it secret because I knew if I didn't I would lose my job with the police force. I have never had a close death in my family and now I am terribly worried about how I'll deal with it when my parents or someone else in the family dies. I have a constant fear that I'll die young. Well, it is only natural: after all I came face to face with death that day.

Rape: An Act of Sex or Violence?

It is perhaps no coincidence that studies initiated in America in the early 1970s by various feminist organizations into the effects of sexual assault on women first identified the phenomenon known as rape trauma syndrome. The discovery that victims of all violent crimes may experience similar symptoms has led psychologists to coin a more comprehensive term, victim trauma syndrome, which encompasses the phenomenon known as post-traumatic stress disorder (PTSD). This is the umbrella term used by the American Psychiatric Association to define a broad spectrum of physical, psychological and behavioural symptoms suffered by war veterans, hostages, survivors of torture and imprisonment, and crime victims. PTSD has emerged as the common bond of psychic experience that links survivors of each and every disaster regardless of its cause. Rape itself is now being seen in a different light. Only now are psychologists – men in particular – beginning to acknowledge what women, especially victims of rape, have always known: rape is essentially a crime of violence and domination which includes a sexual element. Rapists derive their greatest satisfaction from terrorizing their victims into submission with actual or threatened violence, whether sexual intercourse does or does not take place, as psychologists and probation officers who have studied the behaviour of such criminals have repeatedly testified. This also helps to explain why horrifyingly perverse acts of degradation and violence often feature as much as straightforward sexual acts in so many cases of assault on women. When such offences are committed against old women and very young children the notion that all rapists are compelled to assuage uncontrollable sexual urges and release pent up lust becomes a particularly untenable proposition.

The victim's terror of what she perceives to be a direct or implied threat to her life is very often paramount during such an attack. It may transcend even the fear and revulsion she experiences at being forced to have intercourse against her will. This explains why sexual assault and attempted rape may often prove as deeply traumatic as rape itself, or indecent assault which may consist of any number of degrading sexual acts.

The technical difference between rape and other forms of sexual assault is as follows: rape is defined as either partial or complete penetration of the vagina by the penis, whether ejaculation does or does not occur. Penetration of the labia (outer lips) also qualifies as rape. Other acts including sodomy, oral sex, insertion of objects such as a knife, bottle, hand, torch, or pen into the vagina or anus also come under the heading of sexual assault, as does touching of the breasts, bottom or genital area without a woman's consent. It is one of the more inexplicable anomalies of criminal law that rape constitutes a more grievous offence than indecent assault which may get no further than the magistrates' court.

Since sexual offences both symbolically and literally represent the ultimate outrage of violation it is small wonder that for so many women fear of crime is, ipso facto, fear of rape. Apart from inflicting agonizing and potentially long-lasting psychological damage, no other crime has the capacity so to undermine a woman's sexual confidence and diminish her sexual enjoyment, to disrupt the relationships between her and her partner or to destroy her trust in men, especially for very young and inexperienced girls. The popular shibboleths surrounding rape, and the perceived 'stigma' of sexual attack may prevent the victim from talking about her experience openly for fear of inviting moral censure and opprobrium.

When a boy or man is raped, fear that he will be suspected of being a homosexual, or that he will encounter anti-gay bias if he is a homosexual, may cause him to keep the incident a permanent secret. If the attacker was someone known to the victim, as is common in many cases of sexual assault, doubts that anyone will believe the incident really happened or shame or guilt at the thought that they might be suspected of provoking it in the first place may force the victim to stay silent and suffer an even greater sense of isolation. Incredibly, many rape victims do not even tell their spouses or partners for fear of how they will react to the news and how it might affect their future relationship. Parents and other relatives are frequently kept in the dark because victims are afraid news of the rape will either distress or embarrass them.

Age Concern

The emotional scars inflicted as a result of sexual assault can differ greatly according to the woman's age and circumstances. Girls and young women, often by virtue of their sexual inexperience and lack of sophistication, may envisage the experience as a blight which has destroyed their future chances of enjoying a successful sexual relationship. If the girl was a virgin and placed great value on remaining so until she married or fell in love then the horror of being assaulted will come as an especially shattering blow that spells a permanent end to all her wishes and ideals. Many women develop a complete mistrust of men and a phobic avoidance of all sexual activity which forces them to remain celibate for very long periods after assault or can prompt them to explore lesbian relationships. Lesbian rape victims often find it particularly hard to openly discuss their feelings about men and sex after the event, especially if they do not wish to disclose their homosexuality to their friends or family. In some cases disillusionment and bitterness may lead very young women to pursue a promiscuous lifestyle as a means of obliterating the negative experience of rape. In cases where the woman's strongest feelings after being raped are contempt for all men and a desire for revenge, she may come to regard sex as a purely mechanical and exploitative act and even turn to prostitution as a result.

Older women, especially those who are divorced or separated, may find that other people's moral judgement of their past sexual history diminishes their credibility as an 'innocent' rape victim, resulting in persistent feelings of shame and guilt. Women in their fifties or older, caught up in the mid-life crisis, often find that the stigma of rape serves only to intensify existing concerns about their sexual inadequacy. Feelings of devaluation are often most persistent among older rape victims, yet these can prove hardest of all to resolve because they may find it impossible to admit readily their sense of worthlessness.

Physical injuries, whatever their cause and nature, nearly always eventually heal. But invisible wounds may not even become evident until some time has elapsed. Fear, anger, shame, guilt, phobias, a sense of hopelessness and powerlessness are the psychological scars that may persist for months, even years after the event. Thankfully, in the majority of cases, given proper care and understanding, the psychological scarring need not be permanent or irreversible, no matter how long the victim's health has been affected or however extensive the upheaval brought upon their personal relationships and lifestyle. Nor is victim trauma syndrome so complex or confusing as to elude definition. In fact, when you begin to analyse them, certain symptoms appear to take on very consistent patterns and follow logical if sometimes different lines of progression whose origins may be traced back to the very earliest moments of the attack.

3

Fight, Flight or Freeze

He kept hitting me mercilessly. I saw blood gushing, bone jutting from my leg. I could only think, 'I'm being murdered – and no one is coming to help.'

Fred Shortcross

My husband just went berserk. As he jumped on top of me and began punching I thought, 'He's going to kill me.'

A victim of domestic violence

'This is it Shelley, your number's up, you're going to die,' I said to myself. I just prayed I could get out of the car and fall into the road so my body would be found.

Shelley Neiderbach, assaulted in her car

Terror, usually linked to a perceived death threat, is the common denominator of all violent crimes. But how does that terror translate into bodily sensation? Fear, of course, is the ultimate stress response. In situations of extreme danger, body and mind switch automatically to red alert, a state of emergency powered by that primitive evolutionary mechanism the fight or flight response, common to animals and man alike. Such a response cuts across millennia, civilization, race and intellect. The complex chain of biochemical responses that galvanized our primitive ancestors into action empowering them to fight or flee when their lives were endangered by wild animals or marauding tribes is no different to that which produces a panic we experience today should we encounter a mugger or rapist on the streets of twentieth-century New York or London. The mugger may be a relatively new villain come to haunt our dreams, but the fear he elicits is the most fundamentally primordial of all our gut reactions.

In trying to fathom the conundrum of victim trauma which materializes hours, days, or weeks after an attack and takes on a multiplicity of different forms, it is first necessary to examine the immediate impact of the event on the victim and try to place individual responses in their proper perspective – the perspective of fear. It is those responses which will determine our attitudes as non-victims towards the plight of the victim and shape our perceptions of their role in the crime. Certain responses may variously elicit approval, disapproval, or even incomprehension on the part of police, lawyers, the victim's family and acquaintances.

The victim's own assessment of his or her behaviour during the attack is also crucial in determining the degree and nature of subsequent trauma. Although it may not become evident until long after the event, the pattern of victim trauma, no matter how delayed or persistent, is often set from the very first moment of impact, determined by the manner in which a man or woman instinctively acts or reacts when exposed to a sudden unexpected crime. Most outsiders who have never been victimized have little knowledge or appreciation of how fear distorts judgement and paralyses action. Without the necessary frame of reference the victim's behaviour may therefore be interpreted as slow, stupid, compliant, childish, submissive or dangerous. What everyone tends to forget, even the victim, is that victims can rarely be held fully accountable for their actions since these are out of their voluntary control. In extremis, there is little choice but to follow the dictates of primitive instinct. The more stressful a situation the more extreme the self-perpetuating chain reaction of chemical and biological processes that make up the fight or flight response. Those same synergistic impulses – a raised heartbeat and blood pressure, heightened muscle tone, increased flow of blood to brain and muscles, the outpouring of adrenalin and other stress chemicals into the blood, heightened oxygen consumption, shut-down of all digestive activity – that give us the physical drive and mental edge needed to run a race or meet a deadline are also responsible for triggering the aggression and panic caused by violent crime. The stress chemical adrenalin is the chief fear/anxiety hormone responsible for causing such panicky sensations as sweating, a dry mouth, palpitations, and heaviness of the limbs. Studies show that the output of adrenalin is directly related to the degree of unpleasantness inherent in any stressful situation and how in control, or rather out of control, we believe ourselves to be. The more dangerous or frightening we perceive a situation, the more adrenalin is produced by the body. The tendency for excess adrenalin literally to paralyse the body with fright explains why many individuals under extreme stress – and crime victims most of all – should experience loss of control or become immobilized by their ordeal.

Deep Freeze

If we cannot mitigate or moderate our responses to such humdrum everyday anxiety-provoking situations like traffic jams, domestic tiffs, going to the dentist or asking for a bank overdraft, then how can we ever hope to assume control of those same responses magnified a hundred times over through devastatingly frightening circumstances? Taking a deep breath to calm yourself, relaxing your muscles, adopting a positive and rational outlook may prevent you from losing your bottle when the boss is giving you a hard time but these are hardly realistic tactics to consider when someone with a gun at your head is demanding that you hand over your money, or the thug with his arm across your throat gives you the choice of either being raped or murdered. Under such circumstances the term fight or flight seems strangely inappropriate. There is of course a third option – and that is to freeze.

The 'panic freeze' where you literally cannot talk or move and the mind becomes blank is common to a majority of victims, yet it is a response that is largely ignored by the majority of books and articles on stress. Studies that document the effects of stress, in particular how the body becomes aroused in response to challenge and stimulus, unpleasant or otherwise, usually fail to point out how panic or shock can incapacitate the body and numb the mind, thereby preventing the victim from either fleeing or fighting back. Whether the victim does freeze either partially or totally or manages to remain in control of their faculties depends to some extent on the immediate circumstances such as the environment or location, the suddenness and unexpectedness of the attack, the approach of the assailant and whether he is armed or not.

On Guard

Studies carried out in America into the effects of violence show that victims of all crime including rape and mugging tend to display similar patterns of response. Invariably many will ex-

perience a vague premonition just before the crime occurs, an
intuitive hunch that something is wrong which may put them on
their guard. For the lucky few this sensory alarm, provided it
goes off early enough and is sufficiently strong, may go some way
towards preparing the victim for the shock of an impending
attack. Under certain circumstances, for example where street
crime is concerned, split second timing and clear rational thought
may even get some people out of danger altogether.

Justin Munroe was queuing in a bank when armed raiders
burst in and stormed up to the counter.

> I instinctively threw myself flat on the floor in case they opened fire.
> That's exactly what did happen and some people got wounded in the
> crossfire. I am just so thankful I acted fast enough and did the right
> thing.

Should the attacker go in for any verbal preamble before
becoming physically violent the victim, provided he or she can
remain mentally controlled and alert, may even be able to talk
their way out of being attacked. Walking up the driveway to her
block of flats in a prosperous area of Manhattan, Josephine
Gibbon suddenly found herself surrounded by four menacing
youths who began edging in and commenting on the large
bouquet of flowers she was carrying.

> I immediately started humouring them and pretended I was only
> delivering the flowers to someone in the block. I played the poor
> relation and sort of played for sympathy, telling them the flowers
> weren't for me that I was not the sort of person who could ever afford
> anything so expensive. It was a gamble but it paid off. In pretending to
> be a poor visitor not a rich resident I got them on my side by
> persuading them I wasn't worth bothering with and even making
> them think perhaps I was one of them.

Obviously the more sudden and unexpected the attack the more
severe the shock, especially where physical violence – or the
threat of it – is involved. By far the most common initial response
when a criminal strikes out of the blue is shock, disbelief and
denial. 'No, this cannot be happening to me', 'it is a game,
someone is playing a joke on me' and 'it'll end in a minute and
he'll go away' are momentary shock responses familiar to many
victims. Valerie Simpson was buying stamps in her neighbourhood post office when a man standing behind her suddenly
moved ahead of the queue and pointed a sawn-off shotgun at the
clerk.

> He told us all to freeze. I remember staring in total disbelief and
> thinking I think that's a gun but this only happens in films surely or to

other people. It can't be happening to me. I then made a conscious effort not to meet his eyes because I thought that he might pick me out and I might be taken hostage or shot – after all I was at the top of the queue. I wasn't frightened at all until much later. In fact I remained totally cool until he left the post office.

Regressions

Initial disbelief may sometimes quickly give way to a state of severe fright or panic which psychiatrist Dr Martin Symonds, a leading American researcher into responses to violent crime, called 'frozen fright' or 'traumatic psychological infantilism' in which the victim forgets all learned rational behaviour and reverts to the innate adaptive pattern of early childhood. Uppermost in the victim's mind is now one single objective: self-preservation. All his or her behaviour, no matter how regressive, is aimed at getting away and staying alive. Frozen fright may cause the victim to submit readily to the attacker or respond with terror-induced pseudo-calm behaviour that can appear compliant, cooperative, ingratiating, even friendly. In short, to any outsider – and later to the victim who analyses it objectively – it may seem utterly perverse and uncharacteristic. Yet in truth such behaviour, no matter how bizarre it might seem, always stems from the fear of being killed or mutilated.

The longer the contact between the criminal and his victim, as in the case of rape or kidnapping, for example, the greater the sense of hopelessness about getting away or remaining alive and therefore the more infantile and compliant the response to the attacker may become. In one recorded rape case a young girl motivated by terror offered the rapist a glass of water. When the case came to court the judge interpreted that act as an indication of the girl's voluntary compliance with the criminal. In another case a rapist berated his victim for having torn his shirt and not having cooperated with him. She began to cry and apologized profusely. Another woman who was raped then accompanied the man to his car and allowed him to drive her to the nearest bus stop where she thanked him for the lift. When questioned she said she was so frightened that his violent nature might lead him to rape her again or possibly kill her that she was driven to be nice until he left. 'I was so scared I would have done anything. He was quite capable of killing me.'

The effect of frozen fear is evidently to drain any capacity for overt resistance. Typically, most victims, especially women, young girls and children, will concentrate on remaining passive and appeasing rather than upsetting their attacker, in order to ensure survival.

Back to Nature

Martin Symonds draws a vivid analogy between the phenomenon of frozen fear in humans and the similar propitiating, ingratiating and appeasing behaviour pattern of animals when faced with overwhelming violence from other animals of the same species. Young animals in particular expose the most vulnerable parts of their bodies to the aggressors. Even family pets when play gets a bit rough show similar signs of submission to one another. A young dog, for instance, will commonly lie on its back with its abdomen exposed. A wolf adopts the same posture or alternatively will stand still and turn its head away, thereby exposing its throat to the attacker. Invariably this act of submission on the part of one animal prompts the other to cease his attack – a common feature of aggression within the species, notes Dr Symonds. What is interesting however is that while submission successfully inhibits aggression of animals of the same species, the rule does not apply to predatory animals – for instance where a lion attacks a gazelle or a cat a bird. When hunting animals of a different species they attack their prey ignoring any signs of submission. Submission, says Dr Symonds, only makes their work easier. In order to survive, the animal victim therefore has no choice other than to defend himself or die.

In humans, however, the response elicited through submission to a violent attack is obviously less predictable and may vary according to the psychological make-up of the criminal. Anything more active than utter and total submission may spark off extremely violent rage in certain types of offenders with often tragic results for the victim. In acting out his private twisted fantasies the violent criminal is invariably trying to terrorize his victim into submission. This is, after all, the way that he can obtain what he wants, while the feeling of power he experiences in subjugating another person is usually what excites the true psychopath in the first place. This is a consistent feature in the vast majority of all violent and forcible cases of rape, where the rapist is often preoccupied with an overwhelming need to dominate, degrade and control a woman rather than to obtain sexual gratification.

The same rule usually applies to violent street crime. When interviewed, muggers often admit that any slowness or reluctance on the part of the victim to hand over money or other valuables puts them in a position of danger because they might be identified or apprehended by a witness, or even worse by the police. This explains why an attacker will often become enraged and inflict injury on the victims either if he cannot terrorize them into instant submission or as an afterthought once he has obtained their money if he foresees that the victims could possibly hinder his escape by crying for help or giving chase. Muggers, whose *modus operandi* is usually robbery with violence thrown in for good measure, are the ultimate predators. Interviews with criminals who have a record of numerous muggings – up to a hundred incidents or more – reveal a frightening degree of egocentricity, a complete inability to empathize with anyone's needs but their own. Most people's instinct to hand over their money fast is therefore a correct one.

Urban Jungle Law

Muggers who have themselves been attacked and robbed tend in general to observe this law of the urban jungle. Violent criminals, when attacked, usually admit that they remained silent, refrained from arguing or resisting if they felt it was useless and handed over their money promptly. Communication is a crude one-way process for the average violent criminal. Oblivious to the impact of his actions, the attacker sees his victims as objects devoid of identity, merely to be used to gratify his most immediately pressing needs.

Compared to the usually swift dynamic of street crime – a grab-attack-run pattern – the interchange between victim and criminal under more prolonged circumstances can vary according to the degree of danger perceived by the victim. Victims' responses will usually fall into passive or active categories of resistance. Passive patterns of resistance characterized by compliant and submissive behaviour are those that may seem most confusing and mystifying, even bizarre to outsiders. Passive resistance is also liable to cause shame and guilt in the victim when she or he later reviews their responses, long after the danger has past.

How a victim feels about the way they initially reacted to a violent crime will be coloured largely by their success or failure in escaping or deterring the attacker. With hindsight, victims usually recognize that a violent incident such as sexual assault, kidnapping or robbery, was made up of various phases: the early warning and the lead-up stages, the threat, the actual attack or repeated attacks, the possible escape, and the rescue or eventual disappearance of the attacker. The feelings and perceptions of the victim may shift, intensify or dramatically change at any point during these phases. Early attempts to escape, fight back or reason with the assailant may be followed by stronger responses of fear and the urge to survive above all else will then dominate. Increased threats of violence by the criminal may inhibit all rational thought and undermine the victim's normal assertiveness causing them to become crippled by dread at the possible outcome of the event.

Blanking out, becoming physically paralysed or mentally numb to the point where the victim cannot hear or understand the criminal's demands is a classic feature of frozen fright. Unfortunately this reaction can be construed by the attacker as deliberate resistance, sometimes causing him to become more threatening or violent. Mind and body may continue to be incapacitated even after the crime has been committed and the immediate danger is over, confusing and befuddling the victim's thoughts and preventing them from taking appropriate steps to report the incident. In America a man of twenty-nine and his girlfriend were held at gunpoint in her home for six hours. The gunman then told him he could leave. He went out into the street but was so overcome by the effects of fear that in spite of passing a number of shops and office buildings he did not have the confidence to walk in and ask to use their telephone. He therefore walked half a mile until he found a public telephone where he dialled the police and reported the kidnapping. Male as well as female victims of all ages may commonly act like small very frightened children for quite extended periods following a violent crime such as rape, sexual assault, attempted murder or kidnapping.

In Bondage

According to Martin Symonds, as long as there is hope of survival fright will always override anger, giving rise to submissive behaviour. The Balinese, by nature an essentially peaceful people, instinctively often go to sleep when they are afraid. There is a Balinese phrase, 'takoet-poeles', meaning afraid sleep, a state analogous to frozen fright which illustrates this channelling of fear into submission. The close almost interdependent relationship which tends to build up between hostages and their kidnappers is a frequently reported phenomenon. Because the kidnap victim is dependent for their survival on the whims and ultimate clemency of their captor, what develops under certain circumstances is a child/parent transference, initiated by the victim. After a prolonged period emotions become electrically charged. Any signs of kindness on the part of the criminal, for instance allowing a woman to have a drink of water or a blanket to keep warm may assume immense significance for the victim who is grateful for simply being allowed to live. Psychologists sometimes refer to this phenomenon as the Stockholm syndrome. Having regressed through fear to the behaviour patterns of childhood, the victim quickly adopts an attitude of appeasement that is most expedient, be it instant submission, cooperation, even geniality in a bid to protect themselves.

What complicates matters even further in crimes of kidnapping and hostage taking is the delicate, often lengthy knife-edge negotiations between the criminal and either the police or the victim's family which ensue shortly after the initial attack. With the victim relegated to the role of pawn in this game of nerves, the threat of death is used as a lever by the criminal to obtain his desired objective. A hostage is only of use if he or she is alive – but if more than one is being held, as in the recent spate of terrorist hi-jackings of aircraft and the cruise ship the *Achille Lauro*, then any one hostage becomes dispensable. Under extreme circumstances therefore the victim/criminal relationship can take on a paradoxical twist. Relieved at being hitherto unharmed, the victim may begin to view the criminal as his protector, the momentary custodian of his wellbeing, while the police or relatives are perceived as a potential threat if they do not concede to the kidnapper's demands, and deliver an ultimatum or behave in a threatening manner towards the criminal during negotiations. The more terrified the victim the more he may, through a form of self-induced brainwashing, identify with his kidnapper. This bizarre volte-face is thought to have occurred, for example, in the case of Patti Hearst, who having been held hostage for a prolonged period publicly affiliated herself with the political cause espoused by her terrorist kidnappers.

In some cases, although the victim's initial inclination is to fight back, fear may soon gain the upper hand even preventing someone who is physically strong and trained in self-defence from striking out and injuring their assailant. During an Embassy seige some years ago a police officer who was one of the hostages, according to later reports, had developed a very strong sense of allegiance towards some of the terrorists to the point where he reacted negatively to the eventual rescue operation.

Physical Resistance

By no means do all victims submit readily to an attacker. Indeed some men and women may surprise even themselves by the amount of fierce anger and indignation that can erupt within them when faced with a potential mugger, burglar or rapist. This unexpected wellspring of anger is usually responsible for giving them the strength and audacity to fight back, even in the face of formidable odds. However, resistance must be instantaneous and action blindly assertive – to the point of viciousness – in order to catch the criminal off guard and achieve the desired shock response.

Charlotte Barnes is 4 feet 10 inches tall, and a lifelong sufferer of diabetes. However, her reflexes when someone tried to attack her were razor sharp.

> I felt his hand push my back and a tug on my handbag so I swung round and hit him with all the force I could in the chest. He tried to grapple with me and I kicked him and he staggered back, pulling me with him. We fell down on the pavement together and I pushed my hand in his nose and jumped up quickly and just ran. He ran off in the other direction.

The point is that many criminals do not expect a woman to respond assertively when attacked, so if she does they often decide against pursuing their target. Verbal resistance, screaming, shouting, using abusive or obscene language, must therefore carry out the message loud and clear: that the intended victim will stop at nothing to call the police or rouse others to her aid. The threat of being identified by witnesses, tracked down by the police or prevented from getting away is often sufficient to deter some criminals from carrying out a planned attack.

The outcome of physical resistance – kicking, scratching, biting, tearing, punching, using screecher alarms or spraying something into the assailant's face – especially where women are concerned – depends very largely on physical strength, reflexes and split second timing. These are all strategies designed primarily to aid escape rather than overwhelm the offender. The main danger of using physical resistance is that if it is delayed or insufficiently forceful, the victim may be overcome by more force from the criminal. This is why passive resistance is ultimately less likely to endanger the victim's well-being than half-hearted or ill-timed resistance, a point to remember for every victim male or female who feels guilty at not having fought back or who is asked by outsiders why they did not manage to do so. While a man who is attacked may feel tempted to 'prove himself' by taking on his attacker in a prolonged fight often with tragic consequences – especially if dangerous weapons are involved – the clear objective for any woman who resists is to engineer a speedy getaway. In any prolonged struggle with a man, the woman being physically weaker in the majority of cases is almost invariably the loser. If her assailant carries a knife or a gun the instinct not to resist is absolutely the right one – to do otherwise could prove horrific. However, when a woman does strike back, the shock may be enough to deter the attacker. Doreen Stonehouse attributes her quick reaction and strength to her dancer's training.

> He'd come up behind me and clapped his hands over my mouth so I couldn't scream. But my instant reaction was to kick very hard and jab my elbows into him especially the soft bits. He'd got me up by some railings and I clung onto these, lashing out even harder with my legs. He was shortish and slim and obviously unprepared for my strength. He let me go and fled.

In Doreen's case anger was clearly a particularly potent factor.

> After he'd run away I almost felt like chasing after him to get even. There were shock waves of fury welling up inside me. I stood there shaking and yelling at the top of my voice, calling him by every foul name you can think of, I suppose to vent my fright as well as my anger. I think this helped get it out of my system. I reported it to the police. I had very little real remaining anxiety about being attacked again and no doubts about how I'd handled it.

Instinctive anger led Rosemary Grey, an English fashion designer on a working trip to New York, to react in a similarly defiant manner.

> I was alone waiting for the lift on the twenty-ninth floor. The lift door opened and a black man lurched towards me and demanded all my money or he said he'd strangle me. I said no without hesitation. Dammit, I'd just been paid a whole month's wages and the idea of having to part with it infuriated me. Half of me realized I was doing the wrong thing according to the book of rules but I couldn't help myself. I really am surprised that he didn't kill me. He put his hands around my neck and I was prepared to put up a fight but then the other lift door opened and two other men got out and chased this one off.

That Doreen, Rosemary and Charlotte successfully resisted their attackers perhaps testifies to their ability to trust their basic instincts and act swiftly and decisively. Injudicious as it may seem at the time, reacting aggressively, even if it does not help the victim escape or frighten off the attacker, may hold unexpected advantages for the future. There is clear evidence that those men and women who do actively resist their assailant, even if they get injured as a result, tend to suffer fewer psychological side effects as a result. As might be expected, the degree of victim trauma is generally minimal for those who fought back and weren't hurt. Such people generally report feelings of exhilaration and power, of having triumphed or won against the odds.

Psychotherapist Philip Hodson believes that his ability to resist his attacker, a mugger who approached him in a London car park, not only helped him avoid post-traumatic side effects, in spite of the fact that the mugger got away with his money, but also allowed him to assess how he might react were such an incident to recur.

> What was important for me was that I managed to see the guy, and that I was able to express myself both verbally and physically. I now know what I'm capable of for the future should something like this happen again.

Even those who fought back and were hurt appear to enjoy sympathy and social acceptance from the public – though perhaps not from the police who tend to disapprove of victims taking the law into their own hands. The police are unequivocally opposed to victims, especially women, taking on criminals. The official police line is that the risk of incurring injury if you cannot successfully escape or deter an attacker, or if he happens to be armed with a dangerous weapon, is too high to justify putting up a fight, especially for people with no proper training in self-defence.

The Voice of Reason

The idea that it is possible to reason your way out of being mugged, assaulted or raped, and inspire pity or compassion in an attacker or get him to change his mind presupposes that the criminal has normal human emotions and the ability to relate to you as an individual and to respond to your needs and wishes. This, sadly, is a largely erroneous assumption. The majority of hardened violent criminals are deeply psychologically disturbed, predators who act impulsively and have no conscience and little emotional reserve. Trying to inspire guilt in a predatory rapist or mugger simply out to rip off his unfortunate victim is a largely pointless exercise since guilt is an emotion with which he is almost entirely unfamiliar. Predatory criminals who attack without a real motive do not feel guilt or remorse about what they do, only anger and fury at being thwarted and an overriding concern that they might be caught and exposed. They are therefore usually incapable of responding to tears or pleas for mercy and are certainly disinclined to listen to logic.

Responding in this way may indeed have an adverse effect, causing the attacker to become even more enraged at the delay in achieving his desired objective and therefore more liable to terrorize his victim with threats of violence or violence itself. It is usually non-violent criminals with a history of petty sex offences such as obscene telephone calls, indecent exposure and minor assault including touching or rubbing up who are most readily deterred either by pleading or crying or a firm defensive stance on the part of the victim. Sometimes a violent sex attacker though enraged by physical resistance may permit his victim to talk, thus giving her the choice, if she has her wits about her, of manoeuvring herself out of her predicament. In such cases reason is always worth a try.

Saying such things to a rapist as 'I am pregnant', 'I've got my period', 'I feel sick', 'why do you want to do this?', 'I have VD', 'I'm an Aids sufferer', 'I've had a miscarriage', 'my mother has just been taken to hospital' or 'my husband is coming home in the next half hour' will in most cases sadly fall on deaf ears although there are instances where women have used these tactics and successfully avoided being raped. Probation Officer Ray Wyre whose role as a counsellor in the treatment of sex offenders gives him invaluable insight into the criminal mind, stresses that in some cases talking to an attacker calmly and sympathetically, showing you understand his predicament while at the same time trying to explain your fears about being raped, can deter a sexual assailant.

The trick lies in not challenging or confronting the attacker or becoming aggressive with him, since this invariably incites him to further acts of violence, but using reason, infused with empathy. Women who have successfully pulled this off have only been able to do so because the effects of fear, rather than immobilizing their resources, induced in them a chilling degree of mental clarity and control. Trying to find out his name, his job and his background through sympathetic questioning – and even his attitude to sex – may divert him from his initial aim and cause him to regard his victim as an ally rather than an enemy.

The underlying premise is that the criminal does possess a weak spot which renders him susceptible to the victim's approach. Some rapists respond to sympathetic comments about their feelings of rejection and loneliness or their frustration at being unable to control their behaviour. They may react favourably to praise about their appearance or their previous activities. It goes without saying that any woman who adopts this approach with an attacker must be convincing and be prepared to maintain her verbal and mental ingenuity until the attacker tells her to go or leaves of his own accord.

If delay or deterrent tactics fail to work and an attack is inevitable some women have reported that by focusing on positive thoughts connected with their survival they can better endure their ordeal. Concentrating attention on details of the attacker or circumstances relevant to the incident – for example the attacker's clothes, voice, accent, build, bodily characteristics, his car and his numberplate – is obviously going to be of value in assisting police investigations when the crime is reported and may even help to put the criminal behind bars. Involuntary fear responses of an extreme nature can also work in the victim's favour. Fainting, undergoing an epileptic fit, vomiting, urinating or defecating may prove sufficiently offputting in some cases to deter or interrupt an attack.

Second Childhood

Naturally enough it is as futile for any individual to imagine that they will react in an ideal way – or in the case of men a brave 'macho' way – to an attack as it is to later berate themselves for having failed to show courage and fortitude. There will have been no formative experiences in most people's lives unless they have been trained for active combat, survived torture, or a natural disaster, to prepare them for the test of sudden arbitrary violence. In the scenario of attempted rape or murder, kidnapping, and violent assault, there are no roles for heroes or heroines – only for survivors. Such acts of extreme evil perpetrated by another human being can hardly be regarded as a normal test case in which the victim must prove at least their moral fibre if not their physical valour. Those few people – and it must be emphasised that these are a tiny minority – who *do* protest and fight back, escape or deter an attacker, are only able to do so because they have not been paralysed through the effects of frozen fright, but rather mobilized into a hyperactive state of fury. In some cases, victims who first reacted defiantly and fought back unsuccessfully were later overcome by fear and lapsed into submissive and compliant behaviour, which illustrates all too well how anger and fear may co-exist. Anger often becoming converted to fear via a speedy transmutation.

Researchers examining the effects of violent crime note that frozen fright and 'passive' responses to aggression are more commonly seen in women, which explains why those few women who do fight back, as for example the elderly English lady who recently beat off a mugger on the streets of Manhattan with her umbrella, receive what seems a disproportionate amount of praise and publicity. In regressing to the emotional states of early childhood the terror the victim feels now is as deeply real and threatening as the terror they felt at the possibility of being abandoned or punished, and those feelings can cause the very same adaptive responses familiar from childhood of helplessness, panic, shame or anger. Anger and aggression are often the least forthcoming responses because such feelings are often actively discouraged in small children, especially little girls, and thus may be automatically suppressed because they are linked to fears of further punishment.

It has been suggested by some psychologists that men from working-class backgrounds and those who have themselves been criminals are more liable to fight back while those from middle-class backgrounds comply and freeze more readily – a somewhat contentious proposition that fails to account for the vast number of casualties of crime in deprived inner-city areas. Individual responses to crime cannot be measured merely by applying a simple sociological equation.

More credible by far is that early childhood experience and the relationship between a child and his or her parents determines the way individual people react when overcome by fear. The pattern that emerges, faint as it is, suggests that those who have experienced very little or no violence in early life generally behave in a less physically aggressive manner, often attempting to plead or reason with the criminal, expressing themselves verbally rather than resorting to active resistance. Those individuals whose childhood was marked by violence are more liable to use physical patterns of resistance. However, what evidence there is so far remains fragmented and inconclusive, and it is just as likely that, say, a working-class man or woman with early experience of violence will be shocked into passivity through the effects of frozen fright when involved in a violent incident.

4
Victim Trauma Syndrome

When the violent incident is over, the victim, now safe from danger but perhaps still in the grip of frozen fear, often continues to behave in the same pseudo-calm manner they displayed throughout the ordeal. Some survivors, especially young children and people who have been through a very long-drawn-out and gruelling encounter may withdraw into a state of detached calm or near catatonic trance, staring silently into space or assuming a physical pose of tense hyper-alertness as if anticipating further danger. Drained of energy, some victims appear to enter a dream world becoming monosyllabic, utterly mute or unable to answer questions, apparently losing all recollection of past events or else describing the incident in intense detail but in a detached monotone devoid of all obvious signs of emotion.

Others become physically uncoordinated, as if they were drunk or drugged, appearing mentally confused, forgetful and disoriented, falling, stumbling, dropping things, fainting, unable to speak articulately or focus their thoughts. Some individuals, especially those who have experienced an incident that was not especially violent, may give a highly convincing impression of having escaped any ill effects. They tend to remain in control of their behaviour and are able to think rationally and talk coherently to police, bystanders, and friends, even registering surprise if those around them appear more upset by the event than they themselves are, or wondering why everyone is so concerned for their well being.

It is typical for victims at this stage to be on an 'adrenalin high'. The individual is in a sense on automatic pilot and may continue to react with equanimity, buoyed by unusually high spirits for as long as twelve hours or longer after the event. A massive outpouring of stress chemicals, elevated blood pressure, heart rate and muscle tone, increased oxygen consumption all combine to switch mind and body to sustained overdrive. Relief at having survived the danger may raise the spirits even further. This state of euphoria acts as a buffer against pain or discomfort, causing some injured victims to remain oblivious to their injuries sometimes for hours on end. Under stress the body produces powerful morphine-like chemical substances called endorphins that have been associated with increased feelings of elation and the ability to withstand pain. Not surprisingly, therefore, the appearance of normality, especially if kept up for a prolonged period, may end up fooling everyone. Journalist Alexandra Campbell had been woken at 4 a.m. by four men breaking into her bedroom. The leader, who was hooded, pulled her out of bed, cosh raised.

All I remember is thinking 'I have to scream' before the cosh descended on my cheek. I have no more recollection of what happened until my brother came rushing into the room, wakened by my screams. The intruders fled. I got dressed and we called the police and made a report. It wasn't until well into the morning many hours later when I had a bath that I suddenly saw to my horror that I had been extensively wounded with one of my own kitchen knives. There were slashes, cuts and bruises all over my arms and legs, one very deep wound on the inner thigh. When I finally saw my doctor it was too late to have the necessary tetanus shots and stitches. The police, who thought at first that I was uninjured because I had been so totally calm and unfazed by the attack, were utterly horrified at my injuries. My brother and I were both extraordinarily calm for a long time after the break in. We went to work as normal and I felt well enough to go ahead with a prearranged cocktail party for eighty guests the next day.

There is a perfectly understandable tendency for friends and relatives to assume the worst is over and that the victim is really perfectly all right. Of course nothing could be further from the truth. When the numbing effect of shock wears off, the intensity of the victim's reaction can prove cataclysmic.

By the end of the party I was feeling extremely strange; shaky, tearful and jumpy. By the following morning the slightest creak or ordinary sound like the fridge or the telephone ringing just made me fall apart and burst into tears. Hearing the front door bell and knowing there were people outside made me crack up completely. I couldn't do any task for more than about fifteen minutes without falling apart. I was frightened of going into the shops or of using the tube. I couldn't think of anything at all apart from the attack. It was quite impossible to sleep. I had the most horrific nightmares and would wake up at least three times a night sweating profusely and screaming my head off. This went on for at least three months after the attack.

Acute Physical Symptoms

Many victims, especially those who have been raped or physically assaulted or subjected to a long confrontation with their
assailant, react by becoming violently ill. The most typical
reactions early on in the acute phase of victim trauma are
uncontrollable sobbing, screaming, convulsive weeping and
moaning accompanied by physical symptoms such as shivering –
shock causes a sharp drop in body temperature – trembling,
sweating, extreme pallor, nausea, vomiting, diarrhoea, inconti-
nence, tightness and pains in the chest, breathing difficulties, or
fainting. Some victims feel intensely helpless and frightened and
may regress to infantile behaviour such as bed-wetting, thumb-
sucking, clinging to other people, pleading not to be left alone, or
sleeping with the light on. A phrase that crops up repeatedly
according to therapists who have counselled male and female
victims of all ages is 'feeling like a baby'.

The victim may have survived the attack uninjured but they are
now at their most fragile and defenceless and may require
someone to remain constantly at their side for the next few hours
or days to offer protection and support throughout the crisis.
During this early 'impact stage' the victim should not be left alone
especially during the night and will usually feel calmer and less
fearful if encouraged to sleep or rest and remain in a warm
comfortable environment. If a formal statement is to be given to
the police, itself a lengthy and sometimes gruelling procedure,
the victim should be encouraged to do so at home or to wait until
they have had a few hours' rest. Although rape victims should
report the attack and submit to an examination as soon as
possible without having previously had a bath or changed their
clothing, police policy now reflects greater awareness of victim
trauma with the result that there is greater flexibility and a more
understanding attitude towards interviewing and taking statements from victims of sexual assault.

Physical disorders may flare up instantaneously and linger for
anything from just a few hours to weeks on end. Delayed
reactions are not uncommon but all the more alarming, catching
the victim off guard. The force of the IRA bomb that went off
outside Harrods some years ago lifted PC Pam White three feet
up in the air and blew her fifteen feet across the road where her
body hit an iron railing. The woman police officer standing next
to her was killed outright but Pam was physically unmarked.

I remained utterly calm and spent the next two hours dealing with
other casualties and getting on with my normal duties. I just took a few

days off work because I felt perfectly all right. But a few weeks later I developed agonizing stomach cramps. My tummy got extremely distended. I consulted a gastroenterologist who told me it was a spastic colon due to stress and nerves. Then I started to get regular sweats, chest pains, palpitations and shakiness – all the classic signs of a panic attack. I was unable to sleep. The blast had permanently damaged my hearing so I had a constant ringing in the ears.

Key zones of the body – stomach, chest, back, head – are typical target areas where stress and shock wreak the greatest havoc. The stomach and entire gastrointestinal tract is a prime stress site where fear, anxiety, anger, and rage are translated into a full gamut of ailments from cramps, nausea and indigestion to constipation or diarrhoea. Eating can therefore cause severe pain or sickness, and loss of appetite or enjoyment of food is familiar to many victims. Conversely some survivors develop oral dependencies, bingeing obsessively on comfort foods such as chocolates, sweets, biscuits, cakes, buns, junk food or strong coffee. The craving for sweet food may also be triggered by the intense tiredness, depression and lack of energy which commonly result from any prolonged or severely stressful experience.

The need for a 'fix' whether to boost energy levels or calm the nerves may develop into an increased dependence on more addictive stimulants including alcohol, cigarettes and hard drugs. Says Pam White:

> I started to drink quite heavily after the Harrods' bombing. I found that it was the only way I could relax and cope with my fears that the horrific pains in my stomach were possibly due to cancer.

Victimization therefore presents a potential double hazard for anyone with a problem with drink, drugs or overeating since emotional distress may reactivate old dependencies, leading them back down the slippery slope to addiction. Victims with a history of atopic conditions like asthma or eczema, or chronic recurrent stress-linked disorders such as migraine, psoriasis, even epilepsy, may find their condition becomes severely aggravated after the event. Outbreaks either persist for longer periods or occur more frequently and with greater intensity. Hyperventilation, very rapid irregular breathing patterns, the tendency to gulp air or hold one's breath, are also associated with fear and anxiety. Classic symptoms include dizziness, fainting, choking, numbness and tingling in the limbs, chest pain, and inability to concentrate. Sore muscles, niggly aches or sharp jabbing pains in the joints and back, headaches or neuralgia may set in hours or days after the event especially if the victim was physically attacked, bound or gagged.

These acute physical symptoms may occur singly or in any manner of different combinations and can continue to affect survivors for days or weeks following the crime, sometimes disappearing for a period only to return again or give way to a different disorder or a new set of symptoms. A compulsive tendency to relive the incident over and over again – a typical aspect of victim trauma syndrome – may create further mental anguish which in turn amplifies the body's automatic stress response, setting up a self-generating cycle of cause and effect. If the symptoms persist or get worse you should certainly consult a GP if only to put your mind at ease regarding your general health. Worry only generates extra stress and the sooner you can dispel any fears that you may be seriously ill and accept the fact that you are simply at a very low physical ebb the sooner you will be able to rest and recover both your peace of mind and your physical strength. Says PC White, who obtained a medical discharge from the force:

> Knowing that my stomach pains were not due to cancer but simply caused by nerves and stress eventually helped reduce the fear and anxiety about my physical health. I can cope more now because I can understand the cause. I get regular tension headaches and migraines now whenever I am faced with a problem but I recognize that this is part of the stress syndrome. Even now, four years after the bombing, talking about it causes me to come out in a sweat and I get a tight and painful chest and my mouth goes dry. I don't suppose that is something that will ever go away completely.

Post-Traumatic Stress Disorder (PTSD)

PTSD is the umbrella term originally used by the American Psychiatric Association to identify a wide spectrum of psychological and behavioural disturbances particularly endemic among Vietnam war veterans. It now has a broader application and embraces the very similar patterns of distress commonly shared by victims of natural disasters and of all sorts of violent crime. Fear stands out as far and away the most common gut response to violent crime. Almost all the classic symptoms of PTSD – phobias, panic attacks, avoidance behaviour, depression, guilt, nightmares, a sense of isolation, sleep disturbances, diminished self-esteem, denial of events and suppressed anger – have their origin in this most primeval of emotions. Ranging from blind panic and terror at one end of the scale to constant niggling doubts and all-pervasive anxiety at the other, fear is the lynchpin that holds all the other stress responses together.

Fear continues to dictate the victim's behaviour and disrupt relationships long after the incident has passed. Because fear is not something which is easily shared or expressed it can build up inside causing the victim to feel isolated, lonely and abandoned because they are unable to convey the extent of their misery to others. This in turn can breed strong feelings of resentment, creating an urge to withdraw from other people and hide from the outside world which appears fraught with hostility. Many victims fear that they are going crazy or that they are experiencing abnormal reactions. Suspiciousness of others, especially strangers, can colour behaviour and limit activities for long periods after the incident. Noises, loud voices, bright lights, crowds, confined or open spaces and sudden changes of temperature may all suddenly become intolerably stressful. The victim may only feel secure by remaining cloistered in surroundings that are familiar, secure and quiet. Says Alexandra Campbell:

> For a very long time I thought I could hear every single sound in London. A crash of falling scaffolding sounded terrifyingly loud even from about six blocks away. The inability to get a proper night's sleep because of my nightmares had made me completely exhausted and drained away all my resources. It was impossible for me to be in a room full of people, the noise would usually act as a tremendous stress trigger. Although I took two weeks off work, when I went back my concentration was hopeless. I was alternately jumpy and then exhausted so in effect I was only working part-time.

Action Replay

Terror has an extraordinary capacity to dislocate every function, short-circuiting rational thought, subverting normal behaviour, causing the victim to abandon all logic and lose perspective of the true dangers that surround them. The possibility of reprisal or of another attack often looms uppermost in the victim's mind. Victims attacked in their home fear going to sleep or remaining indoors alone in case their attacker returns. The slightest creak, rustle or thud may be sufficient to throw the imagination into overdrive. Only once they have installed bars, grilles, alarms and locks will some victims feel confident enough to return to live and sleep at their home. Parks, country lanes, dark streets, buses, tubes, trains, lifts, car parks, the city streets after dark, and pubs are just some of the ordinary everyday environments that become terrifying no-go areas for some victims who have been attacked outside their home.

Trust in strangers, especially in men, takes the hardest knocking of all especially for women who have been raped or sexually assaulted. Sudden and crippling fears can be stimulated by the sight of weapons, seeing sexual activity or scenes of violence on television and in the cinema, being suddenly awakened at night, being unexpectedly touched, sensing people behind, being confronted by unattractive, tough-looking or seemingly insane people, or groups of men standing in the street. Victims of bombing incidents may react violently to sudden explosive noises or avoid entering target sites such as department stores, airports or restaurants where such explosions have commonly occurred in the past.

Most victims, even those whose immediate crisis reaction is minimal, unwittingly become haunted by the spectre of the past, no matter how strong their will and determination to get on with normal everyday life and put the events behind them. Involuntarily they relive every moment in slow motion and recall every detail of the incident and events leading up to it. This continuous action replay of disturbing images, feelings and thoughts connected with the crime begins to overwhelm the senses. Emotional 'flooding' serves to intensify the victim's state of stress, perpetuating anxiety states, generating panic attacks that no amount of reasoned thought or self-will can control, keeping the catastrophe firmly in the forefront of their mind.

This is by far the most predominant characteristic of PTSD and is in many ways the most insidious of all the symptoms. Escape seems near impossible and the mental images, imagined sounds, and physical sensations constitute a private hell that no one else can possibly share. Vivid dreams and horrific nightmares allow little opportunity to escape during sleep. Disturbed sleep patterns, feelings of exhaustion, anxiety, or panic on awakening, inability to fall asleep or a tendency to wake up in the early hours and remain hyper-alert to every small sound outdoors or within the home seem to be universal problems for the majority of crime victims.

Shame, guilt or fury at having been rendered powerless by the attacker may cause some survivors to fantasize a different outcome to the scenario. Hypothesizing how they might have acted during the crisis if less paralyzed by fear, the survivor evokes dreams in which he or she fights and overcomes the criminal, attacks or humiliates him and emerges triumphant from the situation. While they evoke panic and fear they essentially constitute a catharsis, and these dreams can alter significantly during the course of the survivor's recovery. In the early stages of trauma the victims typically may awake before they can overcome their assailant, later going on to dream the entire episode in full, seeing themselves successfully fighting, injuring or killing him. In other instances the criminal's family and friends now pursue the victim, seeking revenge for his death. As long as they are only prescribed as part of a short-term crisis intervention, tranquillizers or sleeping pills are invaluable in the treatment of these acute symptoms.

Intimate Intrusions

Women who have been raped or indecently assaulted are likely to be assailed by disturbing invasive thoughts about the experience. The subsequent effect may turn out to be drastic and lifechanging in the extreme. Any rape-related 'cues' – stimuli directly associated with the attack – acquire the capacity to evoke very real feelings of anxiety and fear virtually as traumatic as those experienced during the event itself. Within a very short period these symptoms and sensations may develop into full-blown phobias or panic attacks complete with classic phobic alarm signals such as sweating, chest pains, inability to breathe, heightened blood pressure and heartbeat, numbness, fainting, or dizziness. Through their inevitable association with the terror of rape or perceived threat of death these so-called conditioned fear responses might be triggered most frequently, for instance, if the victim suddenly encounters a man she does not know, has sexual intercourse or takes part in certain specific sexual acts which she was forced to perform during the assault.

The fear response might extend to other stimuli present during the attack. These can be numerous, less obvious and will vary according to the individual circumstances surrounding the crime. For instance, if a woman was attacked by a man carrying a knife or getting into a car in a car park within a shopping centre at night, then it follows logically that knives, cars, car parks, shopping centres and night-time may be potential rape-related cues capable of triggering anxiety of one degree or another in the victim.

These cues may be all the more distressing when they occur suddenly and unexpectedly a long time after the incident originally occurred. One woman who seemed to be regaining her confidence relatively quickly after being raped developed a blind panic attack one night months later when her boyfriend kissed her and she tasted whisky on his lips. All her hitherto suppressed memories of the rapist with alcohol on his breath welled up in her consciousness. At a party a girl who had been raped two years previously started to shake and feel sick when one of the guests began to dance with her. The aftershave he was wearing was identical to that worn by her attacker. Her sense of smell had unlocked a train of fearful memories. Another woman insists that her husband shaves before coming to bed because the feel of beard stubble on his face is to her a disgusting and distressing reminder of the unshaven man who raped her.

Avoidance behaviour, often on an extreme and obsessive scale, is the natural corollary to conditioned fear responses. In order to avoid becoming gripped by fear or helplessness, or experiencing panic attacks with all the attendant physical discomfort, the victims will limit their activities and restrict their behaviour, often restructuring their social, home and working lives with quite meticulous precision in order to avoid the risk of encountering further trauma. Says rape victim Sandy Greene:

> Five years after being raped by six youths I still cannot come home alone from work after dark. I spend all my money on cabs during the dark winter months and I insist on having the same driver because I am afraid of getting into a car driven by a strange man. My boyfriend and my family have had to learn not to fling their arms around me or touch me unexpectedly because it is liable to induce the most terrifying feelings of fear and shock.

The more the sufferers abandon their normal activities and restricts their freedom of movement to accommodate this new disability the greater the likelihood of their becoming withdrawn, even alienated, from the outside world. Unresponsiveness to other people, the inability to form new relationships or maintain old ones, reluctance to meet challenges and enjoy life and initiate activities are examples of avoidance taken to its furthest degree.

Mark Chatters resigned from his job as traffic warden after being assaulted twice by a man while on duty.

> I started getting panic attacks a few months after I stopped work. I could not travel in a train. The situation got so bad that I started going to a special training course on how to handle stress and anxiety. This has helped me but I still find I get very nervous and frightened when I go into a crowded pub or a cinema. I am still unable to hold down a job because of the inability of travelling in trains or buses or staying for long periods in a confined space. I can't go on holiday because airports, trains, crowded lounges make me feel very ill. When I do have a bad attack or a bad series of attacks I find that I have to go to bed and stay there for a few days in order to regain my confidence and then I gradually get better. This slows down my whole life and means that I don't have any hobbies or social activities.

Not surprisingly divorce, separation, depression, sexual problems and redundancy, are more common amongst victims once they become prey to avoidance behaviour on a grand scale. The reluctance of many victims to talk openly about their problems inevitably leads to an even deeper sense of isolation and reclusiveness. The number of crime-related cues, far from remaining single and easily identifiable, can multiply over the weeks and months and even years following the event, becoming more generalized and extending to form an amorphous ever-expanding grey area associated with the incident. Thus crowds of people, long ill-lit streets, any confined areas from lifts to trains or aeroplanes, strange faces, may assume a sinister aspect whose menacing qualities are associated however tenuously with the past event.

Some victims find that even thinking or talking about their experience can also undermine their peace of mind. Cognitive anxiety helps to explain why many victims either purposely or unconsciously avoid talking about their experiences. Although in this case the stimuli are all in the mind few would dispute their power of the mind to arouse the body and influence well-being. Victims caught up in obsessive thoughts about their attack – what doctors call catastrophizing – may find themselves in a particularly invidious position. Merely thinking about events brings on irreducibly distressing symptoms of panic, helplessness and anxiety, yet no amount of reasoning or self-control can prevent the victim thinking these thoughts. In such cases the victim is truly in danger of becoming a prisoner of the experience.

Depression

Because depression often develops slowly, dampening the victims' reactions and reducing their capacity to function efficiently, it has an insidious effect on well-being and may be the last symptom of which victims are aware. It can also prove the most pervasive and lingering. Depression gradually and imperceptibly, undermines mental and physical faculties and saps physical energy, causing disturbed sleep patterns, reducing the appetite, making it difficult to come to decisions, and holding the victim back from initiating activities.

It is possible to overlook depression because fear and anxiety are far and away the most noticeable symptoms of PTSD but people suffering from anxiety are invariably also depressed to some degree. Depression and fear develop symbiotically. The victim, frightened of suffering further stress symptoms, phobias or panic attacks, dreads going about their daily activities and ceases to derive joy or satisfaction from either work or leisure pursuits. Following an increasingly restricted lifestyle the 'anxious/depressive' succumbs even further to the downward pull of negative thoughts and feelings. Lack of self-esteem and confidence leads to a further vicious circle of depression as the sufferer becomes increasingly dejected by their own unattractive image and a sense that they are helpless and trapped by the effects that past events have had on their life.

Depression insidiously dislocates the individual's normally balanced perception of themselves and clouds their outlook on the future. Seen through the narrow-angle lens of depression the world can appear menacing and joyless in the extreme. Being victimized can act as a catalyst causing the victim to question who they are and where they are going. Pam White:

> Ever since the Harrods' bombing I have turned from a positive and optimistic person into a pessimistic one. I tend to get very negative about almost everything in life, for example marriage. I now think what's the point in getting married, it will probably only lead to divorce. I continually think about the people who are close to me and what will happen when they get ill and die.

At the age of eighteen John Skinner and his friend were viciously beaten up by four youths late one night while waiting for a taxi outside a pub.

> I am just not as positive as I was any more, if I have an argument I now tend to back off and I think that I might be wrong in my opinions, whereas in the past there was never any doubt in my mind that I was right, that I was sure about what I was arguing about. I find I stay out of the way of a lot of things if people are having an argument or there might be a fight brewing say at a party or a disco. I turn away now. I don't think I'll ever be the same as I was. I am now much more wary even in the daytime when I go out in the street. I used to be tremendously self-confident but a lot of that seems to have gone. I do hope that I get that old feeling of confidence back again sometime.

By reducing self-confidence and distorting perspective, depressive feelings may narrow one's outlook on life to the point of hopelessness. In severe and extreme cases especially where depression is linked to very violent and traumatic crimes such as rape, this can lead to drug addiction, alcoholism and even attempted suicide. The depressed person more than any other distressed victim is in particular need of constant support, encouragement and understanding, having lost sight of the range of options and choices available to them to gain control of their lives.

The type of response and consistency of support given by family and friends immediately after the crime may greatly determine whether the victim ultimately goes on to develop depression. Depression has been found to be far more common in women who have been raped but feel unable to talk about their experience with other people than in those who can discuss the event freely. While it is tempting to attribute their inability to talk openly to the fact that they are depressed it seems far more likely that their depression arises – or is aggravated by – lack of sympathy and understanding. Women who live alone, have no immediate family, and experience loneliness or difficulties in maintaining and making friends are most at risk from long-term depressive symptoms including sexual problems and poor health. The problem, of course, is a self-perpetuating one since depression can slow down the entire process of recovery.

Anger

Many victims are taken aback by the intensity of the anger they feel after being attacked. Anger on such a big scale may be a completely foreign emotion to those who are intrinsically mild tempered, gentle and unaggressive by nature but now have to cope with a bitter, furious urge to seek revenge, perhaps even to hurt or kill their attacker. Because that anger is at first almost exclusively and quite legitimately directed against the criminal who has now probably vanished for good from the victim's life, there can be no satisfactory outlet for these feelings. If for some reason the victim feels inhibited about going to the police and reporting the crime then those feelings may be even more intense. The enforced realization of their powerlessness leads often to a mounting sense of outrage. The attacker has triumphed, causing upheaval, anguish and loss. But what chance has the victim of getting even? Very little, as it turns out, thus heaping additional insult onto injury. This inequitable state of affairs, the gross unfairness of it all, only serves to whip up a further sense of rage.

Anger, when unexpressed, makes for extreme frustrations. The desire for revenge turns into a deep sense of impotence and resentment which may fester and chip away at the survivor's composure, compounding the initial feelings of helplessness and loss of control brought on by the attack itself. Impatience at other people's slow or inadequate responses to the crime, for example that of the police and the courts, can fuel the victim's aggression even more. There is a tendency for some individuals to displace their anger and vent their frustration against the police, hospital staff, GPs, neighbours, volunteers, even friends and family. It is as if someone must be made to pay for their victimization and injured pride. Quite understandably, outsiders finding themselves on the receiving end of the victim's ire may find their patience sorely tested and become openly resentful.

It is at this stage that conflict generated between the victim's anger and hostility and the defensive action adopted by outsiders can prepare the ground for much of the secondary injury described in the next chapter. When fury and indignation are frustrated they have a knack of swiftly turning to bitterness and hostility, especially if the victim feels that he or she had no recourse to retaliatory action and is not receiving sufficient back-up from others who might be able to help them to seek redress for the injustice that has been done. Rage that cannot be fully expressed and legitimately channelled cannot be easily dissipated or resolved. Instead it has the tendency to turn inwards.

Victims who cannot openly express their anger at the perpetrator often start to feel angry with themselves instead, blaming themselves for perhaps precipitating the offence or not having avoided it or triumphed over the attacker. In many social circles expressing anger is regarded as socially unacceptable – especially for women. Many women are still largely brought up to regard anger and aggressiveness as an ugly essentially unfeminine emotion to be suppressed or overcome at all costs. By comparison aggressiveness is accepted as a normal sometimes even admirable masculine trait, outbursts of anger adding a cutting edge to a forceful macho image in the eyes of certain sections of society. Researchers into victim trauma have discovered that overt anger is noticeably absent in the majority of rape victims.

Although it is possible that fear dominates the aftermath of rape and drowns feelings of anger, some psychologists believe that anger is a conditioned response in many women which goes right back to infancy. The premise is that for adults, any threat that cannot be dismissed by conscious action is perceived in the same way as parental threats of punishment for bad behaviour were in childhood. Adults therefore try and control their anger and aggression as they learned to do as children to avoid provoking punishment or disapprobation. In addition, when an adult is humiliated or physically assaulted they may be conditioned to question their behaviour to see what they did wrong. Thus repressed, anger very often re-emerges in the form of guilt and shame, both submissive and acceptably non-violent feelings particularly common amongst women with low self-esteem who find difficulty in asserting themselves. Suppressed anger also surfaces in the form of recurrent bad dreams and nightmares in which the victim often visualizes herself getting even with her attacker.

Denial: I'm Fine, Really I Am

The instinct to turn one's back on disaster is probably the most natural form of self-defence at times of crisis. At its most extreme total or partial lapse of memory indicates the ability of the brain to short-circuit under excessive shock. Forgetfulness offers the fastest escape route from an experience that is too upsetting to talk or think about. A common reaction amongst victims of deeply shocking crimes or a protracted ordeal such as kidnapping is outright denial immediately following the event. Drawing a complete mental blank may be the way in which some survivors react when faced with the added strain of having to answer questions, make statements, submit to medical examination and treatment. At times like these denial is not so much a voluntary strategy as an extension of the very early reaction of shock and disbelief victims display when first attacked. Their attention span, memory and conversation become strictly limited, their ability to follow a simple train of thought is noticeably impaired.

Subconsciously victims may resort to denial as a temporary reprieve from the need to take stock of the damage that has been done to them. Escaping from painful feelings and memories is as common amongst victims of very distressing crimes as it is amongst people who have just recently been bereaved. Victims not only feel out of control, scared and helpless because they were attacked and feared for their life but because perhaps for the first time ever they are at the mercy of a number of very powerful often unfamiliar emotions.

Rarely composed of just one or two single clearly definable symptoms PTSD normally comprises a jumbled cluster of frequently conflicting emotions. Almost universal ignorance about the existence of PTSD on the part of British doctors and hospital staff including the majority of psychiatrists, does nothing to help victims understand the cause of their emotional turmoil or reassure them that their symptoms are normal and will pass. At this stage out-and-out repression or denial of these hurtful feelings may seem the only recourse available. Most therapists are agreed that some denial can prove positively therapeutic, if only as an arbitrary stop-gap when upsetting thoughts and painful feelings flood in and threaten to diminish the victim's already weakened resources even further.

Denial is to emotional distress what sleep is to physical exhaustion: an opportunity to rest and renew one's strength. It is the unconscious saying to the conscious, 'OK, enough is enough, now give me a break. I haven't the strength to take any more of this.' Some researchers into the effects of victim trauma, notably Dr Morton Bard, professor of psychology at the graduate school of the City University of New York, have noted that many victims experience a so-called 'recoil phase' soon after the immediate crisis period is over, as the struggle to make sense of their experience becomes too exhausting. In this phase periods of extreme distress frequently alternate with periods of suppression or minimization of the traumatic aftereffects, analogous to the daily rhythm of waking and sleeping.

Gaining respite from fear and tension by turning their attention away from the problem helps the victims gather their strength and gain a fresh perspective on past events. The most well adjusted people are probably those who acknowledge when and even why they are adopting strategies to help them get through a particularly demanding period – as for example at work – while not losing sight of the fact that they are *still* vulnerable and a fair way away from total recovery. Says Alexandra Campbell:

> Eventually I realised that not thinking about things was stopping me getting well. I had to face my fear, acknowledge that I might very well have been raped or killed if I hadn't managed to scream and wake my brother.

Self delusion is another matter altogether. Those men and women who resolutely refuse to acknowledge the existence of fear, anger, anxiety and helplessness are those most at risk of developing delayed and long term health problems and mental or behavioural disturbances.

It is in such cases, particularly where victims have difficulty in first of all recognizing and secondly coming to terms with and resolving the emotional aftermath that the help of a trained counsellor can prove of inestimable value in ensuring that the victim makes a complete recovery. In the person who has tremendous self-will and is highly motivated, anger, anxiety and resentment may become sublimated into hyperactivity. Some victims, through a surplus of nervous energy, throw themselves into a welter of intense activity in an effort to take their minds off their present misfortunes, concentrating on their work and organizing social and domestic activities. Others seem to adopt a Polyanna-ish attitude of false equanimity, asserting that the event was not really so distressing and assuring everyone around them that they are over the 'worst' and quite able to resume living normally. The impression may be so convincing as to mislead everyone – including the victim.

The day after being assaulted in her home Janet was back at work agreeing to take part in a major project that involved working overtime and meeting a series of strict deadlines.

> I just kept going for weeks making an effort to smile and keep cheerful, go out and socialize, work hard and not be a drag about what had happened. I had lots of energy in spite of bouts of sleeplessness and thought it best to get on with life, I've always prided myself on having a positive outlook on life. Two months later I met up with an old friend I hadn't seen in ages. She asked me how I was and I just broke down, started sobbing uncontrollably. No one had bothered to ask me that in weeks. Great waves of self-pity and resentment came welling up. I realized I'd been blocking off everything. I hadn't faced my feelings so no one else did either. Once I could openly accept how upset and mixed up I was I began to feel as if a tremendous burden was off my shoulders. I didn't have to prove anything any more. I spent a lot of time talking things out with this friend who had been a victim of a hit and run driver. I took time off work also and had a holiday.

Recovery: The Long and Short of It

Unlike physical injury, emotional wounds follow no set pattern of recovery. Long haul or short, each person's recuperation varies, often subject to the vicissitudes of subsequent police enquiries, court appearances, the demands of job and home life. Like any other high stress situation, victimization may tax the victim's capacity for adaptation to the utmost and the rate of recovery may be determined by any number of variables including physical and mental health, temperament, environment. The base line however is determined by the severity of the crime itself.

In cases such as burglary or mugging many people experience relatively little distress and claim to be fully recovered as soon as one week after the event. Some rape survivors report being over the worst a mere three or four weeks afterwards, although a large number may continue to experience symptoms of PTSD for anything from one to four years, although the average recovery period for sexual assault victims is generally estimated to be between six and twelve months. Victim trauma does not, of course, necessarily follow a neat, logical sequence of events and the different phases described earlier can recur or even overlap. Given the ordeal involved in having to make a statement, give evidence, undergo cross-examination, in itself amounting to a virtual re-enactment of the crisis, it is unusual for assault victims to start making a full recovery until any investigations in which they are involved are finally over. Because of the dilatory nature of the judicial system, the all too common last minute adjournments and cancellations, acting as a witness inevitably spins out the agony and delays the task of putting back the pieces for many victims.

In general, the more traumatic the incident, the longer the recovery period. The majority of survivors of serious crime do experience the most severe symptoms in the weeks immediately following the attack, slowly improving over an average three-month period. Some victims of violent assault can continue to experience symptoms for a year or more, with rape victims, especially those with health problems and pre-existing psycho-logical disorders, not surprisingly suffering the most persistent problems of depression, fear and sexual dysfunction. Psycho-therapists working in the field of victim trauma express divergent views on whether it is possible to predict who will have complications in recovering and who not. Research carried out by Professor Dean Kilpatrick indicates that there are clues. Victims with relatively few symptoms and those who are able to cope well and overcome their problems in the weeks immediately succeed-ing the attack usually display few or no aftereffects three months after the crime was committed. The auguries for rapid recovery are therefore often evident at the start of the trauma.

About 25 per cent of rape victims interviewed by Professor Kilpatrick managed to recover within six to twenty-one days following their ordeal. In such women the chance of a relapse or flare-up of delayed symptoms is rare. What is disturbing, however, is that those who do still experience very acute and persistent side effects three months later may continue to be affected to some degree by any number of a wide variety of PTSD symptoms for years afterwards. Other researchers responsible for much of the pioneer work into rape trauma (Burgess and Holmstrom, Sutherland and Scherl) maintain that the tendency for many victims to suppress or deny the trauma initially or very soon after the crisis has passed leads inevitably to delayed symptoms or a later reemergence of PTSD.

5

Why Me? The Search for a Cause

An overwhelming part of the pain of victimization is its apparent
senselessness. Inevitably, in the absence of any discernible
reason for the crime, most victims will sooner or later be
compelled to invent one. Making sense of the incident is all part
of re-establishing trust in society as well as restoring a sense of
control and self-confidence. It also reflects the need we all have to
rationalize powerful and painful emotions like anger, shame and
fear in order to reduce distress. For along with denial, the
tendency to impose patterns of logic on the unexpected and
unfamiliar is a basic self-defence mechanism shared by all human
beings. With their lives already thrown into often considerable
turmoil by the immediate impact of the incident, victims must
now set about first understanding, then accepting and finally
controlling the ensuing trauma or else face the intolerable
prospect of being permanently scarred by the experience. Some
more than others may be able to draw on a personal 'crisis fund'
made up of inner strength and experience of past catastrophes.

Personal Faith

Very deeply religious people inevitably do resign themselves to
crisis, according to the tenets of their particular faith, more
readily than other people. Thus devout Christians gain comfort
from the realization that what happened was simply God's will
and instead of seeking retribution or searching for meaning they
pray for forgiveness for the criminal. Buddhists, having recon-
ciled themselves to the inevitability of past karma will accept
victimization perhaps as due payment of a debt incurred in a
previous incarnation. Even people who believe in astrology may

interpret what happened according to the planetary aspects, finding consolation in the fact that uncontrollable astral forces were at work. Believers in the occult may simply attribute victimization to a manifestation of the forces of evil.

Profound religious beliefs can be a tremendous source of comfort since faith in a supreme power that predetermines one's fate usually obviates the need to reason out the event. On the other hand the sense of injustice and hurt may be so deep for some victims that they question their beliefs or even abandon them – a dilemma shared by many families of murder victims, especially when these were children. But the majority of individuals are brought up according to a fairly simple moralistic creed of cause and effect, which is that good altruistic deeds tend to bring their own reward of harmony and happiness while bad ones reap unhappiness and ill fortune. Therefore, for someone who is victimized, the proposition that we must all take responsibility for our own actions suddenly seems founded on a massive fallacy – namely that we can exercise free will. Becoming a crime victim forces us to acknowledge that there are times when we end up at the mercy of abitrary circumstance, and free will is an elusive chimera.

The Powers of Reason

For many survivors the burning question is not so much why did the criminal do what he did but rather out of all people *why did he do it to me*? Fear and insecurity make up the cornerstone that supports the whole complex of victim trauma. And underpinning that fear is the one constant imponderable – if it happened once presumably it could happen again? That it will happen again is highly unlikely, but the possibility, of course, cannot be ruled out entirely. Before victims can feel truly safe again and resume control over their lives they must inevitably try to establish a rationale for the events that led up to the violent incident. Only by erecting a logical framework, no matter how tenuous, to support a random act of criminal violence, be it a rape, mugging, kidnapping or burglary, can the victim start to regain his or her confidence based on the conviction that it will almost certainly never happen to them again.

What this amounts to is the emotional equivalent to fitting alarms and bars to your home after the burglars have fled in the conviction that a well-protected dwelling, like an alert well-prepared individual, is guaranteed inviolable. Comforting as they may be, most attempts to ascribe a cause to any sudden random attack stem from a certain flawed logic, namely that we can predict the outcome of our actions and remain in control of our well-being at all times. However, there is no getting around the fact that there will inevitably be times and situations in life where we cannot expect necessarily to remain in full control. Yet this is the last thing the victim who has just been forced humiliatingly into a position of powerlessness wishes to hear. The idea that he or she might be rendered powerless yet again is total anathema. To anyone whose confidence has taken a battering, the illusion of complete control can prove a powerful incentive to pick up the pieces of one's life again.

All of us, ex-victims and non-victims alike, must go in for a fair share of self-deception in order to motivate a positive and assertive attitude to life. To live perpetually with fear can turn the everyday activities of urban life into intolerably major hassles. Victimization temporarily destroys a large proportion of that person's ego defences, and these make a vital contribution to our survival in a modern urban environment. They may be hard to rebuild, yet rebuild them one must in order to live a full and productive life once again. Therefore telling yourself 'it cannot happen to me again' or 'it surely will not happen to me because I'm in control of myself and aware of my environment' may seem foolish and shortsighted but is a positive and necessary morale boosting strategy for anyone who does not wish to live their life crippled by a state of nervous apprehension about the possible disasters that might befall them.

Interestingly enough, recent studies into the attitudes which predispose certain people to suffer more or less from victim trauma suggest that those with a distorted perception of their own immunity to danger usually encounter greater problems if they are victimized. These are the people who take the maxim 'it cannot happen to me' to its furthest extreme, exhibiting a tendency to take unnecessary risks, exposing themselves fearlessly and irresponsibly to potentially dangerous situations in the belief that they are either lucky enough or alert and controlled enough to escape any possible hazards. For someone who previously never entertained the slightest notion of fear or vulnerability, trying to grapple with the upheaval caused by a random attack can come as a debilitating blow to the ego. Overoptimism about personal safety prompts comparison with the tendency towards unrealistically high personal expectations – in fact the one trait is frequently congruent with the other. The negative consequences that ensue when a task proves insoluble or a goal unattainable can prove as crushing to the ego as those that arise as a result of a violent crime.

For the normally overconfident with an exaggerated sense of their own personal invulnerability, any loss of control may be perceived as unbearably threatening. This is particularly true as far as many male victims are concerned. It might seem odd that anyone who by nature errs on the side of optimism should have a tough time getting to grips with fear, but a similar tendency prevails in matters of illness and death. In working with patients who are terminally ill, Elizabeth Kübler-Ross found that those people who had lived active, controlling, high pressure lives displayed more difficulty in adjusting to the prospect of death than those who were more passive. Normally confident individuals who perceive themselves as invulnerable precisely because they are aware of the possible dangers that surrounded them and therefore take extra precautions against being victimized, also stand a greater chance of being thrown into emotional turmoil. If in spite of having an elaborate security system you are nevertheless burgled, your sense of outrage and powerlessness is understandably harder to face up to than if you had left your home unprotected.

So it seems that crime victims, whatever their attitude to crime, are often in a no-win situation: the overconfident who did not bother to protect themselves may end up regretfully blaming themselves for their plight while those who acted prudently may be consumed by a sense of utter helplessness.

Self-Blame: Was it Something I Did?

The phenomenom of self-blame is one of the most puzzling and disturbingly perverse aspects of victim trauma. Why almost all crime victims should display an overriding tendency to blame themselves and feel guilty for what occurred to them is a mystery that has long puzzled therapists and researchers into victim trauma. Nevertheless, self-blame and guilt run like a leitmotif through all stages of the aftermath. Such feelings may originate from the belief that the victim was personally responsible in some way for the incident, even if merely by default: either provoking the attack by their behaviour, failing to avoid it, or because they failed to either escape or deal with the offender in a more appropriate and assertive manner. Although it is one of the most common reactions to crime, whether the victim openly admits it or not, such a reaction also seems a complete anomaly to anyone who has ever lived through an experience as terrifying as a violent mugging, rape, kidnapping or attempted murder. But in order to understand how victims construct their theories of self-blame one must also understand their pressing need to come to terms with what occurred in order to ensure their future peace of mind.

The fact that all of us are potential victims is unacceptable to many people – ex-victims as much as non-victims. No matter how great the odds against it, the possibility of a repeated victim-ization continues to haunt the survivor for days, weeks, months, even years after the original attack. By fashioning a neat thesis to account for the past event, victims feel that they can at least rule out any possibility of a repeat performance. Consequently many victims are utterly merciless with themselves to the extent that they will probe deep into their character or behaviour in order to winkle out some suitable defect or anomaly on which to pin their attributions of self-blame.

For many people guilt is an emotion preferable to impotence and rage, and certainly to fear. Feeling guilty because one might have avoided the crime but didn't, or blaming oneself for doing something that precipitated the attack is for many people easier than reconciling themselves to the fact that they actually did nothing wrong and so, by implication, it could happen again. Some victims manage to sew this argument up so tightly that the role of chance or accident is entirely absent from the equation. The victims, typically, will focus their attention on some particular aspect of their behaviour which they regard as instrumental in initiating or contributing to the attack. Therefore actions such as walking or driving in the neighbourhood or along the street where they were attacked, parking their car in the wrong spot, not being more aware of a potentially dangerous situation, travelling on public transport late at night, being out alone after dark in a potentially dangerous environment, accepting lifts or talking to the criminal because he seemed a perfectly respectable human being are just some of the most frequent reasons given by victims who blame themselves.

There is also a tendency for victims to chip away at themselves for failing to be clued up about other people's behaviour. Victims will frequently castigate themselves for showing poor judgement in assessing a person or a set of circumstances or remaining oblivious to possible dangers until it was too late to get away. Burglary and robbery victims invariably berate themselves for not taking sufficient security precautions, for opening the door to a stranger, for carrying too much money on them or carrying a handbag or purse in such a manner that made it easily accessible.

'It was my fault he grabbed my bag. I wasn't paying proper attention to what was going on around me,' says a woman robbed in daylight on a busy street.

'If I hadn't stayed overnight at the party they wouldn't have broken into my flat,' speculates another whose home was burgled during the early hours. But many are burgled while at home asleep like Terence Keeley, or during the day when at work.

'I've only been burgled once at night. The other two were in broad daylight. Every time I come home I expect to find the flat ransacked now – even if it's midday,' says Juliet Holzmann.

Women who were raped or indecently assaulted may become riddled with doubt about whether their clothing, body movement or attitude in some way gave a come-on to the attacker.

In some cases the victim's perceptions may be perfectly valid ones and therefore helpful in making more sense of the crime. This can result in feeling one is again more in control and therefore, theoretically, better equipped to avoid future victimization. By not walking alone at night down a dark street in a high crime area one would undoubtedly, in theory, reduce one's risk of being mugged. Refusing to accept a lift from a stranger in a pub because it is raining and opting instead to take a taxi might well make you a less favourable target for a rapist. But then again it might not. John Skinner and Reg Burton were attacked on coming out of a pub while waiting to get a taxi to go onto a party.

> I suppose that if we had not been waiting for a taxi and had merely walked along the road and perhaps gone down into the underground the four guys who decided to beat us up would simply have not chosen us as targets.

Reducing one's chances of becoming a victim is one thing but it is still no guarantee of complete safety. Some therapists believe that the more logical the line of reasoning the less long-term distress the victim is likely to face, provided their self-esteem is normally fairly high in the first place.

Where self-blame takes on a particularly sinister note is when it is directed not at one specific action but at one's fundamental character. Victims who regard the crime as something which happened because of some intrinsic character defect, a personality flaw which has rendered them incapable of asserting themselves or controlling events around them, stand in danger of becoming increasingly depressed, angry, resentful, anxious and guilty. For those people who have been attacked more than once, the tendency towards self-blame is particularly damaging because it can lead to a perception of oneself as one of 'life's victims' or as having 'a victim personality'. This attitude is reflected in statements like 'something's always happening to me', 'this is just another mess I've got myself into', 'I must be jinxed', 'no wonder I was attacked; I probably come across as someone who can't defend herself', 'I'm hopeless if there is violence around, I just go to pieces' which are typical of many victims. For people with low self-esteem that predates the crime, becoming a victim can seem like the ultimate self-fulfilling prophecy: the crime is seen as a final endorsement of one's negative view of oneself and one's surroundings. In such cases self-blame is extremely counter-productive, slowing down and complicating the whole process of recovery, encouraging the victim to direct all their rage and despair predominantly against themselves.

Off the Hook

Those victims bent on self-blame resolutely refuse to let themselves off the hook. Even if they do not think they directly invited assault through foolish or thoughtless behaviour then the belief that they might have escaped being attacked by some quick thinking and/or assertive behaviour is sufficient to generate remorse. By focusing attention on what they apparently did wrong at this stage – the attack itself – it becomes all too easy to lose all proper perspective of what really took place. Not wishing to acknowledge that they lost control, that rational thought and assertive behaviour were suspended through frozen fright, some survivors now feel intensely ashamed, guilty or furious with themselves for failing to fight back, run away, scream or talk themselves out of the situation. Judging their actions objectively, outside the context of terror, they may condemn themselves for having failed to be brave and strong. But, as we have already seen, no one can count on 'normal' reactions at times of intense fear.

Therapists who have worked with crime victims, war veterans, and even concentration camp survivors, have found that all groups share this tendency to feel guilty about the sort of emergency behaviour required to survive situations of extreme danger – or situations that were perceived as such – in which moral absolutes cease to apply. Symptoms of depression and guilt suffered by soldiers who were involved in active combat can often be traced back to the trauma of being forced to kill cold-bloodedly or maim fellow human beings in order to stay alive. Traumatic events tend to challenge the accepted moral order that runs through society, undermining our basic precepts not only about other people but about ourselves. Therefore a soldier who initially goes into war spurred by altruistic motives, visualizing himself as a fundamentally peaceful defender of freedom with care and regard for his fellow man must eventually come to terms with his own unsuspected ability to inflict brutality. The dichotomy between idealistic attitudes and those required for survival is obvious and cruel; it undermines one of the most basic axioms of life, do unto others as you would have done to you. The child psychiatrist Bruno Bettelheim, imprisoned in a Nazi concentration camp during World War II, observed that ex-prisoners may cope with the pain of past experiences either by purposely forgetting what happened, or by trying to justify why they were the lucky ones who survived. Nevertheless what remains very often is a continual undercurrent of residual guilt. Urban crime, unlike war or prison camps, does not usually call for quite the same desperate measures to ensure survival on the part of the victim. Nevertheless the crime victim is still forced to act in ways he or she may, on later reflection, find deeply disturbing. The trouble is that when 'wartime' behaviour is reviewed under 'peacetime' conditions the need to justify one's actions and rationalize feelings of fury and terror will continue until the victims have come to terms with their ordeal, and accepted that what occurred was inevitable and that they coped with the situation as best they could.

Blaming Other People

The temptation for victims to blame people other than the criminal himself for 'allowing' them to suffer is obviously great. Since the offender is usually not there to be held accountable for his cruelty the frustrated victim may start searching around for another suspect person or institution who might be next in line to take the rap. Blaming the police for not being around at the time the offence was committed or for arriving too late to catch the criminal is common amongst many survivors. People who are burgled may pin blame on the doorman or porter for not having maintained security. Suspicion may be directed at window cleaners or workmen engaged in repairs around the time of the break-in, burglaries may be seen as an inside job or workmen regarded as indirectly responsible for the crime because of their personal negligence. Those involved in street crime might blame pedestrians, drivers, shop keepers, neighbours or any individuals who witnessed the offence but did nothing either to stop the criminal or make sure he was apprehended.

The 'treason' of silence or complacency can prove inexplicable and therefore extremely hurtful to many victims to the point where they have little hesitation in condemning such silent witnesses as being accessories to the crime. Although the instinct to steer clear of dangerous or potentially dangerous situations is certainly natural enough for anyone who values their own safety, to the person being attacked non-involvement amounts to a callous indifference that is hard to comprehend. Yet can the uninvolved outsider who witnesses a violent scene yet does nothing to stop it be accused of indirectly contributing to that crime? If that outsider could have aided the victim promptly without directly endangering their own safety then the answer has to be yes. The way in which many perfectly rational and able-bodied adult men and women will frequently turn their backs on violent or suspicious goings on to avoid 'getting involved' when even a quick phone call to the police might prevent a crime from being carried out is indeed staggering.

The realization that people driving past in their cars had seen him being beaten up and flung bleeding into the gutter, lying there as if dead, was one of the most traumatic aspects of John Skinner's victimization.

> Me and my mate were asssaulted by four black men. We were hit and kicked to the floor repeatedly. When we were down they kept kicking me in the head. I passed out. When I woke up I was lying in the road. Cars were passing but no one had stopped. It was an ambulance that finally stopped and found us covered in blood. I think that was the worst thing about the whole incident. Knowing that a lot of cars had passed me by and I was lying in the gutter, I could have been dead but no one cared. The whole incident reminded me of the story of the Good Samaritan which in this case turned out to be the ambulance driver.

Victims who apportion blame to those who clearly could have helped them but didn't may often be largely justified. But again, such 'silent accomplices', usually faceless and anonymous, are unlikely to be around for long enough to allow the victim the satisfaction of unleashing his or her feelings in their direction. Attributing blame to others, especially if that blame is expressed in an openly abrasive or violent manner, can unfortunately rebound on the victim as they may become alienated and resentful at having to bear the brunt of the victim's rage.

Victims who blame the police or other witnesses are frequently uncooperative and they may find, for example, that the police are then unwilling to report the crime or track down the criminal. Neighbours, volunteers, hospital staff, even friends, if too long in the firing line of the victim's accusations, may themselves become hostile or simply beat a hasty retreat, leaving that person to vent his belligerence elsewhere. When the victims perceive this as rejection by the rest of society, even though it is in a sense self-generated, they may now experience 'second injury', which is described in the next chapter.

Although in some ways verbalizing one's anger openly may be a healthier reaction and possibly more cathartic than suppressing it, it can also prove counterproductive by reducing the amount of sympathy and support the victim's relatives and friends are prepared to offer. A survivor who assumes an attitude of penitent self-blame or a passive acceptance of what happened is likely to generate far more concern and pity than one who displays a more aggressive mood, especially when their accusations are un-justified or their reasons for blaming others largely irrational.

If there is no specific person or group of people to whom the victims attribute responsibility for the crime, they may blame instead certain social ills which they regard as a contributory factor in the rise in crime. Rising unemployment, drug abuse, violence in films and on TV, inner-city deprivation, inter-racial conflict, the decline in so-called traditional moral standards, abolition of corporal and capital punishment are just some of the familiar *bêtes noires* identified by many people as responsible for fostering a more violent environment. The problem with placing the blame for the ills which befall us on society generally is that as these things are almost completely beyond our control they only serve to reinforce most people's sense of personal helplessness. By drifting further into feelings of pessimism and discontent or moods of self-righteous indignation, victims may encounter impatience from those people who do not share their jaundiced view of the world, again running the risk of being driven into isolation.

A Man's World

The implications of having failed to triumph – or at least to hold one's own – in the face of adversity may be shattering to anyone with a normally robust ego, which is why men often tend to suffer greatly from lack of self-esteem after being victimized, resorting to self-blame, especially when reviewing their responses to an attack. Coping with the realization that they may not always be able to defend themselves or control their emotions is particularly tough for certain men. After all, the inability to assert yourself by using your fists amounts to a total antithesis of all that is regarded as desirably 'macho' by so many men. It could be argued that women in general are more familiar with feeling out of control at different times in their life and may even have past experiences of fear, vulnerability, and helplessness – even subjugation and exploitation – to draw on which helps them to deal with the trauma of victimization. Feminists cleave to the rather extreme proposition that we live in a society which designates all women as potential victims. When a woman is attacked therefore she is merely experiencing yet one more manifestation of masculine aggression within a fundamentally violent male-dominated society. Violent attacks by men on women merely reinforce the status quo of a patriarchy based on men's dominance and women's subordination.

Something of a spurious argument to be sure since it obviously fails to address not only the question of female aggression and why more women these days are committing crimes of violence but also why more *men*, especially those under twenty-five, become victims of crime. While no one would argue that women, being physically weaker than men, are a more easy target, the fact that young men, not women, statistically stand the greatest risk of being assaulted is hardly consistent with the thesis of how and why violence occurs as enshrined in feminist doctrine.

Real Men Do

As a result of the almost exclusive emphasis on distress suffered by female crime victims, especially those who have experienced sexual assault, by psychologists involved in researching victim trauma, remarkably little attention has been given until now to the existence of trauma amongst men. In fact there exists a widespread fallacy that men don't suffer, or if they do then probably not as much as women. This view is consistent with cultural myths such as 'real men don't cry' and 'men are not able to express emotion as women do'. Omnipotence is still regarded as the *sine qua non* of true masculinity. Founded as these ideas are on absurdly stereotypical images of men – as reductionist as those pertaining to women – they are at last beginning to shed much of their credibility as the roles traditionally assigned to men and women become less clearly circumscribed and more inter-changeable.

Unfortunately, for some of us, long held assumptions die hard. Therefore the ineluctable pressure on men to be strong, fight back and win, to 'prove themselves' by not giving in to fear, depression or feelings of vulnerability and self-doubt can still prove quite overwhelming. Early childhood conditioning which encourages a tendency not to express these feelings openly is hard to overcome, especially for those men who are not introspective by nature. Yet stoicism is a quality that is usually learnt, not inherent. Many men may not openly express or admit to a sense of guilt and self-blame, which is often just as great if not greater than that felt by women, and may be compounded by shame at having reacted to an attack in a certain allegedly inappropriate way, but there is no doubt that they experience these emotions.

Cult Heroes

After anger, self-blame is the most typical male reaction to being assaulted. Men's need to rationalize their feelings of fury, fear and helplessness or weakness is if anything greater than women's. The impulse that compels a man to castigate himself for having been forced into submission or incapacitated through terror will be particularly strong if his concept of himself embraces such traditional masculine traits as self-sufficiency, assertiveness, dominance and fearlessness. The more credence he gives to the validity of this stereotyped role the harder it is for a man to come to terms with having become a victim. Injured pride can devastate the often fragile male psyche bringing in its wake sexual problems, depression, tiredness, irritability, increased dependence on alcohol and drugs and a tendency to withdraw from friends, colleagues, partners, and other members of the family for fear of being judged weak and inadequate.

Belinda Manuelli and her fiance Bruno were both mugged at gunpoint on a New York street. For three months afterwards their relationship went through upheaval and strain.

> I was shaken by the attack but regained my confidence very quickly. But Bruno suffered terribly, he seemed to regard it as a test. He despaired over and over again at his inability to protect me in particular. Very soon afterwards he became impotent for many weeks and this only made him feel more wretched. Perhaps if he had been attacked alone and not in front of me he would not have felt as bad. It was as if the whole incident had brought his masculinity and his ability to protect me and stand up to danger into question.

The image of the invincible all powerful macho man as epitomized by cult heroes such as Sylvester Stallone and Clint Eastwood dies hard. Men who blame themselves for not having stood up to the attacker suffer longer and more severe bouts of self-punishment than women for whom being seen to remain in control, both literally and symbolically, may not be such a central issue. Sometime, as in the case of Michael Alderman, the event can lead to a complete re-evaluation of self-image.

> I'd always prided myself on having plenty of verbal and mental skills to get out of any potentially risky situation. But when a member of the public suddenly went berserk and attacked me out of the blue in the DHSS office where I was working I was unable to come to terms with my inability to protect myself. Then, some months later, I was injured by a letter bomb. Things simply weren't as I had visualized them. I mean, if you go into the army or the fire brigade you expect to get hurt but not if you are working in the Civil Service. How on earth could I have allowed it to happen? I kept asking myself. I had lots of depression I took a lot of time off work and went back but the fact that I knew it could happen again and that my workmates really weren't that concerned about what had happened made me feel desperately insecure. The bloodstains, my bloodstains were there in the carpet to remind me! In the end I decided I was simply in the wrong job. Once I'd realized I really did not have to prove myself to anybody or even to myself I was able to get on with starting a new life and decided to begin a new career as a psychotherapist.

When a man is attacked along with his family, wife or girlfriend – or indeed any other woman – or is forced to witness their assault without being able to step in and help, and he believes that he, as the stronger sex, should have protected them from harm, then his personal self-image is damaged. A sense of inadequacy mingled with bitterness and frustrated rage directed at himself for having failed in the role of protector adds up to an intensely humiliating experience. After Jonathan's wife was brutally raped when raiders broke into their home, his whole life seemed to fall apart. He lost all interest in sex, started drinking heavily, resigned from his job and developed chronic depression for which he had to undergo eighteen months' psychotherapy. He and his wife are now separated and Jonathan finds it very difficult to contemplate beginning another relationship because of his feelings of inadequacy.

> How on earth can anyone respect me or think I am a real man when I wasn't able to protect my wife and stop her from being raped? The other thing is that I cannot really come to terms with the fact that she was so calm and seemed to get on with her life again so quickly after

that ordeal. A lot of it was sheer self-will on her part, I know that she had problems but she was unable to talk about them openly with me so I feel even worse and more inadequate because I was not able to help her resolve her own personal crisis after the attack.

Having to look on powerless while a woman, often a wife or girlfriend, is raped is an ordeal few men survive without extreme anguish. It is little wonder, therefore, that even if only victimized by association, men who do not fight back or are unable to overpower or chase away the assailant may go on to experience a tremendous sense of inadequacy which can throw their entire life into turmoil. Married and family men whose homes are burgled also have a tendency towards long lasting anger and helplessness at this invasion of their personal territory. Because people who feel inadequate often tend to withdraw from others, even their partners and families, becoming moody, irritable, displaying uncharacteristically erratic behaviour, the resulting conflict within a marriage, for instance, may lead to future trauma even separation or divorce.

Sexual assaults on women also have a disturbing tendency to bring out the worst primitive sentiments in the men they live with. Men who subscribe to the old chauvinistic ethic that wives and girlfriends are a man's property may display a proprietary indignation that someone else has trespassed on their exclusive rights by 'taking their woman'. If a man holds the view that a woman is his property he may express anger that she is now 'devalued' by her experience, and has essentially become 'damaged merchandise'. Such grossly unenlightened male re-actions to women who have been raped will not only retard recovery but create stress and trauma within the relationship.

Male Rape – The Ultimate Humiliation

Although the number of men sexually assaulted each year is relatively low in comparison to the number of women the psychological aftereffects of being sexually attacked can turn out to be quite devastating. Sexual assaults on men commonly take the form of buggery, i.e. anal penetration. Appallingly, the law does not recognise enforced buggery as a serious crime equivalent to female rape, therefore there exist in law, no male rape victims. If the man is heterosexual he may experience severe doubts about his sexual identity, becoming impotent, ashamed, depressed and unable to form new relationships with women. If he has a particularly strong prejudice against homosexuals and feels intense revulsion for homosexual acts his feelings of disgust that his body was defiled and dirtied in a 'perverted' sexual act will be all the greater – perhaps even surpassing the revulsion felt by female rape victims. Concern about why he was picked out by the rapist is overlaid with guilt or anxiety that something about his appearance or behaviour perhaps gave the impression that he was weak, or – worse – that he was gay.

If he is bisexual, perhaps married with a family and his priority is to keep his homosexuality secret, self-blame may be fed by anxiety that his proclivities may become known. Another over-riding fear is often that word about the incident will get around the work environment, vitiating his professional image and causing his position to be directly or indirectly undermined. Self-blame and guilt at having been sexually assaulted may alter the entire nature of his relationships with other men especially if a macho, anti-gay ethos predominates within his immediate milieu. Particularly hard to come to terms with is the self-hatred and emasculating shame felt by men who submitted to violation through terror of being killed.

Like women, men who have been sexually assaulted often do not tell their partners, be they male or female, because they are afraid that the other person will endorse their own attributions of self-blame. Male rape victims become, if anything, more isolated than their female counterparts, thus experiencing more long-term symptoms associated with guilt.

Fuelled by the widespread prejudice and discrimination against homosexuals still rampant in many areas of society, gay men run a particularly high risk of being ostracized by the non-gay community, something which perpetuates the tendency towards self-blame. Society's bias against gays thus generates in male victims well-founded sentiments of either self-pity or defensive rage. Deemed by many to be 'abnormal' or 'sexually degenerate' it is implied that gay men who get assaulted are merely getting what they deserve or, in the case of rape, what they were probably asking for. Sad to say, like AIDS, attacks on homosexual men are often regarded as a form of retributive justice against individuals who lead what many believe to be fundamentally unnatural lifestyles. Says Fred Shortcross, who was nearly killed when an attacker beat him up with a lead pipe:

> I know there is a tendency for victims to feel that everyone is against them but it is not just paranoia – much of it really is true. Most victims I have spoken to since I became a counsellor after the crime in which I was attacked realize the tremendous lack of real compassion or understanding from non-victims in society. If an ordinary straight

man or woman gets victimized it's bad enough, but if a homosexual like myself gets beaten up the reaction in general tends to be so what, so the gay guy got beat up. Too bad they didn't get him. They are all good-for-nothing perverts anyway. Even if people don't say so openly deep down that's the instinctive attitude of most people to gays who are in trouble.

Gay men who are assaulted therefore do have particular cause for bitterness and self-blame, especially when they do not lead an overtly promiscuous, thus inherently riskier, lifestyle and cannot associate the attack with their own provocative or careless behaviour.

Identifying with the Criminal

Although the great majority of victims of attacks by strangers are far too outraged and hurt to think of their assailant in any terms other than evil, immoral, cruel and possibly mentally deranged, a minority will try to explain his actions by trying to analyse what sort of person he might be. People who have been kidnapped and held hostage over long periods of time are particularly prone to develop feelings of sympathy and allegiance towards their captors. Victims in such an extreme state of learnt helplessness must inevitably undergo a period of counselling in order to regain a proper perspective of events. Most victims of everyday urban crime thankfully do not have the opportunity to build up a relationship with the criminal. Often they may not even see his face. But some will be tempted to speculate on his motives and relate these to his social background. While the initial instinct might be to praise such a reaction as altruistic, identification represents yet another, albeit less common, example of the ways in which we are driven to rationalize our overwhelmingly distressing emotions and to make sense of something which is fundamentally senseless.

Saying to yourself 'he probably comes from a broken home', 'he lacked love as a child and rapes women because he can't form relationships', 'he must be very poor', 'he has been forced to steal because of the injustices of society', 'it's the penal system, it doesn't succeed in re-educating criminals' are all plausible concepts which may illuminate the pathology of criminal behaviour generally but can neither explain nor exonerate individual crimes. For with the exception of those who commit a tiny minority of murders, robberies and sexual assaults, few criminals operate according to a ruthless design. Random stranger attacks on property or person or both are frequently opportunistic rather than premeditated. To the average mugger or thief casually on the prowl, or even the drug addict desperate for money to secure his next fix, almost any individual may be singled out as fair game. Furthermore, the 'spoils' of any such random attack cannot be predetermined by the criminal, as attested by the numbers of people often brutally attacked when in possession of mere trifling sums of money or valuables. Crimes committed 'on spec' ultimately defy rationalization, and thus will fail to yield an answer to the perennial question why me? The danger of sparing too much thought trying to create a framework for the criminal's actions when these lack any clearcut objective, is that it deflects anger away from the attacker and sublimates it into orderly logic allowing the victims to believe they have gained mastery over a distressing situation.

Anger, when perpetually unacknowledged and undischarged, has a disturbing way of re-emerging months or years later. The problem about this sort of delayed or residual anger is that it becomes much harder to identify and express once the original cause has slipped so far into the past. When individuals examine what causes their anger or indeed their depression, they often uncover a number of anxiety-mechanisms that perpetuate these feelings. If you feel intensely angry because being attacked made you feel helpless, inadequate and fearful about your future safety or undermined your feelings of self-confidence and pride then not only is it important to express that anger openly but just as important is the ability to acknowledge the underlying loss of self esteem that feeds that anger.

By forcing the victims to come to terms with aspects of their behaviour or character they may find hard to accept, the aftermath of the crime can prove more distressing sometimes than the crime itself. It is this 'Crisis of Self' that often complicates the road to recovery from victim trauma. Very few people can accomplish the job of rebuilding their lives entirely on their own. Yet at a time when victims need all the help they can get the sad irony is that they sometimes encounter forces which may delay or even militate against that recovery.

6

The Second Injury

It would be unrealistic to expect the victim's troubles to end when the crime is over. Their lives are frequently in a state of upheaval, their emotions almost certainly thrown into turmoil. Indeed, for many, far from getting better, things may steadily get worse. In some cases the hours and days following the attack may turn out to be a protracted nightmare, where instead of the spontaneous and unconditional support the victims expect – and desperately needs – to diminish their distress, they encounter instead incomprehension, disapprobation, uninterest and allegations, open or covert, that they themselves might have caused or avoided the crime. If the victims were physically unharmed they may face insinuations that the event was not so serious and that they are over-reacting. Add to this the frustrations of having to put up with the bureaucratic red tape which surrounds the beleagured health, social and police services and the courts not to mention the dilatory off-hand approach displayed by many representatives of these vast government institutions and you start to have a fairly vivid picture of the elements that contribute to what psychiatrist Dr Martin Symonds has termed the second injury.

The sense of being victimized all over again through having to relive the past trauma often first occurs when the victim is asked to make a statement to the police and perhaps to identify the offender. The style of police questioning, especially if hostile, overly-detached or tinged with suspicion, triggers fresh feelings of humiliation, rage or helplessness in the victim. Rape survivors who agree to undergo an internal examination in order to provide forensic evidence may find the experience repulsive and akin to another violation.

Months later, when the victim is just beginning to emerge from the trauma, the second injury caused by having to give evidence in court, undergo vigorous cross-examination and face the attacker once again in court while re-experiencing the full horror of the crime may significantly retard the entire process of recovery. It is therefore easy to understand why so many crimes, even those of an extremely vicious nature, are often unreported.

Real or Imaginary?

Second injury may be sustained on many different levels since the effects can register both consciously and unconsciously and can be perpetrated unwittingly through sheer lack of understanding of what effects a violent incident can have on the individual. Anyone who comes into contact with the victim, from close relatives, neighbours and work colleagues to the police, doctors, nurses, lawyers, trades' people and public service personnel, may inflict secondary injury, especially if they themselves have had no previous experience of being a crime victim.

However, up to a certain point, second injury may be what the victim perceives it to be. As defined by Dr Martin Symonds, second injury is essentially a perceived rejection and lack of expected support from society to an individual who has been injured or victimized. The phenomenon is also experienced by patients who are severely ill or have undergone extensive surgery and must remain in hospital for long periods. Stripped of resources, emotionally raw and therefore more sensitive to other people's attitudes than possibly at any other time in their life, the victims have entered an altered state of consciousness where gut emotions override rationality. The weight victims attach to other people's comments, the value attributed to their actions and the extent to which they are prepared to give credence to uninformed opinion, for want of a balanced perspective of their role in the crime, makes them an open target for even the most veiled and oblique criticism from other people. Does this mean therefore that the second injury is primarily in the mind, a fabrication of paranoid fears or deep personal insecurity?

Far from it. The needs of victims are indeed very real and pressing. Foremost among these is the need to seek reassurance from others that they are now out of danger, that they did not precipitate the attack, and that they did all they humanly could under the circumstances to handle the situation well. The search if not for approval then at least for assurance that they did nothing wrong consistently underlies the victims' drive to reduce their scary feelings of helplessness and restore the self-respect and confidence that have taken such a battering as a result of the crime. The rebuilding of this confidence depends on the efforts of both the victim and those with whom he or she comes into contact. The tragedy is that the reactions of other people, especially those with little or no knowledge of victim trauma, instead of providing a much-needed safety net to break the downward fall of the victim's morale often either initiate feelings of guilt or confirm the victim's existing impulse towards doubt or self-blame.

As we have seen, victims readily subscribe to the theory that they are responsible for what occurred, therefore making things tough on themselves. Other people, by drawing false inferences, can make it tougher still. No matter how innocent or well-intentioned, comments like 'why didn't you take a taxi since it was so late at night', 'didn't you know it was a dodgy area', 'surely you must have realized the danger', 'wasn't the door locked', 'what were you doing in that part of town alone after dark', 'why did you accept his lift', 'what made you use the underground ', 'why didn't you scream', and dozens of others reveal many people's thoughtlessness and their inability to empathize with the crime victim's dilemma.

To make matters worse, questions such as these imply that the victims could have prevented their injuries. To be sure, as outsiders with a broader perspective of a violent incident we may well see how a person's impulsiveness or lack of caution increases the risk of becoming a victim. In the fullness of time, having recovered from the trauma, the victims will no doubt also be able to recognize this and decide whether they can reduce the risk of becoming a victim in the future. Now, however, is not the time to encourage this train of thought. However, just like the victim, his friends and relatives, unable to come to terms with the senselessness of an arbitrary attack, are often compelled to formulate their own putative theory as to what happened and why. The simplest explanation therefore is that by acting in a certain way the victim caused the criminal to commit the offence. Such a conclusion is invariably the end result of a totally misguided line of reasoning. It also demonstrates a marked reluctance to accept the role played by accident and chance in our lives. When it comes to sudden random violence the concept of the victims being in some way the author of their own misfortunes seems entirely nonsensical. Yet by a strange quirk of moral judgement society may succeed in making many victims feel that it is they rather than the criminal who must answer for the crime. Says Alexandra Campbell:

Someone suggested my screaming could have provoked them to knife me. Someone else pointed out I had chosen to live in a high risk area. I felt certain people were looking in my direction for an explanation.

It is extremely difficult to ignore this basic subtext of the second injury. Nowhere is this more aptly illustrated than in the courtroom, where the defendant, after all, is innocent until proved guilty. In trials involving crimes of rape or sexual assault in particular the entire outcome of the case rests on the ability of the witness-victim to establish their own innocence and truthfulness in order to prove the attacker's guilt. Not surprisingly one might be forgiven for wondering who actually is the person on trial, the criminal or his victim. To this day the law on rape still requires judges to warn juries of the danger of convicting on the victim's uncorroborated evidence alone, on the underlying premise that women are prone to lie.

Someone Must Be To Blame

An essential component of secondary injury is undoubtedly blaming the victim. For non-victims to admit the victim was blameless is in a sense tantamount to acknowledging that the event could just as easily have happened to them. Rather than face this fact non-victims usually bolster their own feelings of security by attributing blame to the victim. Moira, a public relations consultant, was mugged at knifepoint when cycling across a bridge linking a very poor area of Manhattan to a more surburban and affluent area of up-state New York.

People asked me almost accusingly what I was doing using that route to get over from the city. The implication was that it was all my fault that I chose to drive briefly through a supposedly risky area on my way over. The point is first of all that this was the quickest route. The others would have taken me over an hour longer. Secondly many people travel by that route daily and nothing happens to them so where is the logic in that line of questioning? My hobby happens to be power cycling and there were some people who even suggested that this was a dangerous sport for a woman to take up and I should not be cycling alone in certain sections of the city. The idea is totally preposterous. A man friend of mine was beaten up when coming out of the side entrance of the Plaza Hotel just as he was about to step into a waiting taxi. Now, are you going to say that he shouldn't have been in that place at that time?

The Myth of Control

The premise that the victims are capable of sound judgement and fast physical reflexes just before or during the attack commonly leads to criticism of the way in which they reacted. The fact that many victims are utterly immobilized by fear escapes the comprehension of large numbers of people, especially those who are unaware of the ways in which stress can diminish physical responses and control. Vicky, who was attacked late at night in a car park by two men who forced her into a nearby alleyway and raped her, was struck by the inability of even her women friends to accept that she couldn't scream.

> They kept asking me why I hadn't shouted and yelled, then someone would have come to help or the men would have been scared off. They couldn't understand that I had no voice. From the moment they grabbed me until after the rape it dissolved away. I opened my mouth but no sound came out. I had a dry mouth, no saliva, so even swallowing was difficult. People just don't think of these things. And in any case if I had screamed who says anyone would have helped me? People usually don't want to know if someone else is in trouble. The men might even have beaten me up or killed me.

Blaming the victim directly or indirectly for not having reacted appropriately adds gross insult to an already massive emotional injury at a time when that person is virtually devoid of resources necessary to rebut any allegations that they might have been responsible. Outsiders tend to assign the role of victim to certain people because of their behaviour, lifestyle or past history. This is a far more insidious form of victim blaming, implying that the 'victim personality' seeks out situations and circumstances, albeit unconsciously, that may lead to negative or damaging consequences in order to reinforce their own poor opinion of themselves. One of the most common theories of criminology is that of victim-precipitated crime, which rests on the premise that some people habitually seek out violent and dangerous situations whether knowingly or unknowingly. Speculations and theories put across by the friends and acquaintances of victims reveal the prevalence of this attitude.

> There you are, you see, she lives in a notorious high-crime area and didn't have proper bars and locks on her windows. Why is it you always hear of these terrible things happening to people in these run-down areas? As a single woman I simply wouldn't live in that part of town.

This was one typical response from a woman on hearing how a

friend living in a so-called high-crime area in south London had been woken up in the middle of the night by thugs who proceeded to stab and beat her up. 'How could he be so stupid as to walk around a city like New York with so much money? No wonder he was mugged,' was the response of one elderly English lady on hearing that her daughter's boyfriend had become a crime victim.

The speciousness of this argument is particularly obvious for two reasons. First, the mugger has no way of knowing whether his victim is carrying a lot of cash or indeed any cash at all. Muggers the world over will attack people largely on spec, getting away with anything from vast sums of money to a few pence or no money at all. Second there exists an unwritten rule in cities such as New York where crime rates are high that you are safer carrying some money in order to placate the attacker and send him on his way rather than risking his wrath by having nothing to hand over at all.

Says Timothy, an English photographer now living in New York:

> On New Years' Eve I was approached by three black men in New York who pulled knives and demanded I hand over everything. I was extremely worried at having only a few dollars. These guys looked really mean. They weren't messing about. They kept asking me to hand over more until they were satisfied I wasn't hiding any extra cash. They took my watch and my rings, my gold pen – the lot.

Asking For It

When women are attacked the implication is often that their dress or behaviour in some way attracted the criminal. Moira is extremely tall and very pretty and was recently hit in the face by a man as she stood in a busy street waiting to meet a friend in the middle of the day.

> Later my work colleagues said to me quite seriously that it must have been because I was wearing white and therefore attracting attention to myself that this man hit me. What am I supposed to do? Just because I am very tall and attractive, purposely make myself look plain and unobtrusive?

Felicity, a very pretty outgoing white girl was attacked by two black girls and a man while out walking with her small son in the middle of the day in Portobello Road, a Bohemian part of London with a large ethnic community.

> They tried to ram me up against a wall with their car, cutting my legs badly, then the girls got out and started hitting me about the face. Then one said, 'She's got a little boy, let's leave her alone now,' and they left. I'm sure it was because I looked very attractive and perhaps quite well to do that day and they resented that. To my mind they attacked me out of sheer frustration and resentment that they didn't have the material things they thought I had.

Later, having heard about the attack, one of Felicity's neighbours commented:

> I bet she was all dolled up like a tart and the local girls resented her trespassing on their patch. She was asking for it, especially a white girl walking in a largely black community.

Another neighbour said:

> She goes about with a smile on her face and a bouncy walk, no wonder she gets attacked. People must think her a pushover and I suppose a lot of men think she's on the game.

Felicity's response?

> I've been told I should dress down, not wear short skirts, smile less, appear to be less extrovert and friendly. But I don't buy that. Yes, maybe that's partly why I stood out, but that's not why I was attacked. I dress up a lot and usually people smile and are friendly back. I don't have any problems. Those sort of people, the criminals, just resent anyone who has something they want and can't have.

The Great Divide

Apart from an inbuilt need, born out of our own insecurities, to construct theories which fit the crime there are other underlying attitudes to victims which can divert our compassion away from their plight. One of these is the primitive fear of contamination by the victim. This concept is not quite as silly as it sounds. After all, what do we mean by the word victim? For good reason, increasing numbers of victim-counselling and self-help groups have stressed a preference for the word 'survivor', semantically more positive than victim which has numerous negative connotations.

The word comes down to us invested with centuries-worth of taboo and contempt. Its etymological roots lie in the ancient sacrificial rite or religious ceremony of expiation. Hence it derives from the concept of the scapegoat, an animal or person symbolically made to carry the burden of all the misdeeds of the rest of the community, thereby protecting them by appeasing the gods' desire for retribution. Traditionally the human victim was someone with no roots in the community; either a young virgin or a stranger. Even to this day the word victim evokes a sense of unease, a feeling of pity tinged with contempt. This primitive response leads us to isolate or exclude the victim, because he or she is regarded in some way as bearing a 'stigma'.

There is a tendency, no matter how deeply someone may commiserate with the misfortune, to look on the victim as a person who is branded as a 'loser'. In feeling sorry for the victim we acknowledge that he or she was forced to submit to the superior strength, conniving and ruthlessness of the criminal. By imputing apparently negative qualities to the victim – loss, submission, humiliation, fear, weakness and helplessness – and positive ones to the criminal – strength, speed, aggression and dominance – some people quite unconsciously may even develop a certain sneaking admiration for the criminal persona while harbouring feelings of scorn for that of the victim.

For confirmation of this poor image of the victim in society one need only look at the modern anti-hero glorified on film and TV, often a vicious gangster, mafioso or urban crook who remains unashamedly uncontrite up to the final reel. The tendency is for our culture to invest certain criminals with an aura of glamour – just think of the Kray brothers, Ronald Biggs or Bonnie and Clyde – and to interpret their crimes as breathtaking daredevil feats of bravura. As a result of this social labelling of winners and losers there is a tendency shared by many, if not directly to shun the company of the crime victims, then at best regard them as objects of pity or deny the validity of their experience because it makes for feelings of unease and insecurity.

Pity is the last sentiment the victims either want or need at a time when they are trying to restore damaged pride and a fragile ego. The tendency for victims to feel like pariahs, outcast by society because they were singled out as the recipient of misfortune, is one of the most insidious effects of second injury. Even animals and young children display this tendency to isolate and exclude the unlucky individual. When an animal who was part of a herd is attacked the others will usually withdraw, leaving the victim an outcast destined to suffer or die alone. Teachers in primary schools often express surprise and dis-appointment at their pupils' responses to the misfortune of a classmate such as a death or illness in the family, or divorce. The child will frequently be ignored, teased and sometimes even struck by classmates who make his or her life a misery. It is as if the other children fear contamination by the tragic event and therefore try to isolate or exclude the victim. This attitude, observes Dr Martin Symonds, causes the victim to feel isolated and helpless and to experience the world as hostile. The victim of crime is therefore often destined to become a victim of society too. In this instance the biggest impediment to recovery can be caused by guilt – the guilt felt by the victim simply at having become a victim.

Get Well Soon

When disaster strikes what else could be more natural than to turn for support and comfort to one's friends and relatives? If those who know us and care for us most cannot be counted upon to offer unconditional support and be trusted not to pass judgement on our fate then who else on earth can? Certainly in the majority of cases, the succour of partners, parents, close relatives and friends is integral in diminishing the severest symptoms of distress suffered by the victim in the period immediately following the crime. However, many individuals soon find that the amount of time and understanding others are capable of giving may prove surprisingly limited. Among relatives and friends there is a disturbing tendency for a victim's responses to the crime – the actual phenomenon of victim trauma syndrome – to be either misunderstood or even ignored. When someone breaks a leg, or has an attack of pneumonia or glandular fever, there is usually a very clear directive passed on by doctors to the patient's family and friends as to the effects of that condition. You would hardly expect someone with a broken leg to start walking about, let alone run up and down stairs. But in the case of victim trauma no such directive exists since there is often a complete absence of awareness that emotional injury has taken place.

Alexandra Campbell was staggered to discover that victim trauma, a phenomenon she was familiar with through living in America, is not recognized in British medical practice.

You do meet the odd enlightened policeman or doctor but this is certainly the exception. Six months after the attack I felt as if I had recovered from a major illness. The only difference there lay in the inability of other people to recognize the nature and the effects of that illness. Anyone who had experienced a life-threatening trauma like a car accident or a major illness on who had suffered the shock of a sudden bereavement was, I found, far more able to respond to my anguish than anyone else. Surely, like any other illness, it is time that victim recovery was examined scientifically. There has been virtually no research, especially in this country, on how best to recover psychologically from a violent attack.

Lack of family support, in particular the sort of unconditional and on-going help the victims now need to aid their recovery, is one of the most devastating manifestations of second injury. At a pinch one can cope with dismissiveness or impatience, say, from the police – indeed many victims may expect as much when they report a crime – but not from those who are close. In the first few days and weeks following a violent crime it is highly unusual for most relatives and intimate friends not to express concern for the victim, to listen patiently and attentively to their constant retelling of the event and to provide a sounding board for their fears and self-doubt. When that person has been physically injured, for as long as there is evidence in the form of bruises, cuts, scars, swelling or disability, there also remains a reminder of the trauma they had to endure. But in the case of someone who was not physically hurt the event, in the minds of the co-victims, soon recedes into oblivion.

Emotional scars being invariably harder to identify than physical ones, the fewer the victim's external wounds the more limited other people's capacity to understand the nature of the trauma or to allow for an indefinite recovery period. People's memories are incredibly short. If the crime was not reported or no charges are made then the victim and those around them cannot even depend on the occasional phone call or court appearance to jog the memory. Consequently, after the initial emotional furore over the crisis, the victim faces an inevitable anti-climax, caught up in a vacuum of intense isolation and expected to resume everyday life as if nothing had happened. As time passes wholehearted support for the victims and the tendency for others to focus attention on their plight begins to diminish, becoming steadily less consistent. Non-victims all tend to carry in their minds an optimum recovery period, expecting the victim to get better according to their schedule. Shelley Neiderbach was the victim of two attacks, the first one involving physical injury, the second in which she was physically unhurt.

> I got far more attention and sympathy from people around me after the first mugging when I was beaten up with a gun and had to have forty-five stitches in my head. The second time when I also thought my life was in danger but the muggers did not attack me, what I got pretty soon was, 'Come on now, you should be getting over this by now. After all you weren't hurt, you are perfectly safe, be thankful you are alive that you weren't beaten up.'

Fred Shortcross, who was severely injured and nearly died as a result of being attacked, agrees.

> The three operations, the transfusion, the weeks and weeks of hospitalization I had to endure were in some ways far less distressing than the long-term aftermath which persisted long after my wounds had healed. This sense that you should be grateful to be alive, that you should pull up your socks and get on with living again, stop dwelling on the past and put all these terrible events behind you, just makes you feel more furious and resentful with everybody around. Because no one really wants to know or listen to your problems you end up bottling them all up inside.

After being raped by six men Sandy Greene found it impossible to gain the support and understanding she needed long after the incident was over.

> Once a certain amount of time has passed there aren't really that many people who are going to want to listen to your fears and problems. What makes it worse is that they themselves often get embarrassed or if they are close to you they get terribly upset, so then you're the one who ends up feeling guilty and having to comfort them. When this happened to me I ended up feeling guilty about my reactions and not speaking about my problems for fear of upsetting the other person.

So, at a time when the victim is just beginning to face the real nitty-gritty of their problem – how to rebuild trust in others and belief in themselves – friends and family may begin to show less inclination to listen to them or start to show ill-concealed signs of boredom or impatience. At this point they may be tempted to imply that the victim is overreacting or displaying an abnormal amount of trauma. Not surprisingly, such responses are usually guaranteed to isolate the victim still further and make them retreat mistrustingly into their own world. The onset of phobic avoidance behaviour, panic attacks and related psychosomatic illnesses, dependence on alcohol or other drugs, and the development of sexual disorders in women who were raped may coincide with this severence of essential helplines by family and friends.

Victims who have denied their negative feelings and perhaps outwardly given the impression of being untraumatized by events may feel forced at this late point to maintain the façade, and go on pretending they are perfectly all right. Early on after an attack has occurred, there is a very real desire in some victims to forget about the event and put their unhappiness behind them. Having displayed an initial reluctance to talk about their feelings and problems they may, however, encounter severe difficulties if they subsequently feel the need to express their feelings and thoughts about what happened. Those individuals who experience delayed trauma or a resurgence of earlier symptoms that had seemingly disappeared may incur impatience or alarm in those around them who had long consigned the entire episode to the past. Ignorance about the time lapses that characterize victim trauma, the phenomenon of delayed reaction, early denial and the tendency for many victims to suffer in silence because they feel no one understands or fear that their reactions may be abnormal, are the chief causes of secondary injury.

In certain cases, the bizarre situation may arise where someone close to the victim, usually a parent, partner or child, appears so upset by the incident that the victims feel forced to suppress their own feelings and refrain from discussing the event in order not to upset that relative. In this case victims may take on an intolerable extra burden of stress which invariably retards their full recovery. It is not uncommon for non-victims to feel 'ambushed' by the strong emotions and behaviour of the victim in distress and then project their own negative reaction back onto the victim when he or she can least withstand the pressure.

Knowing What's Good For You

Second injury may take on even more subtle and insidious forms, for instance where family or friends become overly-presumptuous and project their own subjective impressions of victim trauma onto the victim. In cases where the victims genuinely do not wish to discuss their feelings or past events, well meaning relatives can press them to 'open up' or 'let it out' even when this clearly creates distress. Husbands or boyfriends of rape victims may pressure them too soon or too insistently to resume sexual relations in the misguided belief that this will help them get over their distress. What this often achieves is merely a decline into sexual dysfunction. Victims who want to be alone may find themselves cajoled by well intentioned friends into social activities and when they decline they cause offence. In an attempt to 'make sure this never happens to you again' friends or family members may exhort the victim to move house, take self-defence classes, buy a burglar alarm or a dog, thus increasing their sense of fear and vulnerability even further.

Striking a balance between invasive do-gooding behaviour and detached non-intervention is the hardest challenge facing co-victims. Getting it right depends very much on remaining sensitively attuned to the victims' moods, words, requests and general behaviour without attempting to superimpose one's own interpretation of their needs and desires. Trying to tell victims what is good for them, or how they should behave, is simply another facet of victim blaming, based on an implicit assumption that they are not in control. Low in self-esteem and well aware that they are still vulnerable, this is the last thing that the victims need. Being told what's good for you smacks as much of moral judgement as open criticism and can only serve to augment the victims' existing feeling that they may be responsible for the mess that they are in.

A Friend Indeed

At the other end of the spectrum there exists a nucleus of victims, thankfully small, for whom the prospect of obtaining any form of understanding and support is bleak indeed. Often very old or very young, they may be recent immigrants or foreign visitors living far away from their families and friends, or people who are unmarried and live alone with no immediate family and few close friends who now find themselves entirely isolated, unable to find anyone willing to listen to their problems.

Mentioning their distress either to colleagues at work or to casual and new acquaintances may at worst provoke frank censure – 'well, no wonder you were attacked, you asked for it travelling alone at that time of night' – confusion and embarrassment – 'oh dear, I am the wrong person to talk to, I'm hopeless when someone is in a crisis' – or blatant incomprehension – 'but surely you must be thankful you weren't injured'. At best the victim may be met with polite indifference – 'can we talk about this later? I'm terribly busy right now' – or failure to grasp the point that all the victim is seeking is a sympathetic ear – 'Have you been to see your doctor? He might be able to give you pills to make you feel better. You won't do anything silly will you? I've got the number of the Samaritans if you want it.'

Remarks such as these are indicative of the inability and the unwillingness of many a non-victim to get inside someone else's skin. The buttoned-up, cavalier attitude displayed by many individuals when confronted with someone else's emotional distress illustrates how effectively we insulate ourselves against tragedies that do not directly concern us. Open expression of feeling and the instinct to maintain a controlled front are mutually incompatible and, for many, reserve always wins by seeming a safer bet. Non-involvement serves as a first-rate defence mechanism. Some would argue that this instinct to shrink from any open display of emotion – one's own or anyone else's – is endemic amongst the population of Northern European countries and Britain in particular: the British pride themselves on their stoic stiff upper lip and acceptance of adversity, an attitude completely antithetical to the spontaneous expression of emotion characteristic of, say, the Spanish and Italians.

By and large we do not really want to become too deeply involved in other people's unhappiness because when it comes to the crunch, many of us really don't know how to cope, how best to handle someone else's fear, anger, self-doubt and guilt. The distress of victimization, like the pain of bereavement, has a way of provoking in many people intense embarrassment or confusion. The reasons for this are numerous but fairly straightforward. Most of us feel at heart we really should be able to help those in need. All our instincts make us want to express our sympathy and understanding but, unless we know that person well, we frequently hesitate, not really sure if we should intrude on their grief, usually feeling inadequate and unsure of how to help, terrified lest we commit a *faux pas*. Instead, we make matters worse by saying nothing and turning away. Communicating openly and honestly about other people's feelings as well as our own seems to be by far the most elusive of human skills. Emotional openness and the ability to empathize are gifts not shared by many.

Intense and distressing emotion in others can prove highly distressing for ourselves. Someone else's anger, despair, panic, or depression may trigger similar feelings within ourselves, forcing us to face personal conflict or remember situations we prefer not to acknowledge. Not getting involved is one way of ensuring you yourself don't get ambushed by upsetting memories and feelings. Emotive issues such as death, divorce, violence, terminal illness, loneliness, ageing and victimization touch all of us whether directly or by association, yet these are subjects that nevertheless for many people remain taboo. Someone who experiences conflicting feelings about their own vulnerability, mortality or self-esteem is therefore far from the ideal person to assuage similar concerns in others.

One must remember that someone who has never had a brush with violence often cannot fully comprehend the apparent complexity of a victim's distress or identify his immediate needs. In fact there is little mystique attached to victim trauma, and little expertise is required to alleviate the plight of victims.

What most survivors need is simply to obtain unqualified approval – no holds barred – to feel and act the way they do without having to explain, excuse or justify themselves. What they are searching for is often a tacit validation of their recent experience, a legitimization of their present distress. Expecting a friend, colleague or relative who has been victimized to deny his problems or recover rapidly is in effect to diminish the significance of what he has been through. Negation by others of the significance of what occurred amounts to a hefty secondary injury. Because of their insecurity they very often need the reassurance of knowing that others accept their present dilemma as a normal part of the trauma.

Unfortunately, to most outsiders this seems almost too absurdly simple by far. Surely, we say to ourselves, there must be more we can do, something calculated to make that person feel better, more cheerful and optimistic, make them forget the past and pull themselves out of their misery? Yet in most cases the cathartic experience of talking it out, perhaps over and over again ad nauseam, to be allowed to cry, express panic, anger, apprehension, without interruption or criticism is deeply comforting in itself and protects the victim from experiencing secondary injury. Outsiders often make the mistaken assumption that, like the bereaved, victims don't want to talk about past events because it is too upsetting. At some time or another, even if not immediately the overwhelming desire is to talk.

Finally, there is no escaping from the fact that many of us often will shun a person who is in trouble because their ordeal may have evoked attitudes and behaviour that we find fundamentally anti-social and difficult to deal with. Aggressiveness, self-pity, depression, tearfulness, mistrust of others, and vengefulness are perfectly natural by-products of anxiety and fear which are almost always temporary. Yet for those individuals who are not given the opportunity to share these feelings, rejection comes as the *coup de grâce* which will prolong and intensify that reaction.

PART TWO

Rough Justice: Police, Courts and Compensation

7

The Right and Wrong Side
of the Law

In recent years the police in Britain, as in America and other European countries, have come increasingly under fire for being out of touch with the general public's everyday needs and expectations. Allegations of bias against women reporting sexual or domestic assault, discrimination against ethnic minorities, indifference to emotional distress, reluctance to pursue investigations or press charges typically illustrate what many regard to be the shortfall between the service we expect from the police and what we actually receive. A number of detailed surveys and studies published over the past few years have produced ample circumstantial evidence to sustain such allegations.

But are our expectations too high perhaps or is the police force today really in danger of losing touch with the most pressing concerns and needs of the community? The demise of that stereotyped folk hero, the friendly avuncular neighbourhood 'bobby' immortalized in the popular TV series *Dixon of Dock Green* during the 1950s and 60s is indicative of declining public confidence in the police force. We no longer automatically assume every policeman to have our best interests at heart or even regard him as the dependable custodian of our safety. Those days are vanishing fast, at any rate in the big cities. Sadly, in certain urban communities the rift and ill feeling between some sections of the population and the police is now such that police officers are regarded with hostility, as the potential foe rather than the trustworthy friend and ally.

For one thing, the police never seem to be around when you most need them. Victims of street crime understandably often regard police negligence as a contributory factor in the rise in crime. By their maintaining a higher visibility and patrolling in greater numbers while responding more promptly to calls for help, it is frequently argued, many random crimes of violence might never occur in the first place. Yet the increasingly high and complex workload, much of it time consuming administrative paperwork, now undertaken by police officers has drastically cut down on the amount of time a police constable can spend on the beat, patrolling the streets, pubs and parks to ensure public safety.

The rise in violence as evidenced by the recent wave of street riots, political demonstrations, militant secondary picketing during industrial strikes, football hooliganism has spawned a new, tough breed of police officer in the paramilitary mode. All brawn and aggressive killer instinct, the police constable of late twentieth century Britain, like his American counterpart, is being chosen, it seems, less for his sympathetic man-next-door demeanour as for his ruthless go-for-the-kill aggressiveness. Riot control and mastering the use of firearms rather than the ability to communicate are the new imperatives for survival in the all out battle being fought nowadays by the police against crime and public disorder. What is more it is a battle they sometimes appear in danger of losing as is shown by the poor clear-up rate that seems perpetually to lag behind as the rate of reported crime soars. This fact in itself hardly inspires public confidence in the ability of the police to apprehend offenders and provide protection against crime.

May The Force Be With You

In his zealous determination to combat the rise in crime more effectively, usually due to pressures from within the force and from the government, the new style macho cop is more intimidating, perhaps, than his less action oriented predecessors, a phenomenon which justifiably may foster a sense of unease in people asked to give a statement or to help solve a crime in which they were involved. Because of the pressing need of police forces throughout Britain to recruit more officers, the average age at which many policemen are forced, after a very short period of training and virtually no grass roots experience, to cope with major crimes and deal with victims *in extremis* is now often ludicrously low. Learning how to identify a victim's needs and being able to strike the right balance between an attitude of authority and one of sympathetic understanding takes experience of life in general as well as of law enforcement. In both areas the new police recruit is often a novice, and as a result of his inexperience may come across as officious and uncaring. On the other hand, older officers, just like doctors and nurses whose work brings them into constant contact with other people's suffering, may over the years, have been forced to cultivate deliberately a layer of emotional insulation in order to be able to function efficiently in their job.

The tendency of many doctors, health workers, lawyers and police officers to distance themselves from other people's unhappiness can in many cases make them appear callous, uninterested and even cruel figures of authority. In cases where the victim of a crime is extremely distressed and/or injured, this detached manner in a police officer who is perhaps simply unaccustomed to dealing with a full-blown case of victim trauma may be interpreted as out and out inhumanitarianism.

The way in which the victims perceive their experience of dealing with the police is also coloured by their preconceptions and previous attitudes towards the police generally. They may have found themselves on the wrong side of the Law in the past, or may simply base their views on anecdotal evidence – usually the reports of friends, relatives or neighbours who have had dealings with the police as well as TV and newspaper coverage of police activities. Distorted or sensationalist representation of police behaviour has in recent years contributed tremendously to the wave of anti-police feeling in certain countries. A person who is accustomed to reading reports of the unsympathetic cross-questioning by police of rape victims, for example, or the lack of interest taken in incidents of domestic violence is almost certainly going to feel a sense of surprised relief if the police officer they encounter turns out to be friendly and solicitous.

Whatever You Say

Researchers in recent years have concluded that the vast majority of victims in Britain are indeed satisfied with the way the police responded to their calls for help and subsequently handled the incident. However, some victims do experience a certain amount of frustration when they first call for help. Problems in communicating satisfactorily with the person taking the emergency call may be due to the fact that the victim is in such a state of panic that he cannot speak coherently or give precise details of the address at which the incident occurred. This can lead to confusion and delays and increase the victim's distress. People in extreme distress will often automatically call 999 for help rather than look up the number of their local police station. But victims often assume that 999 calls will get them through to the local police station, not realizing that they are in fact speaking to an operator sitting in a central control room often in a different city or area altogether. Identifying the exact location and referring calls to the appropriate police division may delay arrival of the police.

Other victims have complained of having to emphasize their distress as a means of making police appreciate the urgency of the situation, having to persuade the officer or operator taking the call to take the matter seriously and respond with speed. This may reflect obvious difficulties faced by police in certain areas who receive a high number of hoax calls or reports of so called serious incidents which turn out to be trivial. After the emergency call the victim may have to endure what appears to be a long wait, though police are usually very prompt in responding to calls for help, especially where a person has been physically attacked. However, even fifteen or twenty minutes can seem like an eternity to someone who has been injured and is scared or in a state of extreme shock and distress. Victims also understandably feel that any time wasted by the police in arriving makes it more likely that the criminal will get so far away from the scene of the crime that there will be no chance of ever tracing him or making an arrest.

Initial relief at the arrival of the police may soon give way to dismay or resentment that they are now not treating the matter seriously enough or putting sufficient effort into tracing and apprehending the offender. The victim's expression of distress is often interpreted by the listener, in this case the police, as a demand that something be done as well as criticism of the listener's failure to protect the victim. This is sufficient to strain relations between police and victim. In cases where the victim's distress manifests itself through aggressive behaviour the confrontation can become potentially explosive as the victim becomes increasingly vituperative and begins to shout, argue, and use abusive language, either cursing the attacker or inveighing against the police for their apparent inefficiency or slowness. Any defensive reaction by the police is likely to antagonize the victim even further. Not unnaturally, many police officers resent having to become, as they see it, scapegoats for the victim's wrath.

Dr Martin Symonds's position as chief psychiatric adviser to the New York City Police Force gives him a unique insight into both sides of the problem – that of the police and the victim. He points out that police officers often classify themselves quite justifiably as victims, unceremoniously 'dumped upon' by victims, witnesses, and criminals alike. The police officer who feels unfairly put upon by a disputatious victim who appears overly demanding and ungrateful may develop an inbuilt resentment against the system he works in. Comments from police officers about how they see their role in alleviating victims' distress indicates a tremendous divergence of opinion about the activities they are supposed to undertake.

> How can a victim give to a victim? We are only human beings trying to do a tough job. The public expects us to be superhuman.

> We have a duty to understand the special needs of victims and stop treating them just as witnesses. We owe it to them and to ourselves. That is the only way we can get the public to cooperate with us in fighting crime.

> This notion that we should perform a public service is a load of old rubbish. We don't have the time or resources. Our job is to fight crime and it is up to the victim to get emotional help from their church or doctor or the health services.

So great is the stress and emotional burnout suffered by police officers through the pressures of their increasingly burdensome role that more and more colleges have begun to include communication skills in both initial and advanced police training. Emphasis is on learning how to reassure the victims and neutralize or deflect their anger rather than react defensively. As Dr Symonds observes, ideally that first crucial encounter with the victim should take the form of a 'therapeutic interview' where the police make every effort not to challenge or contradict victims or witnesses especially if they are deeply distressed but offer them support, sympathy and understanding.

Recognition of the causes and symptoms of victim trauma syndrome makes up an important element of this training and helps officers become better equipped to offer support and understanding to victims at this vital early stage as well as avoiding any unnecessary future confrontation. The phenomenon of victim trauma syndrome is obviously particularly relevant in the case of sexual assault victims who on top of their existing distress may be apprehensive about having to relive the incident all over again while giving a statement and being examined by a police doctor. Having perhaps to refute allegations of personal blame or disbelief on the part of police officers comes as the final indignity. Victims of domestic violence, which may or may not also be sexual, face the discomfort of discovering that the police might refuse to take a great deal of interest in their case because it is judged as only a 'personal matter'.

Another intrinsic problem that must be faced by victims, especially in cases of domestic assault, is the very real risk of reprisal, in the form of a repeated attack by the criminal should he find out that the crime has been reported. In most cases of stranger attack the inability of some officers to reassure victims on this point or offer protection against possible retaliatory action can militate against victims making a statement or deciding to go ahead and help the police with their investigations. John Skinner's initial reaction after having been beaten up by four thugs and left for dead in the gutter was to simply go home and forget all about it.

> My main fear was that they might retaliate but my friend who'd been beaten up with me insisted that we ought to make a statement. As it turns out we didn't have much choice. We were in hospital being examined and the hospital had already alerted the police who in fact had caught the men they thought were our attackers. I still didn't want to go to the police station and make a statement. I was scared about doing that and I just didn't want any more to do with the incident. It was 1 o'clock in the morning, I really wasn't in a fit state for it, but they said that we must come along tonight and make a statement. Having caught the chaps they really were keen to do them. Anyway, it turned out not to be as bad as I'd expected. The police were on our side. They were very kind and helpful especially when we had to make our statement. If they hadn't been so cooperative I certainly wouldn't have stuck around trying to help them out.

Michael Alderman, on the other hand, after having been attacked by a man who suddenly went berserk in the office where he was working, came up against frustrations and difficulties both from hospital staff and police.

> The police first of all wanted a statement from me before the ambulance had even arrived. My attacker had got away by then, my face was bleeding profusely, my nose had been smashed in. When I got to hospital they kept me waiting endlessly, then they lost my file and on top of all that they weren't particularly sympathetic about my condition. I then discovered that the police didn't want to prosecute. I couldn't understand that. It seemed they couldn't be bothered, that there was too much important other work to do. I had to make a point of pressing the local policeman on my beat into following up the case. It was such an uphill exhausting process, especially after what I had just gone through, having to fight and fight to try and get justice. I think you've really got to believe in the importance of justice being done to persevere and stick with the system and not be put off by the set-backs. Because I was on such good terms with my local bobby he did end up making sure that charges were pressed.

When the victim does encounter a sympathetic police attitude it is often regarded as integral in reducing the impact of the crisis as well as aiding a speedier recovery. Says Alexandra Campbell:

> The police were terribly worried about me and obviously upset at what had happened. One officer came back later that day after I'd made my full statement because he said he was so worried that I'd seemed so calm. He obviously knew I was in a state of shock and was worried about what would happen when I came out of it. They couldn't have been nicer or more helpful. Unfortunately they never found my attackers. However, I must say that if the case was to be reopened or anything else, God forbid, should ever happen to me where I had to deal with the police I would have no qualms about cooperating and seeking their assistance.

Making A Statement

Several aspects of the crime's aftermath are directly dependent on the first encounter between the victim and the police. The quality of the relationship between victim and police officers will often determine whether the police take the offence seriously enough to record it as an official crime and pursue further investigations and whether the victim agrees to make a statement and, if necessary, act as a witness and appear in court. An unfriendly or offhand attitude by police at this stage can make the victim want to have no further dealings with the law. Undue pressure by police on the victim to make a statement, or to dictate how that statement is worded can add further to their distress and confusion. Too rapid and aggressive questioning about the details of the crime is antithetical to the victim's expectations of comfort and reassurance.

If the victim is willing to make a statement it follows that he or she should want to feel satisfied that the account taken down by the police is accurate and complete. Giving a muddled, unclear or incomplete statement either because the victim is injured, very upset or quite simply exhausted by the experience is likely to add to later feelings of frustration and guilt. In their determination and zeal to nail the criminal, some police officers will often try to rush victims into making a statement and some victims tend to complain that words are being put into their mouth or that their statement is embellished or uncharacteristically phrased.

It is not widely known that as a potential witness you are entitled to write the statement in your own words at your own pace. There is no law which requires witnesses to complete a statement at one sitting, therefore, if you really wish to, you are allowed to leave the police station any time, returning a few hours later or the following day to complete your statement. However, police generally are keen to persuade witnesses to complete a full statement as soon as possible after the event while the incident is still fresh in that person's mind. Witnesses who are worried about forgetting what they have said in their formal statement when they come to appear in court, which may be at a much later date, are entitled to receive a copy of their statement to take away with them. It is worth noting, however, that the police in general seem reluctant to give witnesses a copy of their statement but have no objection to showing them a copy at any time that the witnesses should wish to refresh their memory. If in the future you decide that you wish to withdraw charges, perhaps because you were unsure about reporting the incident in the first place or subsequently realize that you do not wish to go through with a full prosecution and have to appear in court, you must immediately tell the officer in charge of your case that you wish to withdraw and make sure that you sign a formal withdrawal form. Failure to sign this form will result in the case proceeding as originally intended.

On The Conveyor Belt

Complacency in dealing with the victim's complaint and apathetic half-hearted attempts at tracking down the offender are further causes for frustration for many victims. They may feel a bitter sense of injustice that the crime was not considered worth bothering with or that any danger to their well-being was too slight to warrant serious action on the part of the police. Victims of racial or anti-gay crimes report a very strong prejudice within certain police departments which often prevents such incidents being recorded. Women, especially those within the immigrant community who are sexually assaulted, beaten up or threatened by their husbands or boyfriends may have a hard time trying to persuade the police to take action against the offender.

The conveyor belt approach by police and courts where cases are processed as quickly as possible to make room for the next in line, just as with the beleaguered national health system, distresses many victims. They see a direct comparison between the behaviour of the police and the detached, unsympathetic and essentially authoritarian attitudes of many doctors to their patients whom they regard as 'cases' rather than human beings.

The preoccupation with technical efficiency at the expense of empathic concern on a human level is a phenomenon often shared by both the medical profession and the police.

Most damning of all are complaints by victims who have cooperated fully and willingly with the police giving a detailed statement and full description of offender only to find that having secured this vital information the police will now divert their attention away from the victim and refocus it almost exclusively on the search for the criminal. Thus summarily relegated like a bit part player to the side lines of the criminal drama, the victim, superfluous to police investigations, is left to brood and fume at the inequity of the system. Coming in the immediate post-crisis period when victims may just be entering an emotional low and having to get to grips with their feelings of depression, guilt, anger and fear, this cut-off in police communication is experienced by many as yet another form of rejection, further increasing the victim's sense of isolation and emphasizing the fact that they have no real status or accepted role to play in the system. Any delays or difficulties they may encounter with other organizations such as the DHSS, the National Health Service, the Gas or Electricity Board, telephone engineers, banks or credit card companies are likely to exacerbate this sense of injustice even further.

This sense of abandonment is a major component of secondary injury yet it is far from being merely the by-product of raw emotions and a distressed mind. If you consider the victim's peculiar non-status in the judicial system it soon becomes apparent that many victims do indeed have ample and legitimate cause for grievance. For example, even if his or her early encounters with the police were friendly and non-stressful and the incident was taken seriously enough for a proper investigation to be initiated, the victim/witness will naturally enough continue to take an active interest in how these investigations proceed and what they reveal. But the tendency for the police often not to notify victims whether the offender has been caught, what the charges are, if he is in custody or on bail, who he is, whether he pleaded guilty or not guilty, whether the case is still open or closed, if court proceedings are pending or not, will be interpreted at worst as back-sliding incompetence and at best as lack of interest and courtesy. If the police previously seemed to be unhelpful or disbelieving then the victim's earlier anti-police feelings or suspicion that the case has been ignored or forgotten will now be confirmed. If the police initially seemed helpful and caring then the victims may experience profound disappointment at a further betrayal of their trust in humanity. The resulting disenchantment with the police is often a key factor in many people's decision not to bother going to them again should they become involved in any further criminal incident.

Considering that fear of reprisal is often uppermost in the minds of many victims when trying to decide whether to report a crime and give evidence, the ignoring by the police of victims' very real need to know the outcome of police investigations does seem to reinforce the public's disillusionment with the police as agents of justice. Other instances where the police act out of line, seeming to overlook the best interests of victims, are in passing on victims' names and addresses without obtaining prior permission to the local press, sometimes causing embarrassment, anger or fear of reprisals to the victim and the family. The failure of the police to turn up on time or to turn up at all for a scheduled appointment with the victim-witness is another cause for grievance.

One commander with the Metropolitan Police admits candidly that the police are in many ways still operating as if in the dark ages. For instance, in Britain, unlike the USA, there are as yet in most police stations no screens to hide witnesses from suspects during an identification parade so they can see but not be seen. Traumatic as it can be for the victim to have to look the attacker in the face again, this may be nothing compared to the knowledge that the attacker can see them, identify them and may be planning another attack in revenge.

Catch As Catch Can

This divergence between the treatment and service we expect from the police and what we actually receive highlights an irony of the judicial system: although the victim is the person who was wronged, he or she, unlike the criminal, has no statutory rights, and no recognized voice within the system. Once the crime has been committed the victim becomes a potential witness, who may or may not be called upon to testify if the case comes to court and the accused pleads not guilty. Few victims realize that when it comes to the crunch it must ultimately be the decision of the police whether to press charges.

To many victims, especially those with little or no knowledge and experience of criminal law, it can come as something of a shock to discover that their legal status in a prosecution involving rape, assault, attempted murder, or mugging is that of a witness and nothing more, because in Britain the Crown is the prosecutor and therefore in effect the injured party and the crime is committed against the state, *not against the victim*. As a result, the victim-witness can expect little in the way of information about how the case is proceeding and, worst of all, has no solicitor or barrister to act on his behalf.

They are not likely to be given much in the way of advice as to how to act or what to expect when they appear in court. Many individuals may be totally ignorant of the difference between magistrates' courts and crown courts, for example that in the former there is no jury. Lack of comprehension of the legal labyrinth that constitutes the judicial system is the principal source of the stress men and women of all ages experience when faced with a forthcoming court appearance. Says John Skinner:

> I was terribly nervous seeing them face to face when they were standing in the dock. They looked thoroughly tough and experienced; they'd obviously been through it all before. I was asked to give evidence and got confused about what I'd said in my previous statement, worrying that I might say something different now. No one had prepared me for the nerve-wracking experience of cross-examination. What they don't tell you is that the defence lawyer is going to try and pick holes in your statement, make you out to be a liar or an unreliable witness in order to get their client off. It was really getting to me. What also made me incredibly uptight was that my name and address was given out to the magistrate in front of the guys. So I began to worry that they would be able to come after me. I was in there for two hours. It was incredibly tiring. But then when it was the criminals' turn to give evidence me and my mate were told to get out of court. We weren't allowed to hear what they had to say which I thought was extremely unfair. The case is due to come up in the Crown Court very soon now but what's bugging me is that they don't tell you about when you are going to appear in court until probably the night before, so I get nervous just waiting and I don't know when I'm going to have to take some more time off work. This puts me in rather a difficult position with my employer.

Since courtesy in general tends to be scant in the courts it is little wonder victims feel themselves shortchanged by the system. For example, John Skinner ought to have been informed that his address need not be read out in court which would have saved him a lot of aggravation and fear. Witnesses are entitled to pass the necessary information on a piece of paper over to the judge or magistrate.

All Used Up

It is not uncommon for many victims to feel they have been used
and eventually discarded by the police. Having willingly given all
the help they can, many victims rightly feel entitled to support,
respect and reassurance from the police in return. There is, after
all, no getting around the fact that the police need all the
assistance they can get from the victim in order to track down the
offender – and ultimately nail him. As such the fight against
crime is very much dependent on a synergistic relationship
between police and public. The victim, having spent much
energy and time, usually at a period of extreme distress, in
providing this assistance, feels he or she has a right to be kept
informed about the operation and perhaps even to participate in
the investigation process.

Proposed reform to ensure fairer representation for victims
forms the bedrock of the growing Victims' Rights movement in
America and is discussed in a later chapter. But as things stand
now, the quality of the relationship between the victim-witness
and the police varies tremendously and depends very much on
the luck of the draw. Police attitudes may incur either praise or
odium depending on the area of the country, the individual
officers in question, the nature of the offence, the circumstances
and the individual plight and expectations of the victim. The
victim's perception of police behaviour once formed does not
necessarily remain unchanged. What began as a positive experience can distintegrate into a progressively more disappoint-
ing one as is often the case when the victim gets left behind and
forgotten along the investigative route.

As with strained doctor-patient relations so poor victim-police
relations tend to be self-perpetuating because both parties in both
types of relationships regard themselves as trapped within their
respective roles. Like patients – and victims often are also
patients – victims desperately crave insight and information.
They have an overwhelming need to make their own wishes
clear, yet the vulnerability of their position renders them unable
to negotiate a better deal for themselves whether in hospital or in
the police station or in the courts. It is difficult to expect the
public, let alone victims themselves, to change the attitudes of the
police substantially. Like sick patients who seek reassurance and
understanding from their doctors, victims are generally in no
position to assert their needs or fight for what they perceive as
their rights. Police attitudes, however, can be quite crucial in
reducing the victim's acute psychological trauma and can also

help prevent the debilitating secondary trauma many undergo.

Recognition of victim trauma syndrome and the phenomenon of secondary injury can only come about as a result of greater enlightenment within the police system itself. This in turn is dependent on a greater flow of information and closer liaison between the different agencies with which the victim comes into contact: hospital staff, social workers, health visitors, victim support volunteers and the police. Before the police can try more fully to meet the needs and wishes of victims they must first recognize what those needs and wishes *are*. At the moment there exists a yawning chasm between what victims want in the way of fair and respectful treatment by the police and what the police think they want. Narrowing that gap in understanding is an essential step towards securing the public's cooperation in fighting crime: the police desperately need public support in order to do their work successfully.

A lot of the problem hinges on basic attitudes: not only are police, like lawyers and judges, somewhat removed from the personal plight of the victims and therefore unable to identify with their experiences and attitudes, but because the victim is deemed a relatively unimportant participant in the judicial system wherein the offender plays the 'starring role' his needs come low on the list of police priorities. There is no getting around the fact that in the present climate of soaring crime the police need all the help they can get, in particular the good will of victims of crime in order to do a proper job in the detection and investigation of criminal incidents. Recognition of the crucially important relationship between the public and the police has led at least in some areas of Britain and America to a gradual but steady enlightenment. There is growing recognition of the victim's right to be heard. In some cities, for example London and Manchester, police are now routinely joining up with other agencies, in particular the victim support schemes, to ensure that victims obtain adequate backup whether their needs are physical, emotional, financial, or legal.

Special training for new recruits in the causes and effects of PTSD, the setting up of special rape interview suites, and emphasis on gentle, non-judgemental interviewing techniques appears to be paying off as much for the police as for the victim, as the sharp rise in the number of reported rapes and sexual assaults since new police guidelines were implemented indicates. Cynics might contend that police are motivated by the need to get victims on their side in order to catch more criminals. Addressing themselves now so wholeheartedly to the needs of rape victims, many people would argue, is part of a timely and pragmatic move to improve their own public image. Few, especially amongst the police, would refute this claim. So be it. The main thing is, the victim benefits as a result.

8
Victims' Rights: A Piece of the Action

In the great majority of crimes the offender is never caught and victims have little option but to accept that justice cannot be done and this, for better or worse, is the end of the episode. But how much better is the prospect for victims when the offender is caught and brought to trial? The picture that emerges of the victim's subsequent involvement in the judicial system is in many cases grim indeed, often proving as distressing as the crime itself. After a decision has been taken by the police to prosecute the offender, the case is then under the jurisdiction of the courts. At this stage, victims who remain involved with or interested in the prosecution are now confronted not only with police procedures but with all the archaic bureaucracy of the courts and the complex minutiae of criminal law.

It is difficult, if not impossible, to think of any other procedure so guaranteed to inspire confusion, frustration and anxiety as the intricate workings of the judicial system. Moreover, it is a system which appears predominantly oriented towards the offender and in which the victim is deemed relatively superfluous. From the moment that the police decide to prosecute right up till a sentence is finally passed, events conspire to intensify the stress already suffered by the victim. The impression gained at different stages throughout the process is that even if asked to give evidence he or she is a largely unimportant cog in the wheel and therefore liable to be forgotten or ignored by all the other protagonists taking part. Confronted by the lumbering complex machinery of criminal law with its antiquated protocol and formal adversarial system, many victim-witnesses remain unclear or entirely ignorant of how or where they fit in, if at all. In many cases, the victim's active participation as a witness will only be required if the accused pleads not guilty and the case gets as far as Crown Court.

Depending on the nature of the offence hearings may take place in their entirety only in a magistrates' court, or start off in the magistrates' court and then progress to the Crown Court. A man arrested and charged, for example, with rape will within two to four weeks appear at a magistrates' court for committal – a preliminary hearing at which the magistrates decide whether there is sufficient evidence to bring the case before a jury and Crown Court. Although as chief witness for the prosecution, a victim will have to attend Crown Court to give evidence, evidence may or may not be submitted at the committal proceedings. Some committals are very brief, involving only prosecution and defence counsels and magistrates, others, however, resemble a long drawn out dress rehearsal, an enactment of how the case will proceed in Crown Court. If the offender does plead guilty he has the right to change his plea at any time – and vice versa. The defendant may, indeed, even decide to plead guilty on the morning of the trial thus all of a sudden making it unnecessary for the victim to give evidence.

The Long and Short of It

Taking into account the dilatory convoluted nature of the judicial system a period of anything from three months to over a year may elapse before the Crown Court trial takes place, with numerous preliminary hearings not to mention adjournments in between. It is only to be expected that victims often do not feel free to put the whole episode behind them until the trial is well and truly over. The intervening period of suspense coupled with a lack of information about how the case is progressing can create phenomenal mental strain and tension for many victims and their families. What bothers those victims who are not requested to attend committal proceedings is that they are not informed of what transpired during the hearing. They do not know whether the defendant entered a plea of guilty or not guilty (he does not have to enter a plea at this stage and is entitled to ask for legal aid, bail, and someone to represent him) and whether he was remanded in custody or on bail. Bail is frequently unconditional which means the victims feel they or their families may be in danger of another attack. Victims and their families are rarely offered special protection by the courts during this period. Many victims are less upset knowing the offender is out on bail than if they are kept in the dark. Anxiety is a perfectly natural concomitant of ignorance. Says one assault victim:

I wasn't so bothered once I'd found out. At least I knew to be on my guard. It was not knowing if he might or might not be hanging around town that put me on edge.

A criminal case also has the habit of developing and changing sometimes as investigations progress. It is rare for muggers, sex offenders and burglars to be convicted of one isolated crime. Many are discovered to have committed other offences, major and minor, which must be taken into account when prosecution takes place. So, by the time of the trial, the defendant may be facing any number and variety of different charges. This can cast an entirely different complexion on an individual case. If more than one criminal attacked the victim then the picture can become very complicated indeed. Offences of physical assault are rated according to a 'scale' of severity ranging from common assault through wounding to grievous bodily harm. In theory one might expect more and graver charges to indicate a greater likelihood of vigorous prosecution and a stiffer sentence – yet in practice things don't necessarily always work out this way.

In certain cases some or all charges relating to a single incident may be significantly reduced or dropped altogether at the final court appearance because of insufficient evidence. This is often the case in, say, a burglary that was also accompanied by physical assault. The outcome therefore may be an acquittal or a reduced sentence. As the result of negotiation called 'plea bargaining' offenders charged with various crimes may plead guilty to one, usually a lesser charge, on the understanding that the prosecutors will drop the other pending charges. This represents a saving on court time and public money and sometimes results in a more lenient sentence for the offender. Because of the time and expense involved, a court will often decide that a guilty plea to a lesser charge is preferable to going through with a full trial to prosecute the offender for a more severe crime. When, as is often the case, the victim is not in court to witness these developments, the first information he or she receives on the outcome may be a report in the local newspaper. Victims who assumed the offender was being tried for the offence committed against them and then are left to discover for themselves that he is on trial for a different crime will understandably feel that they have been wrongfully ignored and deemed superfluous to the proceedings.

Communication Gap

Victims, whether asked to stand as witnesses or not, have every right to be notified of the decision not to prosecute on some or all of the charges relating to their own case. Victims who are not asked to give evidence but who want to attend the court hearing perhaps with other members of their family may rightly get very upset or angry if they are not kept informed about exactly when the trial is to take place. The police officer in charge of the case in question will have all the necessary details and should, in theory, keep the victim informed, but this does not always happen.

It is very difficult to obtain concrete information on the date of the next hearing, and up-to-date news on whether the case is still proceeding through the magistrates' court or is due to come up in the Crown Court or has been passed on from one venue to another. Cases may be rescheduled due to illness, requested adjournments, or insufficient court time. Requests for inform-ation from court clerks and administrative staff frequently produce very little in the way of definite facts. Cases may be perpetually in transit, the relevant files held up between different courts or en route to Crown Court, and therefore difficult to track down. Unless you have a comprehensive knowledge of court proceedings, the vagaries and quirks of the system are muddling in the extreme.

Victims asked to appear as witnesses frequently get appre-hensive about a pending court hearing. Pre-trial nerves can prove a considerable source of strain and stress for many victim-witnesses. Magistrates' courts do automatically send the victim a witness order telling them that they are ordered to give evidence. But the order does not state the date or location, often throwing the person concerned into a state of nervousness about when and where they should turn up and ignorance as to who will inform them. Again, it is up to the police to forewarn the witness of a pending court appearance. But in cases where the accused states his intention to plead guilty, such a witness order may be conditional rather than absolute, which means the victim will not be called upon to give evidence unless the accused switches his plea to not guilty. Many victims do not comprehend the meaning of the order, are unsure whether it is absolute or conditional and what this really means and may spend weeks or months anticipating a court appearance when in fact their presence was not required at all and the case ended with the defendant pleading guilty.

Just as disconcerting for the victim who knows he or she must give evidence is not knowing precisely *when*. In the case of magistrates' courts and juvenile courts a date for trial is fixed some weeks ahead so the witness may be notified well in advance. But Crown Court cases are scheduled at relatively short notice. Once a case is on the 'warned' list it is liable to be heard on any day in a forthcoming two- or three-week period. The police can then warn the witness when the case is due to come up. If the case is on a 'fixed' list, usually issued ten days before the beginning of the relevant week, witnesses may be given a definite date and time to appear. However, according to whether there is a shortage or surplus of court time, cases may be postponed or else slotted in early, sometimes giving the witness only a few hours' notice. There have been numerous accounts of victims turning up at court at a designated time only to find the case has been postponed at the last minute. Some witnesses are informed late at night that they must appear at Court the next morning. This can cause tremendous aggravation since many witnesses make arrangements, sometimes at considerable expense and inconvenience to themselves and others, to be off work or have their children or dependents looked after, and then have to cancel them or, if summoned at the last minute, resort to a hurried emergency plan. Says John Skinner:

> There was no problem with the magistrates' court. I knew exactly when I had to go and was told well in advance by the police. But I've been on tenterhooks waiting for the Crown Court trial. I know it's sometime this week but I don't know what day. The police say I'll probably be told the night before. Luckily my boss understands but I don't like to inconvenience him too much, my job is too precious.

Getting all keyed up to go to court, then finding the trial postponed can increase the victim's nervousness. Police and witnesses alike complain about the desultory nature of the Crown Court warning system. Frequently police cannot track down a key witness in time or themselves end up being blamed by the victim for shortness of notice, change of venue, or postponement, when this in fact has nothing to do with them.

Civic Gloom

Few courts are designed with due consideration of victims' and witnesses' needs. The average British court building, like so many major institutions, is a depressing monument to civic gloom. Generally the older the building the greater the chance that the victims, their family and friends, will have to wait outside the courtroom along with the defendants, their friends, relatives and counsel. Being forced into such close proximity with the offender, often for lengthy periods not unnaturally, can give rise to considerable tension, ill-feeling, and embarrassment. Seating may be limited, benches and chairs are usually uncomfortable. No provision is made for children and there are often no facilities to obtain refreshments.

In order to protect counsel's impartiality victims are not encouraged to meet the prosecution lawyers before the trial. Therefore if charges are to be dropped the victim will not necessarily be informed until they hear it in court. It is therefore up to police officers connected with the case to act as arbiters in passing on the relevant information whenever possible. This gap in communication between prosecutors and victims is one of the principal causes of dissatisfaction and annoyance with standard court procedure.

It is at this point, when they are at their most perplexed, that victims become most acutely aware of their isolated position and the clear denial of what they see as their right to participate in the process and gain information about the case. What so many victims resent most of all is that unlike the offender, they have no one to represent their interest or to speak for them. Police officers, prosecution solicitors and prosecuting counsel are at court to represent the state, not the victim. Having suffered loss at the criminal's hands what many victims now experience is a loss of identity into the bargain, in effect becoming the invisible man or woman of the system.

In the Box

Once in the witness box victims may be quite unprepared for the detailed extent of cross-examination to which they must submit. In spite of their efforts to answer questions clearly and provide all the relevant information, they may find themselves thrown by interruptions, unexpected or leading questions, and the severe tone of the defending counsel whose prime function, after all, is to get his client acquitted. For the faint-hearted, timid and nervous, giving evidence may amount to an ordeal far more humiliating and nerve-wracking than the crime itself.

A woman who has been raped faces the most gruelling ordeal of all, since in the absence of any corroborative evidence the outcome of the trial hinges on establishing the veracity of her word against that of her attacker. Consequently, the line taken by the defence during cross-examination tends to be far more aggressive, the basic implication being that the woman is lying. Unlike other cases of assault, her character, lifestyle, possible previous relationship with the offender, even, should the judge deem it necessary, her past sexual history, will often be dragged out into the open. To make matters worse, the anonymity accorded to rape victims does not extend to women who were indecently assaulted. In such cases the defending counsel will use every possible tactic and manoeuvre in order to trip up the rape victim and puncture holes in her account of the story with the result that she often ends up feeling that it is she, not the accused, who is on trial and must prove her innocence. To a rape victim often still in a state of severe emotional distress resulting from the attack, the horror of having to recount and relive the past ordeal over again in such great detail in the presence of her assailant and a large assembled audience, possibly made up of many of his relatives and friends, such a courtroom experience inevitably serves to intensify her existing anguish or else reverse the whole process of recovery. Of the two experiences it is hard to determine which is the more deeply distressing – the sexual assault itself or the slow motion action replay the victim goes through in the full glare of public attention.

Another problem facing the victim-witness of all crimes is that the formal nature of courtroom discourse usually does not permit them to recount the event in their own way, placing the episode, as it were, within the context of their own lives. Attempts to get across the true nature of the grievance and extent of the effects suffered as a result of the incident are usually doomed to misfire because the witness, forced to adhere to a set question and answer mode is 'fed' a specific series of questions and often ordered to reply briefly and concisely ('just answer yes or no'). Cross-examination, by its very nature, reduces events and circumstances to black and white absolute terms, leaving no room for any intervening shades of grey. It is clear, therefore, that anyone with confidence and a sharp perceptive mind, who can keep their wits about them, sum things up using cogent and succinct statements without becoming nervous or being caught off guard by the defending counsel, will have a better time of it than someone who is unsure of what they say – or who indeed is still suffering greatly from the effects of victim trauma syndrome. Says John Skinner:

> Nobody warned me about what sort of form the cross-examination takes or how gruelling it can be. I was in there for two hours and it was really starting to get to me in the end especially since I had to look at the attacker face to face across the court. The thing that made it far less traumatic was that the police were so helpful and kept me informed all the way through.

The Forgotten Man

A large majority of victims and virtually all co-victims (the victim's family and cohabitants) however do not end up acting as witnesses either because the defendant pleads guilty or is being charged with a different offence to that originally recorded or simply because they have nothing to add that would constitute hard evidence. Having nothing whatever to contribute to the court proceedings they may find themselves in the invidious position of having been cast as the 'forgotten man' of the courtroom drama. The extent of their predicament depends largely on the effect of the crime on them and how important it is to them to keep tabs on the offender once he is brought to trial. The exclusion of victims from the court process is not merely due to an oversight but to pure intent. In the opinion of one magistrate:

> Victims who do not act as witnesses should really be discouraged to come to court. If they are really curious about the verdict they should go and sit in the public gallery. They have no place in the body of the court. But ideally they should be told of the outcome by the police.

Such an attitude will be interpreted as incomprehensibly harsh and callous, say, by the parents of a child killed by a hit-and-run motorist or a man badly beaten up by a mugger now charged with an altogether different offence.

In some cases sentence is not necessarily always passed immediately after an offender is convicted, but can be given at a later date, so even if the victim-witness was present at the trial and heard the verdict he may not know the final outcome. They will rarely be told the date of the final hearing and it is not always routine police procedure to pass on this information. The Campaign Against Drinking and Driving, a support organization for families of victims killed and injured by drunk and irresponsible drivers, cites numerous instances where bereaved relatives only learnt the outcome of the court case by reading the local newspaper. In one case, a family did not learn that the man who had killed their child had been dealt with for causing her death until two months after the court case, by which time he had completed his prison sentence! Because of this negligence and oversight, families understandably suffer unnecessary extra anguish through being deprived of being present at the sentencing, something they regard as the last act of public support they may offer their lost loved one.

Such accounts illustrate time and time again the fact that

families of people who are murdered or accidentally killed are not even accorded the status of victims within the judicial system. In many, though by no means all, parts of the country, although it has become official police policy to notify victims and their families of the outcome of the case before that case is closed, a long time may elapse before this happens, while sometimes it is something that may be accidentally overlooked altogether. Withholding of information is seen by many victims as the final gross injustice in a long line of inequities within the judicial process.

Seeking Redress

Because there is often no one to inform them of the fact, many victims of violent crime remain entirely unaware that they are entitled to apply for financial compensation. Others often do not apply under the misapprehension that only those who sustained very grave physical injuries or crippling disabilities qualify for compensation. As a result of such widespread ignorance many men and women who are perfectly entitled to claim compensation fail to obtain what could have turned out to be a considerable sum of money which in certain cases might help to lessen some – though by no means all – of the aftereffects of the crime. The plight of the crime victim, as we have seen, revolves so often mainly around psychological and symbolic losses, over and above material ones, that it is unlikely to be assuaged by financial payment. Nevertheless, in many cases, a cash payment may help to offset the losses incurred by the victims through having to be off work, leave their job; or undergo medical treatment or psychotherapy to cope with the effects of victim trauma. In some cases applying for and obtaining compensation amounts to a symbolic act, whereby some of the wrongs done to the victim by the criminal are officially redressed by society.

The organization responsible for making payment is called the Criminal Injuries Compensation Board (CICB). Victims apply for compensation in writing and the board, made up largely of a team of lawyers, decides whether their case qualifies and how much to award. Set up in 1964, the board makes some twenty thousand awards in the UK each year.

Not all injuries are covered by the scheme. For example, you cannot claim for traffic accidents and injuries you are deemed to have brought on yourself. The crime must have been reported to the police but except in domestic cases the attacker need not have been caught or prosecuted. However, if the victim and attacker were living together either within marriage or not, the attacker in most instances must have been prosecuted and the victim, unless a child, must no longer be living with the criminal. All crimes are covered, including rape, mugging, arson, riot, and poisoning. Nor need you be a direct victim. You may also claim if you were injured trying to stop someone from committing a crime, if you were trying to apprehend a suspect after a crime, or if you were trying to help the police apprehend someone. Co-victims may also come under the aegis of this scheme. For instance, widows or widowers of someone who died from criminal injuries or who was injured but died of some other cause may qualify. Other close relatives and dependents may also file a claim, as can a parent of an unmarried victim under the age of eighteen.

Injury must have been serious enough to merit compensation for at least £550. This high figure has led to criticism that the scheme only benefits those who have suffered quite severe physical injuries rather than minor ones. When you apply you must give details of the incident and of your injuries together with losses incurred in reduced earnings and out of pocket expenses. The board may ask for further doctor's letters, police and hospital reports as well as reports from your employer and any government department from which you obtained security or other payments. One glaring anomaly in the present scheme is that it discriminates against those currently receiving social security. Victims claiming over £3,000, not unusual in the case of many injuries, will automatically cease receiving payment from the DHSS, a loophole that claimants often fail to discover until they receive their award. This obviously hits hardest those who are unemployed or single parents.

After considering all the relevant data a board member will decide whether the case is covered by the scheme and how much should be awarded. Claimants are informed of the sum the board intends to award and are allowed the right of appeal if the sum seems inadequate. An appeal involves the victim attending an informal private hearing where three other members of the board look at the case afresh. The victim, however, cannot apply for legal aid to cover the cost of legal representation, only the sum of £50 to obtain advice before the hearing. It may, however, be possible to obtain free legal representation through a law centre or the free representation unit. At the tribunal you will be asked to provide evidence and witnesses to back up your case. The board will cross-examine you, and your evidence will be open to question by anyone else concerned. As a result the board may increase or indeed reduce the award, decide to make an award even if the board member who looked at the case earlier did not do so, or they may reject your application although an award was made earlier.

Though this all seems simple and straightforward enough the one drawback is that the board will want to establish the absence of any contributory negligence in the cause of the crime. The board may also withhold or reduce compensation if they consider that for some reason your life-style or even your character makes you a more likely candidate for victimization. The issue of the victim's culpability, especially in cases of sexual assault, is therefore as relevant in this case as it so often proves to be in a criminal trial. Under new terms laid out in the Criminal Justice Bill (undergoing its second reading at the time of writing) the government intends to implement compensation awards on a statutory basis, conferring on eligible applicants a definite right to receive compensation.

Making Crime Pay: Court Compensation Orders

Some, though very few victims may seek or desire further redress, whether on a point of principle because they see it as their basic right as victims of society or as a means of gaining recognition of the wrong done to them by the criminal. The idea that the offender as part of the sentence should be made to atone for his actions by paying a sum of money to the victim is a relatively new development. While it is theoretically perfectly possible for a crime victim to sue an offender for compensation in civil proceedings, in practice only a very tiny minority ever pursue a civil action because the chances of a satisfactory outcome tend to be slim.

After all, most criminals lack the financial means to repay the victims in full for the losses they have sustained. Many are unemployed and either on probation or doing prison sentences. Their chances of being able to earn enough money to pay such a fine to the claimant are therefore almost non-existent. This point will, of course, be taken into consideration when the victim applies for legal aid to pay for the costs of taking his attacker to court. In some cases, where police refuse to prosecute an offender, as is often the case in domestic disputes, or where the victim believes the outcome of a previous criminal trial to be unjust, the victim is entitled to bring a private prosecution against their attacker which could result in his receiving an award.

However, bearing in mind that the majority of victims usually want to put the matter behind them as soon as possible and perhaps want to avoid having any truck with the law, it is obvious that only in exceptionally rare cases will a victim seriously consider pursuing a lengthy, frustrating and perhaps ultimately unsuccessful private action against their offender. It is only to be expected that victims may feel shortchanged by the system either because the offender got off scot free or was treated too leniently, their responses varying from grudging acceptance and bitter resentment, to outrage and indignation. This post-trial impact may have considerable bearing on the subsequent recovery of those victims still suffering from victim trauma. An unfair, unsatisfactory outcome of a trial can intensify and perpetuate the existing trauma or may indeed initiate fresh emotional upheaval. It is unlikely, however, that pursuing a civil action will do anything more than exacerbate this situation.

However, what is not widely known is that in law the courts are entitled to order the convicted offender to pay a sum of money to the victim to compensate them. A compensation order may be given as an ancilliary order – in addition to another fine, a prison sentence or probation order – or can stand as a sentence in its own right. Again, the major problem in implementing compensation orders is the impecuniousness of many offenders. In practice the likelihood of getting a criminal to pay a significant amount of money, usually made up of regular instalments, is rare. This is why, although due to increasing government pressure more courts are now using their power to order offenders to pay compensation to their victims, the net sum of most orders is in fact very small – usually around £50 and rarely more than £100, though sometimes even less than £20. In most cases, far from being a quid pro quo, compensation can only be regarded as a token whereby the offender is seen to 'pay his debt' to society and to the victim.

The fundamental concept underlying compensation is the intended rehabilitative effect on the offender. This is all well and good in terms of deterring offenders from committing further crimes but does little to make good the injustice suffered by the victim, given the often derisory amounts in question. In cases of physical injury at least there is no way that the sum of a court compensation order in any way matches the amount of money a victim might be awarded through the CICB, although it is worth pointing out that receipt of compensation from an offender does not disqualify a victim from applying for further compensation from the CICB. It is up to the prosecution to decide on whether to apply for a compensation order or not, and if so for how much. Factors determining whether an application for an order is made and for how much are the means of the offender, the damages incurred by the victim, the type of offence committed and whether the offender pleads guilty or not guilty.

Even in cases where the offender does have the means to meet a compensation order, putting a figure on what often amounts more to emotional injury than material loss is an almost impossible task. How do you work out a fair sum that might compensate victims for the emotional anguish and the resulting upheaval within their private relationships, their home and their working lives caused by the offence? The assessment and implementation of orders is riddled with imponderables – not least of which is the absence of any detailed information about the true extent and diverse nature of the losses sustained by the victim. What this highlights once again is the Catch 22 situation perpetuated by the lopsidedness of the judicial system: the information is lacking or largely incomplete because the victim has no voice or right of audience in court.

Courts are given very little in the way of evidence of the victim's injuries and losses, let alone the emotional trauma sustained, which might, amongst other things, provide the necessary criteria for evaluating the amount of a compensation order or indeed ascertaining whether to make one out in the first place. Given that the majority of victims do not even appear as witnesses in court, only the prosecution can ascertain from information given to them by the police whether an order should be made and for how much. In theory, the victim does not have to be in court for a compensation order to be made. Many prosecution solicitors are, however, against court compensation and believe that the victim should instead apply for compensation to the CICB. What is often forgotten is that in the case of many offences the minimum award of £550 disqualifies many victims who have suffered minor injuries from applying.

In many states in America new legislation allows for submission of a victim impact statement, made in writing to the judge by a probation officer or a victim advocate, usually a member of an agency dealing with victims' needs, before the sentence is passed. This gives full details of all injuries suffered by the victim, financial, physical and psychological, thereby providing the vital 'right of address' normally denied to the victim. Interestingly, similar legislation now also exists under Scottish criminal law. At the moment in the rest of Britain the guidelines on court compensation orders are as yet extremely unclear. Whose job it is to make out such orders is not clearly laid down in the statutes and a way of delivering the necessary information about victims' losses to the judge or magistrates has yet to be worked out. It is largely because of this that orders are made out on an ad hoc basis, and payments are usually extremely low. Proposals laid out in the Criminal Justice Bill extending courts' powers to make compensation orders in fatal cases and traffic accident cases are, however, a step in the right direction.

Mediation

Growing awareness of the emotional and psychological harm suffered by many victims of crime has led to the initiation of schemes intended to go beyond mere matters of finance. A number of such experimental so-called reparation schemes, based on those already well established in America, are now currently under way in parts of Britain. These schemes are rooted in the concept of mediation, whereby the victim and offender, if both are willing, may meet face to face for the purposes of reassuring the former and helping the latter face up to the human consequences of his behaviour. Of course, in many cases such an idea may be pure anathema to the crime victim who has no desire to know anything about his attacker or to communicate with him whatsoever. However, in certain instances victims may wish to reassure themselves that offenders are basically ordinary human beings and, more importantly, have the opportunity to express their feelings and opinions directly to the person who is responsible for their plight. If the offender is someone already known to them, mediation can provide a chance to re-establish some sort of *modus vivendi* which may prove valuable, for example, if the offender has been given a prison sentence but wishes to rejoin the same community on his release.

Mediation schemes are usually managed by the probation service, often in conjunction with a voluntary body consisting of men and women with experience of working with criminals and crime victims. Laudable as the concept of mediation might appear, it does seem, once again, that the strongest underlying philosophical thrust is rehabilitation and re-education of offenders rather than redress for victims. Mediation might well be regarded as a form of therapy. But who stands to benefit most; the offender or the victim? The answer, to most victims at any rate, will be self-evident.

Obviously a lot depends on the nature of the offence and the individuals concerned as well as the skill and sensitivity of the individual mediators themselves, but it would appear that few victims, especially those of violent crimes such as sexual assault, could obtain much in the way of comfort or peace of mind from meeting and talking with their attackers, especially when these are hardened violent criminals from a very different environment to their own. Indeed, one might speculate that in some cases the experience could generate further unnecessary trauma for the victim. However, in cases of domestic violence, for example, it is perfectly possible that mediation, especially if managed by a skilled volunteer, social worker or probation officer, may resolve conflicts, in a sense rather like the process of arbitration and conciliation embarked upon by unions and management that are locked in dispute.

Revenge or Reconciliation?

Before his case came up in the juvenile court the burglar sent me a letter saying he was sorry for all the mess he'd made and that he'd like to come and clear it up only he didn't suppose they'd let him. How true, and how iniquitous the system. I wasn't allowed into the juvenile court to say, look, I'm the victim and I'd like him to come back with me now to help me make good the damage. A fundamental flaw in the justice system is that it's geared to punishment not reparation. (Magistrate who was burgled.)

In cases where a reparation order is made by the court, the object is for the offender in effect to demonstrate his contrition in a practical manner, usually by performing some form of service for the victims and also perhaps paying them a token sum of money. Thus it might be arranged for the offender literally to 'make good' his offence by repairing or replacing something he has damaged or stolen or carrying out a suitable task which is of value to the victim. A written or oral apology may also constitute an integral part of reparation. Reparation might therefore prove a feasible proposition for offenders who lack the financial resources necessary to pay off a court compensation order and as either a symbolic or practical act of contrition may appeal to those victims who have suffered more inconvenience than actual financial loss.

As in mediation, reparation can only prove successful if the victims are in accord with the scheme in the first place. A lot of this will depend on their own personal feelings about what has happened to them and whether their primary desire is for revenge or reconcilation and rehabilitation of the offender. Clearly it would be quite iniquitous for the police or the courts to try and foist either reparation or mediation on someone unwilling to receive it. Reparation may go hand in hand with another form of punishment, the payment of a fine, imprisonment or probation, or, depending on the offence, might be considered as an alternative to prosecution linked perhaps with the administration of a formal caution. The object of the experimental schemes currently underway is to discover the value of reparation to all parties concerned as well as to work out the logistics of how and when to integrate such a scheme into the judicial process.

In spite of the primary concept of rehabilitation that underscores all reparation and mediation schemes the positive intent towards the victim cannot and should not be overlooked. Token gesture though it may be, the fact that the impact of the crime on the victim must be taken into account for such schemes to be put into effect seems a welcome breakthrough. Furthermore it is axiomatic that such schemes cannot be instigated without acknowledging the identity of the victim and recognizing his suffering as well as establishing a relationship between the victim and the offender. This is in complete contrast to the court system which is based entirely on a confrontation between the state and the offender and ignores the special needs of the victim. Therefore in order for any reparation scheme to be implemented adequate information about the injuries losses and individual grievances of the victim must first be available to the police and/or courts. In addition the victim must obviously be willing to receive reparation and be consulted as to what form this might take. In principle this would accord victims a definite role and status within the judicial process, in effect opening up the system to include their own perspective of the offence. It can only be hoped that some victims of crime may be repaid part, if not all, of the debt owed to them both by the criminal and society as a whole. A society in which the victim ends up as the forgotten man is by definition, itself guilty of victimizing that individual.

Serving Victims' Needs: The VSS

The speed at which the VSS – the Victims' Support Schemes – have expanded in all areas of Britain in the past decade demonstrates the rapidly growing awareness of both the emotional and practical needs of crime victims. Initially set up in a single experimental centre in Bristol in 1974, there are now over three hundred such schemes throughout the UK, most of these belonging to the government-funded umbrella organization, the National Association of Victims' Support Schemes. Although each scheme is run by paid organizers the bulk of workers are specially trained volunteers – about seven thousand and growing steadily – who undertake grass roots victim support work. As might be expected, the turnover of volunteer work because of the very large number of victims, especially in inner city areas, is enormous. The need for support is proving immense as witnessed by the surge in numbers of victims now being helped by the VSS. In 1986 volunteers helped 185,000 people in person, 65,000 in the London area alone and many more by phone or letter. The figures for 1987/8 indicate a 10 per cent increase in that figure, in tandem with escalating reported crime rates.

The big breakthrough for the VSS, whose primary aim is to provide practical first aid, emotional back-up and essential information to all victims, is the growing cooperation between volunteers and police. In the large majority of cases the police submit the names and details of crime victims to volunteers whose job it then is to contact each victim. In some parts of the country referral is now automatic.

The emphasis is more on nuts and bolts practicalities than on emotional counselling. A large element of volunteer work is made up offering advice on replacing locks and windows, seeking repairs to property damaged in a break-in, getting medical or dental care, and understanding the logistics of the judicial system and how to obtain legal aid and unemployment or sickness benefit. In many cases volunteers may simply sit and talk with victims, offering comfort and a sympathetic ear and off-the-cuff Samaritan-style crisis counselling wherever necessary. The role of some volunteers, however, doesn't stop there. Some are now being specifically trained to offer emotional counselling on an ad hoc basis to sexual assault victims, while a number of male volunteers may be on hand to counsel co-victims, mainly the husbands or boyfriends of women who have been raped.

Other schemes are beginning to train some volunteers in the basics of criminal law in order that more help can be given to victims in court. Indeed, considering the lack of information available to victims who go to court to give evidence, let alone the emotional distress so often experienced by them, it is encouraging to find that a large part of volunteer work consists of advising victims on when and where their case is due to come up and accompanying them to court wherever necessary.

Having recently received a massive injection of government

funds (a sum of £9,000,000 between 1987 and 1989) the heartening news is that the VSS is now beginning to set up committees to study the needs of specific groups of victims, for example the families of murder victims, ethnic minorities and victim-witnesses, with the aim of suggesting improved methods of responding to those needs and improving the system generally. This underlines the increasingly important role played by the VSS as 'middleman', conveying to victims essential information about police procedures, the courts, probation services, and compensation schemes, that might not normally be passed on automatically. This is no mean feat when you consider that volunteers are motivated by humanitarianism, not money. The interchange of information between the VSS and various welfare agencies with whom crime victims and their families might conceivably come into contact is now considerable and growing steadily. Many support schemes have close links with local crime prevention officers, and police and volunteers frequently take part in one another's training sessions.

Nevertheless there are a number of problems that continue to bedevil the work of the VSS, affecting who does and does not receive assistance from volunteers. To begin with, hitherto limited funding has impeded the organization from spreading greater word of its existence in the form of advertising to those most at need -- the poor and the immigrant communities. Because referrals are via the police the VSS faces the problem that as many crimes go unreported, unless victims go to the police they tend to be unaware of the existence of the scheme. According to a recent study only 7 per cent of victims in need of the type of support given by the VSS at present receive it, usually because they have never heard of the scheme.

Police policy on referral differs greatly not only within Britain as a whole but sometimes even within a single police force. While referral may be automatic, say, within the Greater London area, within other forces the offical policy seems to be only to refer volunteers to victims who are deemed 'in need', usually the poor and elderly, especially if they are women. Lack of awareness in some cases of the practical let alone the emotional needs of victims of both sexes and all ages who have experienced all crimes involving violence is still nothing short of appalling. So too is the laxity of referral in some parts of the force. In some cases when a senior officer does grasp the importance of meeting victims' needs and making prompt referrals his frequent absence from the unit often conspires against that policy being followed by other less senior officers. Until the VSS service is extended automatically to embrace a far wider range of victims, and police thinking is less blinkered and blighted by victim stereotyping – the little old lady still ranks as the typical 'deserving victim' – many who might benefit greatly will inevitably escape the net.

From the point of view of victims themselves, however, it seems another problem is the relatively unsophisticated image of volunteers as kind neighbours dispensing nothing more effective than tea and solicitude, a stereotypical labelling shared with other community welfare workers. Although it is true that the rank and file of the VSS is made up of ordinary men and women within the community working from home, there is little that is home-spun about the service on offer. VSS work at grass roots level involves a high degree of expertise in legal, medical, and financial matters backed up by considerable personal skill in liaising with various agencies involved. Also, a point worth pondering is that so far, the VSS is the *only* government-funded body actively committed to reversing many of the injustices suffered by all crime victims in Great Britain.

9
Looking Ahead: A Better Deal?

To have to pin one's hopes for reform on just one single beleaguered underfunded institution like the VSS whose members receive no financial reward whatsoever highlights the lamentable degree to which Britain lags behind countries such as America in establishing a better deal for victims. In the field of victim counselling and treatment for victim trauma syndrome alone, it is obvious how far Britain still has to go in catering for victims' emotional needs. Recognizing the existence of victim trauma is one thing, having sufficient resources and knowhow to treat it is quite another. The differences between, say, London and a large American city such as New York or Boston are significant and numerous enough to consider in detail. Apart from the rape crisis centres here in Britain which might not appeal to all women because their approach to counselling and advice is usually firmly entrenched in feminist doctrine, and the VSS who operate on police referral and do not specialize in counselling, there exists in London at the time of writing no government backed, professionally run clinic or centre where victims of all crimes can receive therapy or counselling for problems associated with their attack.

Now compare this to New York, where anyone who has been victimized is automatically entitled to ten free individual counselling sessions with a trained psychiatrist at the Victim Treatment Centre set up by the famed Karen Horney Clinic. Counselling is also available for parents whose children have been sexually molested. Similarly, the Victims Counselling Services offer free group therapy run by a trained psychotherapist – usually an ex-victim – as well as back-up telephone conselling to all crime victims and co-victims. Both these organizations rely almost exclusively on state funding. The Victim Services Agency, a similar organization to the British VSS, thanks to heavy state funding, provides community-based crisis and long-term counselling and support groups, 24-hour victims' 'hotline service' offering crisis intervention and counselling, essential information about other services, transport to courts, shelters and social services, assistance in applying for compensation and referral to other therapy centres. The agency itself has evolved over a short period from a grass roots voluntary scheme into an efficiently run, high-profile organization with strong effective links with all other agencies that the victim might come into contact with.

In addition it should be noted that the Crime Victims' Board – similar to the British CICB – as well as arranging financial compensation for injuries also provides payment to cover any costs incurred by victims or their families who undergo counselling for victim trauma. Apart from these major government-backed organizations and services there exist numerous victim treatment clinics attached to the psychiatric departments of big teaching hospitals as well as smaller community-based voluntary self-help groups, crisis hotlines, and counselling and educational services in and around New York specifically geared to helping victims get through the aftermath of crime.

What is evident, therefore, is that in Britain, victims' needs go unacknowledged and unmet through uninformed apathy which is endemic in the medical profession, and among mental health specialists in particular. New York is not unique in the type and number of victim services on offer. Important victim treatment centres responsible for initiating much of the early research into the effects of crime as well as the establishment of both long-term and short-term treatment of victim trauma syndrome have long been set up in cities large and small all over America and Canada.

In Britain at present, victims looking for anything more in-depth in the way of counselling or therapy than merely short-term 'crisis intervention' or rape crisis counselling that usually has a strong feminist bias would have to ask their doctor to refer them to a psychiatrist. To obtain psychiatric treatment on the NHS is no easy matter unless you suffer from a classifiable mental illness which is quite obviously not the case for the majority of crime victims. Not only is this a very extreme measure but it is unlikely to do the crime victim much good since only a tiny proportion of psychologists in Great Britain are familiar with the causes and effects, let alone the best type of treatment for victim trauma. Sadder still, if a crime victim suffering PTSD consults the average GP, the response will be to reach for the prescription pad.

In Britain, improved victims' services on the lines of those now burgeoning all over America, can only result through greater awareness on the part of the medical profession and other health professionals of the phenomenon of victim trauma backed up by adequate funding of special clinics to treat the problem.

The Victims' Rights Movement

In America, although the early development of the victims' rights movement seems to have followed a parallel course to that of the feminist movement, as reflected by the setting up in the early 1970s of support groups, clinics and services for rape victims, in recent years the increasingly vocal victims' lobby has gained considerable political muscle. Today, eminent lawyers, judges, politicians and mental health professionals are fast swelling the ranks of victims' lobbyists, once just a small yet fiercely motivated grass roots huddle. What this points to, in hearteningly salutary fashion, is the degree of unyielding zeal and resolve needed to get the message across to enough people and inspire those in a position to implement the necessary changes. From the very beginning, the recognition of victims' invisible wounds, the phenomenon of victim trauma and society's duty to assuage the distress arising from it have informed the ideals of the victims' rights movement.

Today, the aims of American victims' rights advocates, represented by such well established organizations as the National Organization for Victim Assistance and the Victims of Crime Advocacy League, are as much to ensure sufficient government funding for treatment centres and more widespread education about and research into victim trauma as to obtain fairer treatment for victims in the judicial system. Although a lot remains to be done, legislative changes in America so far have proved encouraging, due no doubt in part to the prevailing anti-crime ethic which has impressed on politicians, police and judiciary the urgency for greater grass roots community co-operation in the fight against crime.

Set up in 1982, President Reagan's Task Force on Victims of Crime devoted an entire section of its list of sixty-eight comprehensive reforms to help mental health professionals bring aid and comfort to crime victims. The recommendations included Federal funding of victim assistance organizations, the establishment of training programmes to enable practitioners to treat victims and their families, the study of the immediate and long-term psychological effects of criminal victimization, the creation of direct routine liaison between mental health workers and other victim service agencies, and the encouraging of mental health professionals to work more closely with public agencies, victim compensation boards and private insurers to make psychological treatment readily available to crime victims and their families. Many of these recommendations were incorporated in the Victims of Crime Act of 1984.

The onus in the USA – as it must be ultimately in the UK – is therefore first and foremost on doctors, psychologists and psychotherapists to educate the rest of the community as to the needs of victims as well as on the government to release the funds necessary for the implementation of victim aid programmes. Further proposed legislation, much of it now implemented in parts of the United States, includes the use of video tape interviews and evidence given on close circuit video in the case of children acting as witnesses in criminal trials, and permission for a written or verbal statement to be given by the victim or someone acting on his behalf at the hearing. To ease the victim's immediate plight emergency 'crisis' counselling on the site of the crime and the presence of a victim 'mediator' on 24 hour call at every police station and hospital casualty unit have been suggested. The task force stated that victims have a right to attend and present their views at all critical stages in the judicial process, including the trial itself, bail, sentencing or parole hearings.

Encapsulated in the Victims' Bill of Rights passed recently by New York State are numerous fair treatment standards which make it clear that victims must be kept informed of the progress of the case in which they are involved and given notification about what part they may have to play within it and how they will be asked to contribute. In addition there is tremendous emphasis on the need for victims and their families to have their own private waiting area outside the courtroom, separate to that of the accused, his witnesses, family, friends and counsel. With the passing of the Victims of Crime Act of 1984, it is clear that the vast financial resources and legislation that have for so long gone towards penal reform, the rehabilitation, apprehension, prosecution, compensation and study of criminals, are now in part at least beginning to be diverted towards funding the compensation, rehabilitation and study of victims.

In parts of America the judicial system has been significantly amended to include a fairer deal for victims and their families. In some states training is now routinely given to judges and prosecutors to assist communication with victims and promote greater understanding of their perspective of events. In twenty-three states of America, victims are now permitted to submit impact statements prior to sentencing. In Alabama victims are allowed to sit with the prosecutor at the counsel's table; in Arizona victims and their relatives may comment on plea-bargained sentences. Significantly, seventeen states have laws that prohibit convicted criminals from making money through the sale of newspaper articles, books or films. In addition, more government funds are being released for victims' compensation schemes and victims' services, a trend that is reflected to a very modest degree in Britain in the new Criminal Justice Bill.

A Better Deal?

Although victims' rights is not yet an important political issue in Britain, largely because so far there exist few activists sufficiently committed and energetic enough to make their voices heard, it would be unfair to dismiss summarily all British authorities and community agencies as nihilistically opposed to the prospect of reform. The wheel at last appears to be turning, albeit somewhat creakily, from an attitude of complacency to one of concern. The establishment of rape interview suites, greater training for police officers on the effects of PTSD, proposed legislation for tougher action on domestic violence, the use of live and pre-recorded video tape interviews with child witnesses to be used in court as evidence in sex abuse cases are some of the very recent changes that signify growing awareness of victims' needs. One senior police official looks forward to the day when all victims are permitted to give a videotaped police interview immediately following their ordeal, to be used later, if necessary, as evidence in court.

In some cities, most notably Manchester, special rape care and counselling clinics that are staffed and equipped to treat victims' physical and emotional needs while cooperating if necessary with the police to provide forensic evidence, are being set up within major teaching hospitals. Hospital-affiliated rape clinics which offer every type of medical service and back-up therapy to victims are based on similar American and Australian models initiated in the 1970s to facilitate greater community under-standing of the problems of sexual assault.

NHS finances, however, will ultimately dictate where and how soon such clinics are set up in Britain and how extensive their services will be. It is to be hoped that the trend will continue for modern newly-built courts to include separate waiting areas for victims and improved facilities as part of a generally brightened-up, more cheerful environment. In a bid to clarify the conditions of witness orders some magistrates' courts now follow a policy of adding a few explanatory notes to the order making the conditions clear and enclosing a telephone number for queries. Confusion and worry due to incomplete or non-existent inform-ation regarding court processes, dates and other details of cases, could well be minimized if not dispelled altogether by the employment by the police of a victim liaison officer and routine dispatch of computerized letters to victims keeping them informed of proceedings. Although there exist leaflets explaining the work of the VSS and victims' entitlement to compensation available from the police, booklets and pamphlets written in clear layman's terms explaining the intricacies and conditions of the judicial system would also go a long way towards helping victims who get caught up in the system.

In France, victims and their families – who are incidentally allowed to join a civil action to the state's criminal action for which legal aid may be obtained – may learn all about the system in a paperback book that has so far sold well over 100,000 copies. In Denmark and Norway rape victims are now permitted their own legal representation in court. Above all, victims should not have to go to inordinate lengths and employ their already depleted resources to obtain the necessary information. There is obviously a vital need for essential documentation on victim trauma syndrome, compensation claims, and victims' services, to be freely available in the form of simply but comprehensively written leaflets, say, at libraries, hospital casualty units, police stations, and DHSS offices. Singly these may sound like minor measures and modest changes, but taken as a whole they could be the start of a significant decline in the prevalence of secondary victimization. Only by recognizing crime victims and bringing them back into the mainstream of the action against crime can all citizens finally begin to look forward to a fairer balance of justice.

PART THREE:

Recovery: Coping with Long- and Short-term Effects

10
Recovery: Instant Crisis Strategies

High stress situations have a disconcerting way of disrupting communications between mind and body. When a crisis strikes, so overwhelming and prompt is the response by the body's autonomic nervous system in taking over bodily functions that the term 'going on automatic' takes on new dimensions. For the most part being in shock can in fact work to your positive advantage. By slowing down mental processes the shock response temporarily suspends all strong and distressing emotions and allows you to focus your mind on contacting the police, describing the incident, getting in touch with friends or relatives and making any other important arrangements which might well include anything from getting in carpenters and locksmiths, cancelling cheque and credit cards, and telephoning insurance companies to organizing medical treatment for yourself or others.

The police and the local hospital are the principal operatives in any major crisis. Working together or independently hospital staff and police are responsible for providing you with a comprehensive first aid service covering medical intervention, practical advice and comfort and all the information you need following the crisis. If you have been injured or wish to see a doctor, the police will inform you where to go and in serious cases notify the hospital that you are coming or even take you there themselves. It is also the job of the police to provide you with the names of carpenters and locksmiths if your home has been broken into and is now unsafe or to arrange for such services to be carried out without delay.

If it is very late at night and there are no public transport services or if you are in a state of extreme shock you should be offered transport back to your home or to the hospital from the police station. If the police cannot provide transport they should ensure that either a friend or acquaintance or a victim support scheme volunteer is available to accompany you. In some cases where the victim's clothes have been torn or soiled during the attack arrangements to obtain a change of clothing should also be made by the police with the help of the victim's family especially if he or she has been asked to stay on at the police station to give a full statement or, in the case of rape victims, to undergo a forensic medical examination. Passing on information regarding the help offered by the VSS, the local rape crisis centre and other victims' 'help lines' should be an essential part of police emergency operation.

Rape victims who agree to undergo a medical examination for forensic purposes may ask to see a woman police surgeon and can also have their statement taken down by a woman police officer. They may also be permitted to call on their own doctor if necessary to conduct this examination. In the special rape interview suites now being set up in some London police stations, women who have been raped are encouraged to relax in surroundings that are comfortable, private and quiet to reduce the ordeal of having to go over the details of the attack. If you have been raped you should immediately go to the police without first bathing or showering or, if you were hurt, having your injuries cleaned up. Torn or soiled clothing must also be brought along as further evidence of the attack. This is necessary because the police require as much hard evidence as they can get their hands on in order to prosecute the assailant if he is caught. In most cases, for want of necessary evidence, rape is sadly a notoriously difficult case to prove.

At the new rape interview suites you may have a shower after being examined, lie down and have a rest if you feel extremely tired and can be given fresh clothing to wear while making a statement – a process which can last anything from two to twelve hours. Do not worry if your home or the place where you were attacked is a long way away from a police station that has a special rape unit. You can ask the police to drive you to the nearest centre if you feel unable to face the rough and tumble of an ordinary police station.

Dream World

The principal effect of being in shock is that bodily sensations either become dulled or may temporarily be severed altogether. If you have been physically attacked and had sustained injuries you may either be totally unaware of them or unaware of how extensive they are. Conversely, many people who have been physically violated and sustained cuts, scratches and bruises may overreact to the sight of blood and swollen tissues, convinced that they have been seriously injured. Head and facial cuts, blows to the nose and mouth, grazes on shins and any other bony part of the body all tend to induce profuse bleeding. The tissues around the eyes, nose and lips are particularly sensitive and are liable not only to bleed and bruise easily but also to swell instantaneously, making the injuries seem far worse than they are. Says John Skinner:

> My sister and my mother both got terribly worked up when they saw all blood on my clothes and my face. My mother got terribly angry because she thought that the thugs had caused very serious and permanent damage in beating me up. She felt I'd be left with scars, but once it was all cleaned up and began to heal she could see that in fact the injuries were relatively minor, although I did have to have an operation on my nose which had been broken.

If you are suffering from any wounds that continue to bleed freely after you have cleaned and dressed them you should go immediately to your nearest hospital for further treatment. This may include having stitches and anti-tetanus injections and more elaborate dressing of the wound. Facial swelling and bruising can be reduced by applying ice cold compresses to the affected area. If you sustain a blow to the nose, eyes or head which causes undue pain, prolonged numbness, dizziness, blurred vision, nausea, fainting or a severe and prolonged headache it is absolutely essential to consult your doctor or the casualty department of your nearest hospital immediately.

Minor concussion, a dislocated or fractured jaw, a fractured skull, broken or fractured nose, damage to the eyes are all too common aftereffects of being hit in the face or on the head. The degree or severity of the damage may not be immediately evident, so if you think you were badly hit, but are not sure how badly, you must seek immediate medical help to establish the exact nature of the injury and prevent any more serious aftereffects from developing. A severe blow to the face or head necessitates very prompt attention to rule out the possibility of damage to the neurological system. In most cases, however, bruising, minor fractures and concussion are the commonest injuries and should give no cause for concern. Any damage to the back, chest, stomach, groin and legs should also be taken seriously. Persistent numbness may mask the injury done to you and therefore it is essential to undergo a thorough examination perhaps even a scan or X-ray to determine whether any internal or structural damage has occurred. Breaks and fractures must be treated and set as soon as possible after the injury to prevent the bones from knitting together in misalignment and thus causing a permanent deformity.

If you have been raped or sexually assaulted you should undergo an internal and general examination even if you decide not to report the incident to the police. Although there may well be no cause for alarm you may want to set your mind at ease regarding the likelihood of having contracted a sexually trans-mitted disease or having become pregnant. Many women are unaware of the fact that it is possible to develop an infection such as gonorrhoea without showing any symptoms at all. For this reason alone – and because the risks of developing subsequent complications and of passing on the disease should it remain untreated are very high – it is essential to obtain a full medical check up soon after you have been raped. Centres such as the Pregnancy Advisory Bureau or the Genito-Urinary Departments and Special Clinics (i.e. VD clinics) attached to many large teaching hospitals offer the fastest facilities for both testing and treatment of all sexually transmitted diseases.

The risk of pregnancy is usually eliminated by prescription of the morning after pill. If you don't visit a doctor immediately after being raped but become worried a few weeks later that you could be pregnant, you may wish to have a pregnancy test and undergo an early abortion if the test is positive. Performed on an outpatient basis, an abortion at twelve weeks or less is relatively untraumatic and usually involves a very rapid procedure called vacuum aspiration. It is important to remember that the sooner you have an abortion after becoming pregnant the lower your chances of suffering emotional side effects such as depression linked to the loss of the foetus, as well as any internal compli-cations. Treatment for sexually transmitted diseases, as for pregnancy, tends to be preventive. If you wish you may receive two injections of an antibiotic that will automatically remove any risk of developing gonorrhoea.

After effects of the rape may, however, not become apparent until some days or weeks after the incident. Vaginal discharge and itching sometimes accompanied by irritation and redness around the vulva and anus may be due to a candidal infection, thrush, which can be treated with anti-fungal pessaries such as Canestan, creams and by taking a course of Nystatin tablets to kill off any vestiges of the fungus in the gut. One important often forgotten feature of thrush is its tendency to flare up at times of stress, illness and as a result of taking antibiotics – circumstances which could all apply to women who have been sexually assaulted. So be patient. The condition may persist or recur after initial treatment and it may not be directly caused by the rape. Trichomoniasis and nonspecific urethritis, however, may well be caused by sexual assault. Symptoms of NSU include a yellow-green discharge with an often offensive odour, itching or vaginal irritation and burning as well as frequency of urination. Antibiotics will usually clear up the disorder and care must be taken to complete the course to prevent reinfection. Because these conditions are easily passed on, your husband or boyfriend may also take antibiotics in order to cut out the possibility of a recurring cross-infection.

In theory it is possible to contract other less common disorders such as Chlamydia, venereal warts or herpes as a result of anal, vaginal or oral intercourse, but in practice the chances of actually doing so are highly remote. However, if you are worried that you might have contracted any of these you can arrange to have the necessary tests carried out at your local hospital clinic. Any sudden or persistent vaginal bleeding or abdominal pain, lumps in the genital area, or pain on passing urine should be reported at once to your doctor.

The possibility of contracting AIDS may now also be added to the burden of fears suffered by rape victims, both male and female. Again, the likelihood of a woman developing AIDS is rather remote but the fear is perfectly justifiable especially in cases where a woman has suffered cuts and wounds to the anus or vagina and where anal penetration has taken place which would theoretically make a woman more susceptible to contracting the virus from a man who is infected. So very great is the medical profession's concern now about the spread of AIDS in all sections of the community that no doctor in his or her right mind would dream of summarily dismissing such anxieties as foolish or neurotic. So if you are worried that you could have been exposed to the virus you can set your mind at rest by having a blood test to ensure you are antibody negative a few months after the rape has occurred. It can take up to 3 months, occasionally longer to produce antibodies to the virus after infection.

If the assault involved anal penetration, lacerations to the rectum may not become evident until you move your bowels, therefore any bleeding or pain should be reported to your doctor even if it occurs after you have already been fully examined. If the tissues of the anus, vulva, vagina or perineum were damaged during the rape the area will probably continue to feel sore for some days after. This is almost certain to have an effect both on your desire for sex and your sexual enjoyment for some considerable period after the attack.

The Big Turn Off

An all too common problem experienced by rape and indecent assault victims is going off sex for a time, usually due to a physical revulsion at the idea of anyone touching them after they have been sexually abused. The whole idea of sexual intercourse or of certain sexual acts may become repulsive to certain women. They may have come to regard their bodies as soiled or defiled as a result of the attack. A feeling of shame may lead them to want to keep their bodies covered up. Many rape survivors develop an involuntary tightening of the vaginal muscles when trying to have sex. Largely triggered by fears connected with the rape, any annoyance or anxiety because of this, whether expressed by the woman or by her partner, is calculated to make matters worse. Rape victims and their partners must be prepared for the fact that a certain amount of pain and discomfort during sex or the inability to participate in straightforward intercourse is perfectly normal in the weeks following the traumatic incident. Research shows that almost all rape victims admit to a tremendous loss of trust, and feeling of ambivalence towards men after being attacked. For some women all men may now be suspect and therefore are potentially on trial.

The fundamental underlying conflict is that most women expect men to be protective, yet recognize that men are also potential aggressors and sexually exploitive. Sexual assault finally confronts a woman with this reality. To enjoy sex, especially good sex, a woman must first be able to feel comfortable again about the context of when, how and with whom she has sex. She needs to be able to regain pride in her body and confidence in her sexuality. While still consumed by feelings of anger, shame, and a sense of revulsion at being used, soiled, rendered powerless and treated as an inhuman object, a woman will find it well nigh impossible to regain the ability to relax that leads to spontaneous erotic sensations. Nor can she regain these feelings entirely on her own. It is up to her partner to be as supportive, patient and loving as possible in the weeks and months after the crime.

Studies show that the majority of rape or attempted rape

victims get sexually turned off to one degree or another for often very long periods. A man who tries to pressure or cajole a woman into resuming full sexual relations after she was raped is almost guaranteed to sabotage both their chances of recapturing their full sexual enjoyment. Having sex immediately after being raped is not like getting back on a horse again after being thrown. No matter how loving the approach, sexual intercourse cannot be regarded as a rite of exorcism. The fear and sense of humiliation, far from being automatically dispelled, will on the contrary almost certainly be compounded by the woman's anger and resentment which may extend to men in general and all sexual acts – even sex with someone she loves.

If you have been sexually assaulted the last thing you need at this stage is to feel guilty, angry or worried at your partner's responses to the crisis. Arguments like 'let's do it now, it will make you forget, you will feel good about your body again' may sound well intentioned enough but are almost invariably motivated by a strong streak of self-interest. Such comments also indicate either a naive inability to understand the woman's predicament or else a callous determination not to share her problems.

Taking the Lead

Paradoxically, in many cases those women who can resist such pressures and manoeuvres and instead manage to assert their immediate sexual needs and desires – or lack of desires – stand by far the greatest chance of regaining their sense of control and self-esteem. 'Giving in' to their partner's sexual demands is calculated often to intensify a woman's feelings of helplessness. Problems ranging from complete abstinence caused by absence of any interest in sex to diminished desire for intercourse are categorized as disorders of the 'desire phase'. Invariably, due to the stress of conflicting emotions conscious or unconscious, regarding one's own sexuality and perceptions about men and their sexuality, these may include an abhorrence or nervousness at taking part in certain sexual acts, most commonly oral and anal sex if these were included in the attack. Other women may feel quite prepared to have sex with their partners but find they derive little enjoyment and are frequently unable to reach orgasm. Again, a sensitive and caring partner can help re-establish the feelings of relaxation and spontaneous abandon so necessary to full sexual enjoyment. Specific sexual positions, body smells, the odour of alcohol, having sex in the dark, the feel of the partner's beard, are other turn-offs for certain women if in any way reminiscent of the sexual attack. These rape-related 'cues' have the capacity to induce negative responses ranging from uninterest and uptightness to disgust, fear or a full blown panic attack. In the majority of cases these responses tend to become less frequent and debilitating in the months following the event, eventually disappearing altogether.

Very persistent chronic sexual disorders, however, nearly always respond well to professional counselling. A previously sexually assertive woman may decline to take the initiative in lovemaking. Much depends on the couple's previous sexual relationship. Women with long-standing, well established relationships tend to suffer fewer long term sexual difficulties than those engaged in casual affairs. Women who have no relationship whatsoever at the time of the sexual attack may often feel safer by withdrawing into a period of self-imposed celibacy until they meet someone whom they can trust and feel comfortable with as a sexual partner.

How quickly a woman recovers from such problems depends largely on how easy she finds it to talk about the difficulties arising from the attack as well as on the amount of support and understanding provided by those closest to her.

Stress-Related Physical Disorders

Mysterious aches, pains and odd sensations that appear out of nowhere are a very common by-product of severe psychological distress. Even if you were not physically harmed during the attack you may develop any number of inexplicable symptoms in the following days and weeks. Coming so soon after the crime when you are feeling at your most vulnerable and low, a natural reaction is to suspect that you are developing an illness. Fears of developing a serious disease or illness are common amongst people who are emotionally distressed and reflect already prevalent anxiety and depression. In addition, there may be sufficiently persistent symptoms to validate these fears. The point is that under extreme stress many people become physically extra vulnerable. Emotions such as fear, anger, depression and anxiety may affect any number of bodily organs and systems. Stress and emotional shock can throw the body's delicately synchronized hormonal system into violent upheaval causing some women to menstruate irregularly or cease menstruating altogether, exacerbating symptoms of pre-menstrual tension, and intensifying menstrual discomfort and pain.

The body's immune defence system may become significantly weakened by the effects of severe or prolonged stress which explains why periods of emotional trauma often coincide with a bout of flu, an attack of herpes, bronchitis or a severe cold. To make matters worse, anyone caught in the throes of victim trauma syndrome lacks the resources necessary to fight many of these symptoms.

Inability to get to sleep or to sleep through the night undisturbed is a major source of physical and psychological distress among victims. Deprived of the rest they so desperately need their physical and mental resources can become depleted even further. This is the one occasion when sleeping pillls or tranquillizers, provided they are prescribed for a limited period only, can help many victims overcome the worst symptoms of exhaustion. Anger, fear, depression are all emotions that in themselves drain the body of its energy and other resources. Lack of sleep is calculated to wear down bodily strength and reduce the brain's capacity to function even further. Taking a mild sleeping pill such as Dalmane or Mogadon for no more than three or four weeks will not set you on the road to addiction but will allow you to regain the mental alertness and physical stamina without which you cannot put things into perspective and reassert control over your life. If you don't like the idea of taking drugs or are frightened of not sleeping well after coming off the sleeping pills it is well worth experimenting with such natural alternatives as calcium or dolomite (a mixture of calcium and magnesium) tablets or tryptophan, an amino acid which induces sleepiness and relaxation, or herbal extracts such as passiflora and valerian.

Because in many ways you are as physically and emotionally fragile in the weeks following a crime as someone who has just been bereaved or gone through a major life threatening illness or surgery, you will be susceptible to any number and variety of physical upsets. This is not a cause for alarm but for caution. Treating yourself with extra care and gentleness at this period can help you along the road to recovery faster and more smoothly and with minimum disruption to your life, work and relationships. Eating regular meals and a well-balanced diet can prevent you from becoming ill.

Off Balance

Remember that because shock invariably jolts and jars the normal process of thinking, judging and decision-making, the period after an attack is not an opportune time to take on important new commitments or make major decisions involving work or personal life if you can possibly avoid them. Don't take un-necessary risks – a shock or crisis makes people more accident prone, less liable to react quickly and effectively to alarm or danger. Driving a car, playing certain sports, operating complex machinery, doing anything that requires a high degree of dexterity or coordination may prove more of an effort than usual. Be patient: don't make too many excessive demands of yourself and don't allow others to push you back into everyday life before you feel you are well and ready to do so.

Making clear-cut decisions or carrying out tasks which require a lot of mental concentration are infinitely more difficult for someone who is either very anxious or depressed. Pushing yourself too hard and then getting upset or angry at yourself for being dim or slow is merely counterproductive, heaping stress upon existing stress and leading to further mental blockage. Try to take your mind off matters relating to your work or the problems in your immediate environment. Distracting yourself by taking a holiday, visiting friends, reading books, or going to see films can help to dispel obsessive thoughts and worries. Gentle forms of activity such as swimming, walking and yoga, because these are unforced and rhythmic, can help to calm the mind and relax the body.

Osteopathy and acupuncture either independently or com-bined can – provided you go to an expert practitioner – work wonders in reducing back pain, headaches, migraine, elimin-ating muscular soreness and stiffness and generally relaxing the body. Anyone who has suffered a blow to the head or a wrench involving the neck and head should try to consult an osteopath who is also trained in cranial osteopathy. This is a branch of osteopathy that focuses specifically on the bones and joints of the head and face in relation to the spine. Any stiffness or dislocation of the cranial bones which might occur as a result of whiplash injury, for example, can have far-reaching repercussions on the spine and may also produce visual and hearing disturbances, severe headaches and facial pain. A course of acupuncture which works by bringing the body and its symptoms into balance may counteract stress-related ailments including headaches, gastro-intestinal disorders, insomnia, nausea, and muscular spasm.

What Do Victims Want?

It is often hard for a victim to impress the urgency and precise nature of their needs upon others. We have already looked at some of the personal causes underlying many people's inability to give freely of their time and support. As a victim it will alas soon become evident from whom you can expect the sort of unconditional acknowledgement of your needs so vital to your complete recovery. Study after study into the aftereffects of violent crimes such as rape indicate that it is not so much the immediate level of trauma following the incident that determines the length of the recovery period but the amount of ongoing outside support and help the victim can count on often, in the days, weeks and months afterwards.

Other people's reactions of impatience or embarrassment when faced with your desire to talk, to cry or to seek reassurance may turn out to be your cue to apologize for being a drag or simply to withdraw into silence rather than insist they hear you out. In this instance there is little else you can do but accept that this person does have a problem in coping with your distress. Though it is not much consolation, that person is probably feeling guilty as hell at not being able to offer more help.

However, the problem is theirs – not yours. What's difficult is avoiding the tendency to interpret such a reaction as an outright personal rejection. Try instead to seek out those people you remember as having been helpful and supportive when you were in difficulties in the past. Don't apologize for the fact that you feel angry or be ashamed as you are likely to burst into tears or need to retell events over and over again. You have a right to feel and behave in this way. Feeling frightened and helpless is a perfectly normal reaction. You are fully entitled to feel and express any strong emotions that arise, and if in the early stages after the crisis you need your relatives and close friends to help you overcome the worst symptoms try not to be diffident about expressing those needs and making demands on people's time and energy.

Try not to be on your own for long periods in the first few days following the event, especially in the evenings and throughout the night when you are most likely to feel afraid and become disturbed by nightmares and sleeplessness. If you live alone get someone to stay with you for a week or two or go and stay with them. Says Alexandra Campbell:

> I stayed with friends for about three weeks after the attack during which time they had to put up with my waking up screaming blood curdlingly around twice or three times a night and jumping out of my

skin during the day, as well as having to listen to both my and my brother's incessant need to go over and over the incident.

Forewarn your close friends or relatives that you may need to depend on them as a security team over the coming days or weeks, for example to help you out with the shopping if you are afraid to go out, to pick you up from work if you cannot face using public transport or if the streets after dark seem too menacing for you in your present condition. In many cases those close to you will also be feeling very distressed at what happened and worried about your well-being. This does not mean that they can accurately determine what your present needs really are or how they can best help you through the trauma. Verbalizing your fears and thoughts rather than putting a brave face on things and telling everyone you are all right will help others support you.

Many women in particular encounter a problem in recognizing that their needs are legitimate or that they deserve to have those needs met. Often brought up to be selfless and nurturing, satisfying other people's needs before their own, some female victims will need others to validate their distress. Women who appear strong, capable and normally resilient may be those most unable to voice their fears. The more unduly high their own expectations of themselves as well as the expectations of others around them, the harder it may be for them to acknowledge their distress.

A Woman's Lot

For a woman who has always regarded herself – and been regarded by her partner, parents, children, and other relatives and close friends and colleagues – as an unstinting provider and a prime source of comfort, suddenly to be confronted by her own neediness and desire to be nurtured can conjure up almost irreconcilable inner conflicts: how can she depend for a change on others when others have always depended on her? Acknowledging the validity of those needs is a prerequisite to fulfilling them. The problem is that you may not feel inclined to ask for help if help is not immediately forthcoming from those around you. So, if someone asks you how you are and feel tell them. Try to resist the urge to put on a brave face or an image of how you think you ought to act. This may prove difficult at first for friends and relatives who have always seen your role in life as being strong and in control.

Difficult maybe, but not impossible in the majority of cases. Tell those people you feel close to that you need them to sit down and listen to you. Talking is far and away the most important outlet for victims. If someone criticizes your handling of the attack or passes judgement on your behaviour or actions as being responsible for initiating the incident then try not to let their remarks fuel any feelings of guilt. If you can give a full account of what happened and how you felt during the attack without becoming too upset then do so as clearly and concisely as possible. This can often remove any traces of incomprehension or confusion from other people's minds and convey the extent of the crisis you have been through. It can be difficult for even the most well meaning and sympathetic persons to comprehend fully the nature of a crime such as mugging or rape and its impact on the victim, especially if they have never encountered any such experience before. They may feel it is up to you to open up about your feelings, and wish to avoid upsetting you by broaching the subject or asking you how you feel.

This can easily be misinterpreted as uninterest. Once you let someone know it's all right to talk – in fact it's essential as far as you are concerned – you will be surprised at how most people's inhibitions vanish. The embargo we place on our emotions can often be due as much to our desire to protect others as to shield ourselves. When recounting your story don't allow others to interrupt or sidetrack you or try to draw you into an argument. Some people may feel tempted to butt in with their own experiences of ill fortune in the belief that in listening to their own saga of woe you may forget yours. In the early stages of a crisis the opposite almost invariably applies. This is not a time for you to take on board other people's problems and difficulties. Right now, similarly, try to avoid the company of people who tire, irritate or drain your energies no matter how much you like or care for them. At this moment it is your needs alone that are paramount. This is not selfishness but fundamental to crisis intervention. In granting yourself the right to express your emotions and seek support from others you are also tacitly admitting that there is an emergency on – and you need all the help you can get in dealing with it. After all, if you had just broken your leg no one would think it strange if you complained of pain from time to time and needed help in getting around. Why should emotional injuries be any different?

A Holding Environment

Psychotherapists use the term a safe 'holding' environment in describing what victims most need in the aftermath of crime. Essentially this environment allows the victims to talk freely and frequently about their experiences without risk of being blamed, judged, criticized or having others impose their own interpretations and definitions about what the victim experienced or what he or she needs or should do now. Requests for help should be met unquestioningly and any impulse on the part of relatives and friends to project their own distress about what happened onto the victim should be overcome wherever possible. Victims should be 'welcomed back' into the safe world and told that everyone is glad they are alive and uninjured, and that they handled the situation well whether they managed to fight back or not, and that they did nothing wrong. This can greatly dispel any tendency the victims might have to blame themselves for what happened.

The victim needs to be reassured that their reactions are normal rather than being urged to calm down, be reasonable, pull themselves together, stop crying or be thankful that things are not worse. People in shock cannot always talk openly about the incident or spontaneously express their feelings. By telling them that you are there to listen and to help should they wish to share their feelings rather than forcefully trying to pull the experience out of them you will help them relax more easily. It is helpful eventually for the victims to talk through their theories of attribution whether these make sense or not – these are all strategies by which the victims seek to regain control of themselves and their lives. Arguing with the victims about the illogicality of self-blame or shooting down any other attributions of blame as silly or implausible can cause them to feel isolated and perpetually vulnerable for want of a 'handy hook' on which to hang the incident.

Not until the survivors have integrated the event into their overall experience of their life do they have sufficient confidence in their autonomy to be able to acknowledge the role that accident and chance play in life. If it appears that the victims are on a 'guilt trip' and prone to give themselves a particularly hard time for what happened, gentle diplomacy and comforting words rather than upfront impatience or worry are more likely to steer them off this course of self-destruction. Any positive aspect about the event or the victim's role in it, no matter how minor should be brought out and stressed by the co-victims in order to foster the victims' self-respect and the renewed belief in themselves without which re-establishing their normal life is impossible. It helps to assure the victims that they are resilient and remind them that they have all the resources necessary to survive the present trauma. Going to other extremes and implying that the event has rendered the victims weak and ineffectual, unwell or more vulnerable can have a disastrous effect since it makes them feel stigmatized and doubly doubt their ability to get back on their feet and resume control.

Being over protective, a natural instinct if the person who is suffering is very young or elderly, can be counterproductive because it may sabotage the victim's attempt to regain control of life. Listen carefully to the victims and observe every change of mood and impulse – these will tell you how they are going about the business of putting back the pieces. Be alert and patient and let the victim be the one to state his needs rather than assuming you know them already or superimposing your own beliefs and theories about what's best. Over zealous solicitude, even if well-meaning, can be almost as counter-productive as criticism or blame since it implies the victim is deemed incapable of knowing how best to run his life – an attitude that serves further to undermine already shaky self-confidence.

11
Putting Back the Pieces

Unlikely though it may seem at the time, it is possible to emerge from the experience of violent crime a stronger more confident person than you were before. Because intense stress and trauma inevitably force many people to challenge long-held assumptions and reconstruct their perceptions of themselves as well as of their environment, the opportunity for gaining greater awareness and ultimately for attaining personal growth and change exist, and should be grasped.

Far from falling apart, many victims, once they recognize that they can turn a negative experience to a positive one and begin to explore ways to do so, become stronger more self-aware human beings as a result of the crisis. Alexandra Campbell believes that her attack gave her the opportunity to embark on what amounted to an intensive course in greater self-awareness.

I had to do so much to get myself back together again after the incident that I became much more clued up about the links between stress and my physical well-being. I am now much more sensitive to the way that stress affects my health and can treat the symptoms and get rid of them earlier on. I have also become aware of how a major crisis such as a criminal attack acts as a catalyst in bringing other suppressed symptoms to the surface. In this case when they do arise you have a fresh opportunity to deal with them, something you might normally never have had. In this way you learn more about your problems, your reactions and your attitudes. Above all, what was necessary for me was to make a conscious decision not to become a victim of life because I had been a victim of crime. You do actually have the choice but sometimes it's not that apparent. Knowing you have that choice gives you a tremendous sense of personal strength. I have much more faith now in my ability to cope whatever happens.

Company director Lawrence Woodward, who was viciously

mugged while out jogging, claims the incident led to a far greater awareness of everyday big city hazards.

> I am now acutely aware of other people around me when I am out walking even during the day, especially when I am in a crowd. I now register the faces and attitudes of people walking towards me. It's like a development of a whole extra sense. I've become aware of things to a degree that I would never have contemplated ever, before I was attacked. It'll certainly be a long time before I ever go jogging after dark again. I am nervous even when jogging during the day and I found it necessary to push myself in order to overcome that fear, which I have now largely done.

Another mugging victim, Tony King, claims that being attacked gave him an invaluable sense of awareness of potential hazards and dangers which means he can now avoid situations long before he is directly confronted by them.

> Whenever I see suspicious groups of people or gangs of youths or I notice somebody peculiar on a bus or train or I get an inkling that an upheaval or fight may occur I instinctively turn my back, cross the road go away, get myself right out of the possibility of any harm which may befall me. Whereas once upon a time I might have walked around more absentmindedly, my ears and eyes not fully alerted to what was going on around, now the antennae pick up every message, no matter now subtle.

However, becoming more positively aware of one's behaviour and sharpening one's perception of the environment is no simple matter. It usually entails hard work, patience and courage to examine aspects of one's behaviour and personality that one might normally be tempted to keep under wraps. Personal growth is never easy and can prove painful – but the rewards reaped in terms of confidence and strength normally far out-weigh the effort and upheaval involved.

A Friend Indeed

Any crisis can deliver shattering disappointments as well as positive, unexpected surprises. Be prepared, for instance, to face up to that old adage of not knowing who one's true friends are until one is in trouble. Some come up trumps, others fall by the wayside. Thus your friendships may now come under supreme test. If your trust in other people has taken a hefty battering because of the attack what follows is a period of make or break. How readily your friends rally to your aid is not only a decisive factor in how those friendships progress in the future but in how readily you regain trust in others. While certain friends may be deemed to have failed you by being incapable of true understanding, less obvious people in your life can restore your waning belief in humanity by turning out to be staunchly supportive throughout the crisis.

When this occurs the resulting review and cooling off or even ending of certain friendships, though initially sad, can impart an exhilarating feeling of having cleared the decks and gained a clear overview of the true value of certain relationships. During the aftermath of the crime it will become pretty clear to you who you want to be with because they make you feel pretty good and who to avoid because they seem to contribute nothing positive to your well-being or may even consciously or unconsciously undermine your recovery. When Pam White was caught in the Harrods' bombing she was then living with her boyfriend, himself a police officer.

> In the police force you are not supposed to show your feelings so I had to put on a brave face at work. But I wasn't even able to let myself go and express my feelings at home. My boyfriend kept telling me I should be grateful not to have been killed like the other constable standing next to me. He couldn't understand my fears and doubts and kept telling me to get on with life and put it behind me. Very soon we split up. My needs and his lack of understanding caused a tremendous strain between us.

One dominant anxiety shared by many victims is that they will be unable to put their lives back together again and may remain permanently scarred by events. Yet far from finding your resources non-existent you may indeed discover yourself mobilizing inner strengths and capabilities that you never previously knew you possessed. Loss of self-confidence may prompt you to question all manner of things about yourself. But the positive constructive approach to self-analysis lies not in berating and blaming yourself for what you regard as demerits or gross inadequacies but in emphasizing what you know to be positive qualities that were evident at the time of the attack. Focusing on one's strong points is an obvious morale-booster, but the problem is that most victims, by dint of other people's negative reactions and an already severely punctured ego, are so demoralized and guilt ridden that it hardly occurs to them to view themselves in a positive light. Caught up in such a double bind, some victims may find themselves diverted from the true road to recovery.

Positive Strategies

After the worst symptoms of the crisis have passed you will be able to analyse more calmly and rationally the different ways in which you could take greater control of those parts of your life which now seem unmanageable or which you now realize perhaps you never really put much thought into managing before. With hindsight you may perceive that certain elements of your working, social and home life, your relationships, activities, and self-image are not as cohesive as they might be. Gaining control over those disparate strands is an integral part of making sense of your life and feeling good about who you are again.

By making definite changes or initiating positive actions at this point in your life there are numerous ways of overcoming feelings of helplessness or being out of control. These may or may not be directly involved with or related to your experience as a victim. Installing a better security system in your home, moving to another part of the country, moving home, ending or re-examining your relationships with others, changing jobs or insisting on greater safety precautions at work, altering your style of dress, altering the way you move, use your voice and generally express yourself, becoming physically fit, learning self-defence, learning more about your environment, giving up alcohol or drugs, becoming more interested in sexual, social, or political issues related to crime, helping other victims, training to become a counsellor or setting up a self-help group, or joining or creating a pressure group are just some of the productive steps you might take. Says Tamsin, who was raped at the age of fifteen:

> Feeling totally helpless and angry at the world led me to become interested in what positive ways I could break the bonds that I felt tied me up in society and limited my role and activity in it. I started joining a lot of feminist consciousness-raising groups to become more aware of the socio-economic issues surrounding crimes against women. This turned out to be tremendously inspiring. My real desire is to try and help other victims to channel their negative feelings into something positive. There is so much energy in an emotion like anger and you can do a lot of good things with it. I applied to join the Samaritans but was told I was too young so I am now taking courses in psychology and rape trauma because I want to start a self-help group for other victims. I have begun in a small way because I am helping and counselling another rape victim, a girl who is just fifteen – the same age that I was when I was raped.

Coping Strategies

The ultimate goal of recovery is to achieve what therapists call a full integration of the experience of victimization. This occurs once victims have reached a state of mind and being when the crime is no longer the controlling factor in their lives. This can occur very soon for some victims and much later after a long and complicated period of recovery for others. It is in effect the end result of a deep inner process of reconstructing a balanced view of one's self that incorporates all one's newly gained knowledge and experience. Before this can occur some victims may have to work systematically through the most distressing and persistent feelings arising out of their reaction to the crime.

Trying to rush recovery is a counterproductive and pointless exercise. However, certain emotions are harder to handle for some people than others. The strategies victims adopt in trying to recover vary tremendously while as time passes most people tend to draw on different resources, switching tactics depending on how depleted or energetic they feel at various phases of their recovery. The victims' behaviour is usually guided by very clear instinct and personal need and any criticism or judgement of their actions may inculcate in victims further feelings of guilt frustration, and low self-regard. As a victim or co-victim you may recognize some of the typical coping strategies demonstrated by individuals suffering from victim trauma in the chart below. Apart from an exclusive adherence to self-destructive mechanisms, such as drugtaking, there is no right or wrong way for victims to cope with their problems. Interviews with victims show that some may draw exclusively on one set of strategies while others may employ many different modes of coping depending on how they feel at the time.

Behavioural Symptoms Most Frequently Exhibited by Victims of Crime

Avoidance
Sleeping a lot, not thinking about what happened.
Avoiding people, places, situations that could be a reminder of the attack.
Trying to forget it ever happened.
Trying to ignore all thoughts and feelings about the attack.
Getting more involved in religion or changing religions.

Keeping busy, distracting oneself from being bothered by the experience.

Nervous/Anxious

Changing one's habitual way of doing things especially in one's daily routine.

Crying, screaming, giggling a lot when alone.

Openly screaming and crying in front of others.

Snapping at people for no reason, feeling irritable and as if about to explode.

Eating, drinking, smoking more than usual.

Taking drugs (like valium) to help relaxation.

Developing dependence on a counsellor/social worker.

Staying at home.

Cognitive

Trying to rethink the situation, see it from a different perspective.

Seeking more information about violence/rape and other people's experiences.

Going over the assault repeatedly, trying to work out why it happened and what occurred at each stage.

Trying intellectually to understand what happened, and why the experience has caused these feelings.

Going over all the positive things one did and which helped ensure survival.

Talking to a therapist or counsellor.

Expressive/Positive

Taking concrete actions to make positive changes in one's life.

Giving oneself permission to feel certain emotions and considering any feelings to be normal and healthy.

Directly showing one's feelings in front of others.

Talking to friends and family about one's feelings.

Doing things for oneself just because they make one feel good.

Examining one's life activities, relationships and priorities and getting rid of things that are not really important.

Telling oneself and others that one is determined the attack will not ruin one's life or lead to emotional defeat.

Helping other people who have suffered a similar experience.

Self-Destructive

Blaming onself for what happened, going over all the things one did wrong, holding oneself responsible for the attack.

Snapping at others, being irritable, feeling one is about to explode.

Refusing all offers of help, dismissing other people's enquiries
and sympathy.
Drinking a lot of alcohol or taking other drugs more than usual.
Eating or smoking cigarettes much more than usual.
Thinking about killing oneself.
Attempted suicide.

In the period shortly following the crisis many victims find it
easier to sidestep the emotional issues raised and instead engage
themselves in initiating practical changes in a bid to restore their
self-confidence. People who have been burgled or attacked at
home often find that installing a new, more effective security
system helps immediately in making them feel safer. Alexandra
Campbell and her brother spent over £4,000 on having bars,
burglar alarms, and panic buttons installed and being connected
to a central alarm station.

> Everyone kept asking how we could bear to stay in the house but logic
> told us that such an attack could occur in any other house, so actually
> moving made no sense but spending a lot of money to feel secure
> made all the sense in the world.

Confiding in the security adviser or locksmith responsible for
carrying out these installations may confer tremendous benefits
on someone who is deeply troubled by the experience and needs
to talk about his fears to someone knowledgeable about crime
prevention. In New York City the Victims' Service Agency
recently initiated a scheme called the SAFE programme whereby
a rota of locksmiths with special training in how to recognize and
alleviate the symptoms of victim trauma syndrome are on 24-
hour call. Locksmiths, who are often the very first people victims
see after the crime, can, like the police, in theory, make ideal crisis
counsellors. Victims often have an overwhelming need to be
reassured by crime experts about their chances of being victimized again and someone whose job involves security seems
ideally suited to provide this reassurance. After all, an important
step in recovery is to remove the threat of another attack as soon
and as effectively as possible. Says Alexandra Campbell, 'It is
really ironic that I obtained so much guidance and good sense
from the security expert rather than from the doctors.'

Make or Break

If victims have been pestered by obscene or mysterious phone calls and are worried the burglar or attacker may be keeping tabs on them changing their telephone number is the most obvious strategy to remove this source of fear. Moving house may seem an extreme measure in counteracting feelings of vulnerability but it is a highly significant act for many burglary victims. For a fair percentage, moving home, leaving the area altogether, or choosing to live in a block of flats rather than a house is the only way in which they can ever start to feel safe again. Important too is the symbolic meaning of starting anew, cutting one's links with past troubles and ill-fortune. After Terence Keeley was burgled while trapped alone in his bedroom police insisted that he had an expensive burglar alarm installed.

> It didn't diminish any of my fears. I used to sit up all night listening. I couldn't sleep for nervousness. I am a rotten sleeper anyway and the alarm system meant that I couldn't freely walk about in the house and make cups of tea and sit and read and turn on the television. Finally I decided to sell up. From the moment I walked out of that house and moved out of the area into a new flat I started to enjoy life again.

Realistic Fears

Many women who were sexually assaulted find their working environment unbearably menacing after such an incident. If the attack occurred at work or the perpetrator was a colleague or someone associated with her working life, then the reasons for this are obvious. Survivors may find it impossible, especially early on after the crime to work in the company of large numbers of men, particularly if they feel intimidated by either covert or openly sexist attitudes or have been threatened by sexual harassment. For many women there is a very subtle and fine dividing line between the implied endorsement of masculine aggression which is the subtext of many sexist jokes, salacious comments or innuendo, and such extreme examples of male violence as sexual assault. The sexual assault victim, because of her experience, becomes far more acutely sensitive to the whole theme of dominance and aggression that colours many men's attitudes towards women. For many women sexual harassment and sexual assault can be interpreted as being part of the same continuum of sexual violence, an uneasy reminder that we live in a society that tacitly sanctions the exploitation of women. Many women feel threatened by the undercurrent of masculine aggression present in certain predominantly male working environments. All the signs are that although few women complain or quit their jobs and the majority put up with sexism in order not to be considered unsuitable for the job, very few are unaware of the insidious effects of 'office sexism'.

A large study carried out recently by a national magazine suggests that a general feeling of constant fear is part of a working woman's life. Women whose jobs bring them into contact with criminals, the mentally ill, strange men or areas of high crime –for example social and health workers, and estate agents – or who have to do shift work and go to work in the middle of the night, are obviously faced with a far higher degree of risk to their personal safety than someone who works a regular nine to five job. The temptation to change jobs or resign after becoming a victim – especially if the attack occurred while you were on your way to or from work or carrying out your job – may come as an obvious solution to victims whose fears are directly connected to their employment. Changing jobs may prove to be a positive step, but resigning could be interpreted as a cop-out all round.

Becoming more aware of the ways in which you can and should protect yourself against the risk of attack is, on the other hand, a step calculated to pay greater net dividends in helping the victims feel they have done something productive in overcoming adverse circumstances. Learning to drive or getting a car, if you can afford it, delivers you from the stresses and possible dangers of using public transport or walking the city streets at night. Best of all, if you feel your job is inherently risky, is to persuade your employers to take steps in protecting the safety of all their personnel. For example, following complaints by staff working at the BBC Television Centre in London about the high rate of crime in the surrounding area, free transport has been made available after dark to take employees anywhere within a mile radius in order to get a taxi, or get onto public transport.

Resigning from one's job and taking on a safer but less satisfactory one may also seem to many women an essentially retrograde step, an admission of defeat which only serves to undermine further their already frail self-esteem. It is rarely possible to consider the wisdom of any major decision when one is under severe emotional stress. Conflicting and hurtful feelings invariably lead to clouded judgement and spur of the moment actions which may later be regretted. If in doubt don't decide is the guiding maxim for anyone coming through a crisis. It is far better to stall any major decision until you feel calmer and more in control than to act on blind impulse and then later to blame yourself still further for having erred and made a 'mess' of your life.

Turning Point

There are some individuals who when faced with a crisis instead of turning away will instead confront it as a challenge to be met or a project to be completed on route to full recovery. This style of total immersion though prompted by very strong emotions and the overall urge to gain control of one's life and make sense of things relies very largely on intellectual input. Victims who approach recovery in this way are often highly self-motivated perfectionists as well as analytical by nature. Imposing order on past chaos includes talking over events and feelings connected with the attack. This presents something of a problem, at least in Britain, since the opportunities for one-to-one counselling or group therapy for victims other than those who have been sexually assaulted are almost non-existent.

Rape victims may find an outlet for their need to articulate and discuss their feelings through one of the rape crisis centres or by joining a feminist organization such as the Women's Therapy Centre. Many women find themselves becoming increasingly interested in the broader issues pertaining to violence, crime and victimization following an attack. The need to understand how the police and the judicial system operate can lead to a greater awareness of the complexity of the deeper issues underlying secondary injury.

If the victims have reported the crime and become involved in the criminal process they may feel compelled to immerse themselves in criminal law and begin talking to other victim-witnesses to seek confirmation of their own beliefs. This involvement is rooted in the need to seek validation of powerful feelings of outrage, anger or dismay at the apparent inequities of the judicial system and the absence of any statutory victims' rights. This realization that others are suffering the same amount of secondary injury, if not more, because their needs are not being met by the system can act as a powerful incentive to many victims in attempting to redress their grievances.

Like ex-patients who have been very ill and whose stay in hospital opened their eyes to the suffering of others, victims may be driven by the same missionary zeal to improve the lot of others who have encountered similar distress. There is often an over-riding need to share one's experiences with other victims and set one's mind at rest that one's own reactions far from being abnormal or unique are common to the majority of survivors. Relief and gratitude that one has survived the attack also serves as a powerful motive to help others who may be less fortunate.

This leads many ex-victims to become victim support volunteers or rape crisis counsellors and even to try and gain a political voice within the community.

How personal distress can be channelled into positive altruistic action with potentially far-reaching benefits has been proven by Shelley Neiderbach, one of America's leading victims' rights activists. A victim of two muggings, Shelley is the founder of New York's group therapy centre, the Brooklyn-based Victims' Counselling Services, which has become a crucial lifeline for casualties of all crimes from rape and burglary to attempted murder. As both a psychologist and a crime victim, her understanding of victim trauma is a wide one.

> Five years after being robbed by two men who beat me over the head with a gun, a guy robbed me at knifepoint in the hall way of my apartment. Though I wasn't physically injured I was emotionally shattered. I experienced phenomenal rage and fear. I couldn't go out into the streets for weeks later: I was crippled with fear. Even though I was a qualified psychotherapist I couldn't handle my own feelings, they were so intense and frighteningly powerful. It was hard for me to believe that I was the only victim struggling with emotional issues of rage, guilt and helplessness and I wanted to know how other people were dealing with the traumas that beset them. I really thought I was going crazy. Although I had access to a wide variety of therapies I felt this route was somewhat insufficient. I needed desperately to talk to other victims, only others who had been through similar experiences might understand the crisis I was going through. Because I wasn't hurt people kept expecting me to be over the crisis. They got impatient or couldn't understand if I started to open up about my problems. I hunted around New York for a victims' equivalent of alcoholics anonymous, a sort of muggees anonymous, and failed to uncover such an organization. So I decided to start one.

For the first two years Shelley built up her counselling service and held group therapy sessions for victims in her own home, abandoning a lucrative private practice and muddling through for four years without financial backing but with encouragement and advice and help from other therapists, health professionals and doctors who referred victims to her. Over the years she has gained full government funding and increasing respect and support for her centre from the police and government officials.

> Many victims either cannot talk about their distress because no one wants to listen or else are unable to open up and admit they are distressed. They often want to forget their experience as soon as possible. Once they come to the centre and find other victims feel the same way the relief at finding they are not the only one is immense.

Counselling is specialized, intensive and short-term and uniquely focused on the problems of victim trauma. However, even victims who have no background in psychology, medicine or therapy can train to become counsellors. Having been through the experience, provided they have integrated their feelings, ex-victims are of course uniquely suited to counsel other victims.

A Suitable Case for Treatment

In theory the route to recovery appears manifestly simple and straightforward. The catharsis which results through articulating one's thoughts and venting one's emotions within a supportive holding environment in itself serves as an anodyne powerful enough to heal the most damaged psyche and restore the shakiest self-image. Or it may not. For some people being victimized acts as a catalyst, dredging up forgotten memories of crises long past, painfully opening old wounds and resurrecting emotional conflicts which may be traced back as far as early childhood, yet which the victim had hitherto efficiently suppressed. For example, children who were sexually abused or assaulted, if later victimized as adults may re-experience all the agonies associated with their early years. Where one traumatic incident reactivates the memory of another earlier and possibly far more painful episode, the recovery process for the victim can prove fraught with hitches, reversals and hold-ups. While attempting to deal with the present source of distress victims may battle in vain against a rising tide of memories from the past. On the one hand they try desperately to repress the earlier hurt yet on the other they are compelled to relive the childhood nightmare.

For Mariette being raped by a man she had just met at a party at the age of twenty brought back all the horrific memories of her childhood when her father would regularly have intercourse with her.

> I have never been able to talk about it. This recent rape made me feel that it was my father who was doing the same thing again. I feel so terribly ashamed. I feel as if I am just there to be used by men. It seems as if the past nightmare is repeating itself once again.

Others may become trapped in a time warp in which the present crisis pales into insignificance in comparison with what is a terrifying reconstruction of the past. In such cases of double victimization the victim nearly always needs expert help in

resolving both sets of problems in particular any earlier unresolved traumas. Victims who have lived through previous
crimes of violence will invariably find it very difficult, even
impossible, to discuss their feelings with those around them. Yet
the danger inherent in this second trauma is that it will lead the
victims to ignore or repress their present reactions thereby
augmenting an already simmering substratum of pain and
unresolved distress.

If the childhood experience involved sexual abuse, especially
by a parent, residual guilt and shame may easily prevent the
victim from mentioning the incident to anyone, even a close
family member. This extra burden can prove quite intolerable for
many victims. Suffering in secret isolation can lead many
second-time victims to depend increasingly on drugs or alcohol
or develop obsessive-compulsive disorders such as gambling,
anorexia or bulimia. The total freezing of all feelings stemming
from past and present victimization can also cause a tendency to
withdraw from other people, decreased activity – for example
sleeping or staying in bed a lot, or not leaving home – and creates
an increased risk of phobias, depression, alcoholism, drug
addiction, and suicide attempts.

Victimization in adulthood can evoke other disturbing incidents from the long distant past, not just violent ones, and strike
a chime somewhere far back within the deepest recesses of the
sub-conscious, rousing any number of puzzling or troubling
sensations associated with past events. This phenomenon
accounts for the fact that if you talk to a group of victims there will
always be one aspect of the crime that will bother one person and
not another. For instance, if the victim lost a parent in infancy
perhaps as a result of death or divorce, and now feels that no one
came to his aid during the ordeal of the crime, he may have
particular problems associated with the issue of abandonment
and attendant feelings of helplessness.

Feelings of helplessness, vulnerability, fear, dependence and
anger – which are all common responses to being attacked – are
also the most basic of feelings we experience from early infancy.
Need and helplessness characterize a baby's earliest relationships. It is during the early formative years that we learn either to
express freely or else to suppress our instinctive feelings of anger,
rage, pain and fear in order to ensure that our infant needs to be
loved and protected are met. As we grow older, further
conditioning may reinforce the negative or positive 'tag' that we
attach to those emotions. Consequently we grow up inhibiting
some of these emotions, and find ourselves unable to express

them spontaneously or openly to others or even sometimes indeed to ourselves. This is why for some people there is nothing 'natural' about showing anger, admitting to fear or guilt, or declaring a need for revenge.

In certain victims such feelings, because of their association with early trauma or childhood conditioning, may be ineluctably bound up with punishment or disapproval. Many women, for instance, if taught as little girls that showing anger or losing one's temper is unfeminine or unattractive will have trouble admitting these feelings as adults. Similarly men whose childhood upbringing was guided by a prevailing macho ethic – 'real men don't cry' – may find themselves deeply troubled by purportedly unmasculine emotions such as fear and helplessness. This sub-text of victim trauma is something that many victims fail to address on their own, largely through an inability to understand or identify the underlying problem that is impeding their recovery. In such cases the guidance of a trained counsellor can prove invaluable in helping victims work through any unfinished business arising out of earlier crises.

Unravelling the Spiral

Counsellors such as Shelley Neiderbach observe that the tremendous variations in the order of symptoms displayed by victims is one of the most puzzling aspects of victim trauma. Most victims exhibit a symptom spiral that must be fully unravelled before full recovery can commence. Some will have little trouble, perhaps, in expressing anger initially, yet others may only experience this emotion as the final strand of the psychological skein. Patient probing, reassurance and encouragement on the part of a counsellor, perhaps coupled with the confidence imparted through hearing the experiences of others, usually helps overcome any resistance a victim might have towards confronting the most troubling feelings.

Many victims cannot begin to exorcise their feelings of distress until they have been able to relive the past crisis in a safe supportive environment – a phenomenon also common to many war veterans suffering from PTSD. Through detailed analysis of the exercises undertaken as part of the therapy, Shelley Neiderbach has come to the conclusion that whatever victims handle worst they handle last. Therefore the psychological state of the crime victim may deteriorate as it spirals downwards towards that which poses the most emotional difficulty, be it a feeling of fear, powerlessness, guilt or anger. Once the bottom of the spiral has been reached all the symptoms become greatly alleviated as the most troubling one has been exposed and worked through.

The benefits of undergoing specialized counselling or group therapy are therefore obvious: left to work out the effects of the trauma on their own any victims who approach an emotional no-go area and instinctively hold back from fully admitting or expressing certain feelings because these are too disturbing stand the risk of simply blocking them out and carrying some effects of the trauma into their future lives. However, by confronting the most vulnerable aspect of their personalities, and seeing that it is possible to regain full control of their lives victims may experience a sense of emotional relief that can have a revolutionary effect on their lives. Even victims whose trauma is not compounded by past experiences may benefit from specialized counselling. Those who cannot rely on support of family or friends are obvious contenders for therapy, and even those who do encounter sympathetic attitudes may find people's support and patience beginning to wane and give way to incomprehension or impatience in the weeks or months following the crisis.

What If?

There is little mystique about victim counselling, be it one-to-one or group oriented. Unlike ongoing psychoanalysis or general psychotherapy treatment tends to be intensive and short-term, usually about six to twelve sessions of one or two hours that focus on feelings and issues directly arising from the crime. Therapists stress that victims must not be encouraged to form relationships of dependence with their counsellors or the group but must be encouraged to lead independent and autonomous lives as soon as they have worked their way through the trauma. The counsellor's role is frequently one of interpreter and guide, helping victims understand the fundamental causes of their distress and directing them towards the various options available to restore order and harmony to their life.

Short-term crisis intervention immediately following the crime usually helps victims avoid the worst repercussions of the experience. The principle goal of therapy is to restore to the victims their ordinary coping skills which are often temporarily knocked out of commission by the severity of the shock.

Specialized victim counselling and group therapy – in which six to ten people are led by a psychotherapist or counsellor who has also been a victim – provides survivors with that much-needed holding environment in which they can openly express their feelings. Co-victims usually attend separate sessions in which they can voice their own problems and questions, and be given extensive information about victim trauma.

At this point it is only fair to point out that apart from a certain amount of emotional counselling available to rape victims no such professionally run organization exists in the UK at the time of writing. In order to undergo psychotherapy to help you get over PTSD you must ask your GP to refer you to a psychiatrist or private therapist. This prompts another caveat. Mental health professionals, let alone GPs, who know about PTSD and are well versed in the aetiological complexities of victim trauma syndrome or who have had first hand experience in treating the disorder are at present very few and far between in Britain.

In elaborating on the types of treatment and areas of focus within victim therapy I must stress that the information is based on therapies and treatment models currently available in various parts of the USA.

Victims attending group therapy at Brooklyn-based Crime Victims' Services have experienced all sorts of crimes from rape to mugging and attempted murder. Clients are both male and female and the groups are mixed. Those who are withdrawn or inhibited are encouraged to talk more openly about their feelings, others perhaps for the first time feel free to over-dramatize or retell past events repeatedly. The patience of many counsellors or therapists unused to dealing with victim trauma may be worn to a frazzle by victims' tendency towards over-expression – therefore knowing that they are free to do this without irritating the listener may be deeply comforting to the victim. Victims are also encouraged to keep a diary or make cassette tapes recording their innermost feelings, doubts and conflicts. They are then encouraged to read these out in the group – an immensely helpful aid for those who find it hard to talk about their feelings on cue.

Role-playing and psychodrama are integral aspects of group work. Those victims who experience very vivid and distressing nightmares are also sometimes encouraged to act out those situations. Much of group therapy consists of victims acting out hypothetical dramatized situations to encourage expression of frustration, anger, resentment and indignation which might be levelled at the attacker, the police, the legal profession or outsiders whom the victims perceive as having let them down.

Knowing that the assailant was not caught, or if he was that he only received a minimal sentence or got off free can generate a deep sense of injustice which must be dispelled before the victim can make a full recovery.

Victims experiencing helplessness or shame and anger at not having stood up to their attacker now have the opportunity to go over past events and restage the scenario to accommodate their own alternative and ideal reactions. One exercise in particular expressly addresses the thorny issue of getting even with the attacker. Victims are asked what they would say or do if their attacker walked into the room right now. Graphic and violent in the extreme, the invective discharged in this exercise attests to the explosive nature of many victims' pent-up hatred.

> If the perpetrator of the crime came into this room right now I think I would kill him. If I could get his knife I would cut him into a million little pieces. I would then leave the pieces at the bus stop. Maybe the people who ran away would see him.

> If the perpetrator of the crime came into this room right now I would fucking bite his nuts off! I'd take his head and bash it into the tile floor! Maybe then I'd feel better. I want blood! I'd probably scream a lot. I feel hate, hate, hate! Because these people changed me and they are probably out right now hurting other people and laughing about it. These fucks don't have the right to breathe! There is no justification for hurting other lives. They need to be put to sleep like rabid dogs! Only I'd wish them painful degrading ugly death.

For victims with chronic symptoms of PTSD that persist long after the event or become worse instead of improving, treatment may be specifically tailored to treat pathological symptoms such as agoraphobia, panic attacks and obsessive compulsive behaviour which may severely restrict the victims' freedom to live normally. The aim of crisis intervention is to mobilize the victims' resources so they can cope with the problems arising out of events. Techniques such as hypnotherapy can be immensely valuable in helping sufferers control their fears and anxieties. In those cases where the shock of the incident has caused the victim to block out mentally most if not all of the event, hypnosis, by encouraging deep physical relaxation and raising levels of confidence, can unlock whole chunks of memory hitherto consigned to oblivion. Achieving recall is important because it is necessary to understand the sources and individual cues for one's anxieties before one can begin to address the symptoms.

In cases where chronic physical tension and mental strain are responsible for stress-related symptoms, for example migraine, backache, spastic colon, chest pain, breathing difficulties, addiction to drugs, alcohol or cigarettes, bio-feedback therapy may help the victim control the physical responses associated with such symptoms. Autogenic training is also used extensively nowadays by both doctors and therapists to counteract the effects of stress. Both these systems can help in teaching victims how to control a number of biological functions including heart rate, blood pressure, muscle tension, oxygen consumption, body temperature and the digestive system which can be extremely useful when stress symptoms threaten to become unduly chronic and debilitating.

Stress Inoculation

One of the most multi-faceted and well thought out treatment 'packages' designed specifically for victims suffering chronic long-term PTSD is stress inoculation training (SIT) devised by Professor Dean Kilpatrick, director of the Crime Victims' Research and Treatment Centre in Charleston, South Carolina. So successful has this treatment proved in curing victims of fear, anxiety and phobic avoidance that one can only hope fervently for the speedy introduction of it in Great Britain. The treatment draws on a cognitive behavioural approach to the management of crime-related fear and anxiety. The first-century stoic philosopher Epictetus observed, 'It is not the things themselves that disturb men, but their judgements about these things.' Shakespeare's Hamlet also had a fair idea of the power of thought over our feelings: 'There is nothing either good or bad but thinking makes it so.' The rationale for cognitive therapy is rooted in the belief that negative feelings such as depression, low self-esteem and fear arise from distorted thinking and misinterpretations of reality. This proposition is congruent with the crisis theory that underpins much of victim trauma syndrome. The habit of negative reasoning results directly from victimization: a rape victim concludes that because factors *a*, *b* and *c* were present during the assault any future situation in which either *a*, *b* or *c* is present is potentially dangerous and therefore may lead to another attack. The value of cognitive techniques in treating victim trauma is that they neatly demolish this premise, thereby straightening out the victims' distorted perceptions both of themselves and of the world.

The goal of SIT is, however, not the elimination of anxiety but its management. Yet once their negative patterns of thought are effectively broken, victims may once again resume activities and re-enter environments previously avoided because they were reminiscent of the attack. SIT therefore encompasses a very realistic approach to anxiety as an unavoidable but controllable aspect of life. Within this conceptual framework, victims are taught exactly how fear affects bodily functions, jamming or re-routing the conduits between emotion, physical sensation and behaviour. The particular ways in which this manifests itself in the victim's own case in relation to the attack is examined and analyzed in great detail. The rationale is not hard to grasp – once you understand and accept how fear manifests itself in your thoughts, your body and your behaviour, controlling that fear becomes a less daunting proposition.

At this stage exercises to achieve muscular relaxation and breath control are taught to help counteract the physical manifestations of fear. The confidence gained by the victim in mastering these primary coping skills which he or she can then use at any time in any number of situations and settings to overcome the worst symptoms of anxiety such as palpitations, dry mouth, sweating, and shortness of breath is in itself consider-able. Knowing that fear and anxiety are normal learned responses which can be controlled usually comes as a tremend-ous relief to those who previously believed there was something wrong with them or feared that they might be physically or mentally ill. Recognizing which aspects of the crime are likely to trigger crime-related fear later – by a process known as classical conditioning –helps the victim see why they come to experience profound panic or anxiety in response to apparently innocuous stimuli.

Following this stage of training the victim is taught how acting out different responses, rehearsing dialogue and actions in preparation for being in a particular situation can provide the means of learning new forms of behaviour and language to replace the old negative ways. Anxiety has been described as a repeated stress rehearsal for a catastrophe which will probably never occur. SIT provides dialogue, action and plot to change that into a rehearsal for a pleasant and constructive scenario with a positive end. For example, a woman might describe one of her problems as feeling put down or dismissed by one of her male colleagues at work whenever she asks him for his cooperation. As part of the training the woman and the counsellor playing the male colleague act out a typical situation, intermittently receiving feedback, encouragement and suggestions from the counsellor about her voice, posture and style of conversation. Every time the woman re-enacts the scene she becomes progressively more assertive, so gaining confidence. Other problem situations which elicit fear and other negative feelings in the victim are similarly played out with the counsellor during therapy. Having gained confidence the victim is then encouaged to do her homework, putting the skills she has learnt into practice for real.

Modelling

Another skill similar to role-playing is 'covert modelling' whereby rather than acting out hypothetical problem situations the victim instead visualizes them mentally, successfully confronting fear- or anxiety-provoking situations. Anyone who has practised meditation using guided imagery – where you see yourself winning a race, relaxing in a beautiful stress-free environment, overcoming illness and disease – will get an idea of how mental powers can be channelled to attain well-being and confidence using such techniques.

Another vital component of SIT is thought-stoppage, aimed at breaking habitual negative thoughts, overcoming the compulsion many victims have either to go over and over mentally what they perceive as the negative elements affecting their lives or blighting their character, or else becoming obsessed by hypothetical future catastrophes. Here the idea is to learn how and when to shout 'stop' aloud whenever these negative thoughts occur. Eventually victims are capable of breaking the train of non-productive thought simply by saying no silently to themselves. Thought stoppage can be utilized to overcome compulsive ritualistic behaviour such as the checking and re-checking that many burglary or assault victims go through whenever they leave or enter a room, go to bed, or prepare to come into or depart from their home.

Following on from this technique comes 'guided self dialogue' which is probably the most important of all the coping skills taught in SIT. The victims are taught to focus on their 'internal dialogue', subliminal messages pertaining to ourself and our environment that we unconsciously play over and over again in our heads like an internal tape-recording. Any irrational, counter-productive or negative dialogue is identified, challenged and substituted by rational productive and positive dialogue. A series of questions, answers and statements germane to the victim's self-image in situations which hitherto have been interpreted as stressful or unpleasant make up the framework for reprogramming this internal dialogue. The statements are geared to fit each of the victim's target fears and are written out for him or her to practise in between therapy sessions.

Once the victims have acquired all these different coping skills they are encouraged to practise them constantly, singly or in a variety of different combinations in everyday situations, utilizing whichever seems most appropriate at the time. All the skills work synergistically, each one enhancing the action of the other. By choosing which skill or combination of skills to employ, victims rapidly acquire a greater sense of control over themselves and their environment.

When offered a choice of two different types of therapy, straightforward one-to-one counselling and SIT, the majority of victims attending Professor Kilpatrick's clinic invariably choose SIT. Its obvious appeal is its specificity and comprehensiveness. The focus on self-dialogue – something victims find hard to explain in ordinary therapy – seems particularly appealing.

Although SIT is, at the time of writing, not available in Britain another system of therapeutic intervention called Neuro-Linguistic Programming (NLP) is now increasingly being used by therapists and psychologists in the UK to treat a variety of problems. NLP is a hybrid model that incorporates numerous components including hypnosis, mediation, linguistics, body movement, behavioural and cognitive techniques which, packaged together, are used by therapists to treat emotional and sexual disorders, phobias, stress-related ailments, over-eating and addiction. Used by a therapist with sufficient knowledge of the aetiology of victim trauma syndrome, NLP, because of its emphasis on mental reframing and internal dialogue which encourages individuals to perceive problems and situations in a different more positive light, could prove helpful in overcoming certain symptoms of PTSD.

PART FOUR:

Prevention and Awareness

12
Accentuating the Positive

A question that preoccupies many researchers into crime is whether there are certain inherent characteristics that make some people more liable than others to become victims. This proposition forces us, somewhat uncomfortably, to confront the whole issue of accountability that obsesses so many victims following a violent incident.

In trying to make sense of an entirely arbitrary motiveless attack we juggle with numerous hypotheses: had I not walked but taken a taxi I wouldn't have been mugged; by wearing trousers and gym shoes instead of high heels and a tight skirt I would not have attracted the attacker's attention; double locks on the windows would have deterred the burglar. Maybe so, but again, maybe not. The mugger could have struck as you were getting out of the taxi; a determined rapist will not be deterred because his intended victim wears jeans; the burglar failing to gain entry through the window may decide instead to break down the front door. Looking at crime purely fatalistically one might conclude that whichever way one analyzes it, you can't win. However, most of us have an inbuilt attitude to crime and violence which is based both upon our personal experience of handling potentially dangerous situations and on our confidence in our own ability to assert ourselves and control events. Anyone who has ever been threatened or attacked will have gained a very accurate measure of their reflexes and emergency resources. Simply knowing through past experience that you have it in you to scream, run, hit back at someone or keep your cool while assessing the potential outcome of dangerous circumstances provides a tremendous confidence booster for the future. Knowing that your experience has made you more alert to possible dangers and more aware of your own actions stacks the cards against the likelihood of a future similar crisis occurring or catching you off guard. Awareness and a sense of being in control are not, as many might think, synonymous with total absence of fear. Rather, achieving a manageable working balance between rational realistic fears, a greater awareness of your own environment and self-confidence is the key to being streetwise and safety conscious.

Eliminating the Negative

But where to begin in building confidence? Fear may be specific or all pervasive, traceable to past experience or vague and unidentifiable. Women especially may be subject to particular fears associated with certain specific environments, and to more widespread all-encompassing anxiety about their inability to control any unpleasant chance events. Such anxieties are almost invariably linked to a poor self-image and lack of assertiveness that extends into all other areas of life including their domestic and working environments. The inability to assert one's wishes clearly and positively is usually reflected by self-deprecating behaviour which invokes negative responses in others thereby reinforcing that person's existing insecurity. Unassertive behaviour therefore in itself can set up a negative cycle of feedback which serves to perpetuate that person's lack of confidence and self-esteem.

The problem with negative attitudes or unassertive behaviour is that they are very often unconscious habits we have acquired over the years. Hesitant or confused speech, a timid weak voice, slouched posture, uncoordinated tentative movements, a nervous or blank expression, defensively aggressive or childlike mannerisms are all calculated to create in others an impression of lack of confidence and unassertiveness, whether in fact such impressions are fully justified or not. Mannerisms, after all, can prove highly misleading. Where a person's appearance and behaviour are at variance with his inner perceptions and feelings this usually indicates that that person has lost the ability to view himself objectively, as he comes across to others. However, as with negative thoughts, negative behaviour can be transformed into positive assertive habits.

Interestingly enough, in a person who does suffer from nervousness, shyness, self-consciousness and the inability to assert himself freely, mastering more assertive patterns of speech and body movement can often result in a dramatic inner transformation of attitudes. The spin-off is similar to that experienced by people with emotional problems who have been chronically overweight for many years and yet manage to derive a new and positive outlook on life as soon as they lose weight and become more attractive. This is due largely to the overwhelming power of external appearance.

It has been estimated that as much as 70 per cent of the conscious and unconscious messages we transmit to others are conveyed not through speech but through the silent and subtle intricacies of body language. This is most evident on our first contact with another human being. We meet a stranger and our first impressions, invariably the strongest, are formed instantly according to the current cultural code by which we invest meaning in a person's looks and actions. Depending on individual prejudice and the criteria applied, the verdict we pass on those we meet may turn out to be entirely fair or wholly unjust but it points to the consistency with which most people are taken in by the external 'image' projected by others. Studies show quite conclusively, for instance, that women who, according to society's guidelines are deemed physically attractive, have more social relationships, and enjoy more high-profile, prestigious and higher-paid jobs than those regarded as unattractive.

Women confined to hospital suffering from psychological disorders begin to behave in a more optimistic and positive manner when they have been instructed how to improve their appearance by applying make-up and styling their hair. Much of this positive behaviour, however, is due to the patients' reactions to more positive, approving attitudes from other people with whom they come into contact, such as hospital staff. Self-image, therefore, has a powerful effect on human behaviour – your own and that of other people. It follows therefore that by feeling positive about yourself – and more especially acting in accordance with those feelings – you will transmit that sense of control and personal strength to anyone who might be tempted to attack you, causing them to reconsider or back off instantly when they see you are not a pushover. However this still prompts the question whether the risk of victimization may ever be fully eradicated? No amount of environmental awareness and self assertiveness can be wholly guaranteed to eliminate the possibility of an attack, only to reduce the odds by a significant margin. Those who claim otherwise are either whistling in the dark or being foolishly complacent. It cannot be sufficiently stressed that the information included in these last chapters is only meant as a guide to reduce the likelihood of victimization – nothing more.

People-Watching

So how exactly does positive behaviour manifest itself to the outside world? Look down any busy city street. You can spot them without fail. The confident and assertive appear 'all there', their wits tuned sharply to the here and now, fully aware of their environment and sure of their place within it. Young, old, male, female, smart, not so smart, they appear to own the street on which they walk. At first glance, directness of purpose is most readily manifest in posture, facial expression and style of walking. As unaware as we ourselves may be of the signals we emit with each characteristic step, swing and tilt of the body, to others the minutiae of body movement convey a wealth of significant information.

Take, for instance, your average mugger, eyes peeled to spot easy prey. Though unlikely to be well up on the esoteric vocabulary of 'body-speak', a sixth sense allows him to identify his target simply by the way he or she walks down the street. At least, that seems to be the conclusion of a fascinating if disturbing study conducted recently in America by Betty Grayson, Professor of Marketing and Communications at Hofstra University. Her research to some extent debunks the widely held theory that it's your age, looks, sex, the location and time of day or night which set the scene for a rape, robbery or some other physical assault. Over and above such undoubted contributory factors it now appears that there is also a correlation between people's movement patterns and the possibility, however slight, of becoming the victim of an attack. To identify the signals people send out when walking in the street and assess their potential meaning, Professor Grayson used a hidden video camera to film a broad cross-section of men and women of all ages walking along a New York street. She then showed the individual film profile to groups of prisoners convicted of violent crimes at Rahway Prison in New Jersey. The inmates accorded each person a 'muggability' rating from 1 (a pushover – would offer least resistance to attack) to 10 (steer clear – would offer most resistance).

In a second, more illuminating part of the study, the same tapes were analyzed by the Labam-Bartenieff Institute of Movement Studies, pioneers in the notation and analysis of every facet of body movement. They corroborated Betty Grayson's theory. Out of twenty-one different types of movement that were codified, including several that are usually considered of prime significance in urban survival and anti-rape classes, five distinct-ive types of movement emerged as apparently crucial in signalling vulnerability. The distinct come-on signals common to all those individuals who had been singled out as easy targets by the criminals were:

(1) Taking unusually long strides (stride was measured relative to overall body size in terms of leg movement and weight shift, not in terms of any absolute number of inches). In contrast none of the potential non-victims made unusually long or short strides.

(2) A tendency to lift the feet when walking, adopting a flat footed style in contrast to the non-victim types who tended to swing their feet and incorporate a smooth heel-toe stride.

(3) Swinging the same arm and leg forward instead of in opposition to each other.

(4) Walking 'gesturally' – moving an isolated part of the body such a a limb, hand or foot – instead of 'posturally' – in a smooth integrated fashion.

(5) Upper and lower body moving at cross purposes to one another, such as when the body is rigid from the torso up while the lower half swings along freely. Potential non-victim types usually exhibit a figure eight like sway of upper and lower body.

Such traits, according to movement analysts, are indicative of people who without even being aware of it are ill at ease or simply out of touch with their bodies. This has less to do with grace and poise than with using integrated movements and consistency of rhythm and style. A person who feels comfortable within his own body appears to have an organized quality about his body movements. In contrast the jerky, uncoordinated and gestural movement of potential victims seems to communicate unsureness, and lack of awareness. According to this study, at any rate, this might well be picked up by the criminal as a signal of that person's vulnerability and therefore a cue to attack. It is worth pointing out, for example, that one of Grayson's findings was that women wearing high heeled shoes tend to make the typical 'victim type' step while walking since their heels keep them from swinging their feet in the heel-to-toe manner of non-victims.

Future findings in this field of research could well prove invaluable in the fight against crime as well as in creating training methods for reducing a high-risk person's susceptibility to assault or alerting someone who in fact does feel perfectly confident and in control to the fact that they are projecting an altogether different image.

Body in Mind

In an environment that you suspect may be dangerous, especially after dark, both men and women – but women in particular – should observe a few cautionary tactics while walking.

(1) Increase your speed, keeping it brisk and purposeful. Don't veer from one side of the pavement to the other, walk straight and keep to the outer kerbside well away from dark doorways and alleyways yet not too close to parked cars.

(2) Avoid making eye contact with men, especially if the street is relatively deserted. Keep your eyes level and focus on the direction in which you are going.

(3) Sharpen your peripheral vision – but do it surreptitiously. Instead of looking around you in an obvious manner to ensure that no one suspicious is near you or coming up beside you keep your head level but try to dart regular sideways glances especially when waiting to cross the road or approaching a dark alleyway or cross-street, a tube entrance, a pub or a disco.

(4) Don't swing your handbag or smoke a cigarette while walking in the street – both habits give an impression of easy accessibility and insufficient personal control.

(5) When confronted by a group of men keep walking on by without looking at them. If they try to engage you in conversation, ignore them. If asked for the time say you don't have a watch or announce the time swiftly and articulately without slowing down or breaking your stride.

(6) Coming to a halt when someone tries to engage you in conversation makes it all too easy for them to confront and trap you. If asked for a light say you don't have one and carry on walking.

The whole idea is to maintain your normal rhythm, style and pace of walking as if arriving at your destination is your chief imperative and no one is going to stop you. To achieve that effect women may find it helps to put extra swing and speed into their stride, placing each foot down extra firmly on the pavement as one would if in a great hurry. An integrated style of movement should, however, stop short of being mannered. Acting 'confident' is only likely to attract attention.

There is no need to adopt an aggressive machismo swagger or stride forth defensively along the city streets as if primed for active combat. Quite the contrary. It is that very mean menacing aggression which characterizes the attitudes of many young urban men – when for instance obviously spoiling for a fight – that is often responsible for initiating a potentially violent confrontation. There is little doubt that over-aggressive body language rather than defusing a potentially violent confrontation may actually inflame it, as any pub brawl, disco fight or furore on the football stands demonstrates. Integrated movement, on the other hand, essentially reflects a relaxed yet alert body.

Taking up sport or any form of regular exercise is guaranteed in most cases to help you develop greater physical assurance and bodily coordination. Women in particular often move according to how they visualize their body shape. Keeping fit through any form of regular exercise and in particular improving muscular tone and strength by taking up weight training, dance or aerobics classes or any of the martial arts is virtually guaranteed to cultivate suppleness, improved reflexes and muscular strength. It goes without saying that if you have ever entertained ideas of being able to flee rapidly from or fight any potential attacker you are unlikely to have sufficient resources to do so if you are extremely physically unfit.

Face Values

Also characteristic of those who project a confident image is a certain congruence of voice, facial expression and body movement. Someone with a purposeful brisk stride rarely mismatches this with a confused or blank facial expression. It is unusual for a man or woman who speaks cogently not to back up the words with assertive gestures and postures. When all modes of self-expression are coherent and integrated one with another for maximum impact, there is less chance of a person who is really aware and in control of his actions being misread. While individual physiognomy dictates largely what type of expression each person's face assumes when he or she is out walking, driving their car, sitting in a train or waiting for a bus, it is as well to be aware of what impression this 'look' may have on others – and to try to alter it where necessary. Tension, fear, and nervousness usually come across in the eyes: staring, a vague wide-eyed expression, rapidly shifting glances, and frowning mostly convey lack of confidence while a relaxed forehead, candid open eyes – the sort of look that says 'I'm at home here, I feel good' – invariably suggest self-possession. A relaxed mouth, neither openly smiling nor tightly disapproving, reads the same way. Pouting, lip-biting, gum chewing, and nail-biting not only attract attention but can indicate anything from nervousness to simple-mindedness. In an environment you feel could be slightly dodgy – the tube late at night, a run-down inner city are, around the pubs at closing time, assuming an attitude of slightly bored indifference, the sort of expression that says 'I've seen it all before' adds extra weight to your self-possession. Wearing a walkman personal stereo set provides perfect cover because your hearing is engaged – a first-rate put-off to anyone wanting to strike up a conversation – while your vision remains firmly hooked into the here and now.

Practise these expressions in the mirror – learn how to become a good actor by analyzing how your different facial expressions can come across. As any method actor will testify, even just assuming a look of confidence or good humour may go a long way towards inspiring such feelings within you.

Vocal Powers

An integral aspect of overall image, the voice is something that can let down even the most apparently self-confident man or woman. Women in particular who have squeaky high-pitched, breathy or faint voices may find it difficult to act assertively or to elicit the right response from others even if they actually feel they are being assertive. Talking too quickly, or not projecting the words audibly and distinctly are often signs of nervousness or tension in the jaw, neck and throat muscles, and also reflect an inability to breathe deeply and rhythmically. Such handicaps can usually be overcome by learning to relax and becoming more aware of breathing from the diaphragm using the entire lung capacity rather than only the upper chest.

The throat, mouth and therefore the voice are the first areas to be affected by nerves. If tightness in the throat is likely to rob you of your full vocal powers then practise first, consciously tensing the neck, face and jaw muscles, then letting go. Taking short breaths and emphasizing the out breath every time you breathe rather than gulping in too much air, which tends further to increase feelings of anxiety or nervousness, will help you remain in control of your breathing and your voice. Remember that you do not have to speak loudly to appear assertive, but you do need to talk distinctly and inject a firm note into your voice.

If someone is rude, attempts to chat you up, makes an obscene comment or goes on pestering you in an environment where you cannot get away such as a crowded underground train or bus, then the best tactic is either to ignore that person or to respond with a firm peremptory put down. This is not a test of politeness or tact, so don't be afraid to sound rude. Women in particular often have an inbuilt abhorrence of being insulting, seeming aggressive or hurting someone's feelings, so they often get caught up in unnecessary confusion by trying to be nice. Yet most men do not expect women to respond forcefully or to use rude language as a man might do. So if and when you do it will almost certainly deter anyone who is being a nuisance from pursuing their tactics further. If the first sharp 'no' or 'leave me alone' doesn't work, rest assured that a clearly delivered 'fuck off' or better still 'fuck off at once or I'll call the police' will do the trick. Following this up with a sharp dig in the ribs with your elbow or a kick on the shins should hit the message home.

Above all, avoid the temptation to pretty up the message by taking a 'please would you mind not doing that' approach. Pleading or politeness have no place in such an encounter. In more extreme circumstances if someone is about to attack you physically, you should try to scream as loudly as you can. Ironically, though screaming might seem to be the most natural and spontaneous thing to do, many women are horrified to find that when the moment comes they cannot scream no matter how hard they try. This is because nervousness and fear make the voice literally 'stick' in the throat, especially in someone who is not normally voluble. It may sound silly, but if you have never discovered whether you can scream spontaneously you should practise – or at least exercise the vocal chords by singing very loudly in the highest possible register. Even if it proves difficult at first, you may eventually surprise yourself at the sound that comes out. That sound might at some time prove instrumental in saving your life.

Telephone Manners

Women are virtually the exclusive recipients of that quaint euphemism, coined by British Telecom, the nuisance call. Modern technology has given today's offender a broader scope to shock and traumatize. In the past if he failed to get a reply chances were that the caller wouldn't bother to try that number again. These days he may have ample opportunity to record repeated indecent messages on an answering machine, perhaps learning the identity and whereabouts of his victim from the outgoing message.

Obscene calls represent a sinister invasion of privacy and can be responsible for causing tremendous emotional trauma. With increasing numbers of women now living alone, obscene calls are becoming worryingly commonplace. According to a recent report 10 per cent of young and middle-aged women, especially those who are separated or divorced, receive obscene calls in any given year. Over half these women are pestered by numerous calls rather than the isolated one-off and this seems to be a predominant feature of the offence. The calls are more than just a nuisance, and tend to turn into an insidious form of torment and menace, generating anxiety that the caller, especially if he knows the woman's identity and address, might be watching her movements and may go on to perpetrate a more serious crime.

Although there is no discernible link between receiving obscene calls and becoming a victim of sex crimes, such fears are completely understandable. If someone attempts to harass you over the telephone, making repeated obscene suggestions or attempting to draw you into an intimate conversation, use the same tactics that you might do when confronted in a street by an offensive stranger. It is believed that one of the reasons why women are often revictimized by the same nuisance caller is their inability to come up with a sufficiently swift and adequately assertive rejoinder. Just banging down the receiver may deter him for only as long as it takes to redial your number if he is really persistent. Don't get caught up in a conversation just because you don't want to be rude and don't answer his questions. If his opening gambit is sexual – and it usually is – then a contemptuous put-down delivered in a sharp authoritative tone before you replace the receiver will almost certainly be sufficiently humiliating to put him off for good.

If you own a telephone answering machine, when recording your outgoing message make sure you talk in a firm, neutral tone and at a measured pace including the minimum amount of information about who you are. Do not give your full name – in fact, try to omit your name altogether – your address or, if possible, even your number. This may be difficult if you use the machine to record business as well as social calls. When you answer the telephone in person do not give your name or number, just say hello and wait for the caller to respond. If there is no response or you begin to hear heavy breathing, groans, gasps or anything out of the ordinary don't carry on saying, 'Hello who is that?' Just hang up. Never indicate to the caller that you are alone at the other end of the phone. The chances are that that person won't call back. Should the calls persist keep a whistle or better still a screecher alarm by the phone and blow it down the mouthpiece sharply, then hang up immediately. This will certainly shock the caller and may even temporarily damage his hearing. Very distressing and persistent calls should be reported to the police or the operator who may be able to arrange for you to have your calls intercepted. In very extreme circumstances it may be worth your while, for your own peace of mind, to consider changing your telephone number. If you are a woman living alone do not enter your full name in the telephone directory, only the last name and an initial.

Dressing the Part

Everyone has their own idea of how smart, sexy or glamorous they want to look and which fashion styles make them feel their very best. Wearing very outré and revealing styles, favoured especially by the young and fashion-conscious, may present a problem in certain environments especially if worn after dark when some men might automatically equate a woman with a certain look – say a short tight skirt, fishnet stockings and high heels – with one who is 'on offer'. To dress frumpily out of fear of men's possible reaction, to don shabby army-surplus gear, bovver boots and shun make-up and jewellery simply in order to look purposely unattractive and thus hopefully avoid getting into trouble is however, to go to unnecessary extremes.

If you have trouble at work with male colleagues who annoy you by passing sexual comments or even resort to more offensive forms of harassment, then it makes sense to wear clothes that are not too revealing or skin-tight, which some men could take as a sign of 'availability' or provocation. Flashy jewellery may be regarded as glamorous by some people but to others who aren't up on the latest fashion trends too much glitz and glitter may come across as overly sexy or slightly tarty. When making your way alone in the evening to a dressy occasion try to cover up your finery with a simple coat or shawl in order to avoid attracting too much attention. Very high heels impede your progress if you want to walk fast or if you should need to run, so a good bet is to wear a more comfortable low heeled style and change into your dressy shoes when you arrive. Interestingly, some crime researchers have noted that the 'tick-tack' sound made by metal tipped stiletto heels on the pavement acts as a come-on to some sex attackers. Always try to dress down when out at night alone or in a high crime area, especially if you have to take public transport. Don't wear any obvious, snatchable items of jewellery. If on your way to or from a party put them in your bag until you get to your destination.

The one fashion item that needs some sensible forethought is your handbag. Whatever the design, access – especially for someone standing next to you – should be as difficult as possible. Keep money and valuables in the deepest and furthest recesses of the bag, if possible inside a compartment that can be zipped up. Bags which can be opened easily or have a flap which someone could easily lift are a pickpocket's delight. Don't swing the bag loosely from your hand or shoulder as someone might easily grab it and rip it away from you. The safest way to carry a bag is over your shoulder with the strap slung diagonally across your chest so the bag lies against the body, preferably not at the side or back, but towards the front of the hip. Try to choose a bag that has a strong and fairly wide strap so that it cannot break if someone tugs it. If you carry a purse or smaller bag inside a larger tote or shopping bag then make sure this is safely zipped up and your valuables are not lying directly underneath the zipper.

If you have had your bag or wallet snatched in the past and are nervous about this happening again, you may feel more secure carrying your money, cheque book and credit card – these should always be separated, by the way, never in the same wallet or compartment – in a money pouch inside your jacket or coat or even in a secret compartment sewn onto the inside of your clothes. Knowing that your valuables are secure helps you relax and therefore will allow you to walk around in a more confident manner. This is a particularly valuable strategy for anyone travelling abroad, especially in countries where pickpocketing and mugging are rife, with foreign tourists singled out as prime targets. If you can also carry your guidebook, map, dictionary, camera and all other paraphernalia that identify you as a foreign visitor – and therefore eminently worth ripping off – well under wraps, you may well avoid ruining your travels by becoming a crime victim.

On the point of dress for travellers abroad, it is as well to remember that the rule of dressing down will always reduce women's risk of getting mugged or sexually assaulted. Plunging, low-cut, sleeveless sundresses, bikini tops, very skimpy shorts, see through blouses and dresses are a distinct turn-on to the average Latin Arab or Asian male in the street. Remember, what may be regarded as perfectly acceptable, respectable and trendy at home in the USA or the UK may be interpreted as outrageously provocative in other societies and cultures, causing some men to take up what they regard as an open invitation to approach you or to attack. If in doubt as to which clothes are not worn by respectable women in the country that you are visiting, consult the local consulate or tourist office in your home town *before* you go. Rules on dismissing men who try to chat you up or make an indecent approach apply equally in foreign countries – if not more so. Pretend you do not understand even if you do. If caught up in what could prove to be a 'tight' confrontation, point to a ring on your finger and say you are about to meet your husband or fiancé – a ploy calculated to cool the ardour of any would-be Romeo.

On the Run

When Company Director Lawrence Woodward was beaten up by two youths while out running on the fringes of Hyde Park, police in trying to establish a motive for the attack pointed out that muggers tend to lurk in the streets and parks near the big luxury hotels in big cities, waiting for rich visitors who sometimes carry money on them while out jogging or walking. Just because you are a runner and therefore seem fit and nimble does not mean you cannot be attacked. So don't wear ostentatious expensive-looking sports clothes that attract attention and do not carry valuables, especially not in a visible pouch or purse. Be sure to leave your jewellery at home. The rule applies to both men and women. Women who go out jogging wearing expensive-looking or extra-feminine and sexy gear – shiny tights or skin-tight catsuits – revealing satin shorts, very startling colours – are unfortunately far more likely to attract potential muggers than those togged out in regulation navy blue or grey tracksuits.

13
Safety First

One of the more disturbing aspects of the growing fear of crime is the underlying sense of helplessness which prevents many people from actively taking responsibility for their own safety. Studies indicate that very young and elderly women who habitually express concern about the possibility of becoming crime victims in fact do little to mitigate those risks. Worse, they may remain entirely unaware of how many avoidable risks they encounter in their daily life. Amazingly, even those who were previously victimized or came close to it continue to be oblivious of the simple commonsense strategies that would not only make their lives safer but also cut down on their pervading unease and apprehension. It is almost as if, for some people, fear were a self-perpetuating handicap which by dislocating judgement and distorting vision encourages an exclusively negative view of events past present and future.

This might explain why, according to a recent survey, women who have been attacked are no more diligent about taking personal safety precautions than those who have not been, and in many cases may be less so. Very young women under the age of eighteen are often far less careful than older women which tends to suggest a lack of awareness that they represent the highest risk category. All in all, it is as if past experience were totally at variance with present knowledge.

As crime figures soar there has been increased focus by the media of late on the unacceptable dangers faced by women who work. Suggestions about how to counteract these risks range from training in self-defence and the use of firearms to stricter vigilance on the part of employers in protecting the safety of female employees. Some of these possible strategies seem plausible enough, others smack of an alarmist overreaction virtually calculated to whip up an unnecessary paranoid seige mentality. The last thing most working women want, having at last won long sought-after equal opportunities within the work-place, is to be deemed as high risk and therefore in need of special care and protection from employers. Unfair as this might seem, there is a very real danger that by stressing their vulnerability by asking to be made a special case, women may lose out to men when being considered for certain jobs.

Even more unjust in the opinion of many women is the suggestion that it is they who must modify their behaviour and appearance, in short be penalized because of the aggressive or aberrant behaviour of men. Nevertheless having now achieved equal status with men it would surely be iniquitous for women to be discriminated against because of their inability to protect themselves. Any victory in being made a 'special case' because of implicit weaknesses would prove a Pyrrhic victory. More to the point, employers do have a certain responsibility to ensure wherever possible the safety of *all* their staff, male and female, young and not so young, black and white, senior or not so senior, especially within those professions where both sexes may be equally at risk. The more obvious of these are the social services departments, all areas of the health service, public transport, the police and where employees find themselves frequently caught up in potentially high risk situations. However, rather than rules and regulations and stricter safety legislation what all of us probably need, male and female, employer and employee, is greater schooling in the sharpening of wits and instinct with regard to potentially violent or dangerous situations. For instance, greater awareness of the diverse factors that contribute towards violent confrontations can help us defuse a potentially explosive situation before it even arises. In learning how to decipher the clues and messages – verbal and non verbal – sent out by people who might prove to be violent, knowing how to anticipate and recognize danger while feeling confident in our ability to avoid or deal with it is probably the most potent form of self-defence. This is why safety, like charity, begins at home and in the street.

True safety consciousness is a state of mind and indicates a perhaps more than average level of awareness of yourself, other people and of your environment, commensurate with real risks rather than imagined dangers. It therefore does not entail having to become defensively paranoid or psyche yourself up every time you go out in the street or respond to a ring at the door. On the contrary, just like those people who project confidence and control because they are at ease in their bodies and comfortably assertive in the way they interact with others, so those who are by nature safety-conscious automatically adopt commonsense strategies in their daily activities as a matter of habit, motivated as much by levelheadedness as by imagination and the ability to think ahead and put themselves into other people's shoes.

What this boils down to is having that extra edge of awareness and recognizing when a potentially risky situation or set of circumstances does arise. In contrast, adopting a permanently suspicious aggressively mistrustful attitude towards every new person you might meet, being continually on the defensive against possible threats of violence, doubting the trustworthiness of strangers and new acquaintances reflects an attitude born almost exclusively of fear, which invariably breeds more fear and imposes countless limitations on freedom.

Home Safe Home

Lax home security coupled with absence of forethought together account for the very high incidence of casual break-ins. Police continually point out that a large number of burglaries could be prevented if people bothered to analyze the weak areas of their home, adopting the burglar's point of view. How would you get into your home? Which are the most accessible points of entry and those offering the greatest chance of unobserved access? Does the house look inhabited or does it seem obviously empty? A house or flat that is slightly secluded and has blind spots such as a garden which cannot be fully overlooked or a hidden back door or window, is far more vulnerable to break-in than one which stands in a busy street, overlooked on all sides by neighbours. Corner properties, detached houses, basement or top floor flats are therefore most 'burglar friendly'.

It goes without saying that both front and back doors should be fitted with a good lock – if possible an automatic deadlock that is morticed, i.e. set in the woodwork of the door – which cannot be opened without the use of a key. A door chain, viewer and intercom or video are necessary extras to enable you to vet strangers before you speak to them or let them in. Having good quality door locks fitted to a poor quality door is obviously a self-defeating exercise. Ensure that the door is sturdy, the hinges secure and that the door frame itself is strong enough to resist collapse if someone tried to kick in the door itself. Steel cladding is expensive – between £250 and £450 per door – but well worth the expense if your home is in a vulnerable position.

Entry in more than 50 per cent of domestic burglaries is through a window, so these should be fitted with bolts that are opened with a key. Double-glazing acts as a deterrent but does not preclude forcible entry. In some cases a burglar alarm may make the intruder think twice about trying to force his way in, but this is by no means always the case. Many burglars confess that alarms do not bother them and stress that they would persevere in trying to break in and neutralize the alarm. Bars and ornamental grilles over such obvious access points as skylight windows, patio or balcony doors will certainly maximize security if you feel this is not an undue affront to aesthetics. An obvious compromise is to install a collapsible steel gate which can be pulled back from the window or door when you are home and locked into place when you go out.

An alarm that is linked to the local police station provides good all round cover, as does a hidden sensor installed in the garden or close to the front door which if activated by someone stepping over a certain boundary sets off a bell or switches on lights in the house so scaring off the intruder. Far more off-putting than alarms, in many cases, is the presence of a seemingly fierce dog in the house. Dogs that are very large, vigorous, and that bark long and loud frequently act as a deterrent because burglars fear that they will be injured and possibly immobilized and that the barking will alert someone's attention and they may then be caught.

Remember that burglars will invariably try to break in when they think the house is uninhabited. A major percentage of burglaries are committed by day, when people are at work. A radio or TV left playing, preferably tuned to a talk programme, during the day or when you go out in the evening, lights switched on in the hallway and one or two of the main rooms help to create an impression that someone is in. Better still, invest in a couple of time switches so that lights and radio are set to come on at different times of day or evening. It is particularly important to set up such a front when you go away on holiday and leave the home unattended – a prime time for burglars to break in. Remember, about 75 per cent of all burglaries are opportunist – the criminal happens to walk by and acts on impulse because a certain property seems a good bet.

Burglars often live near the house they break into and may recognize the signs that indicate tenants are away on holiday, i.e. lights off or newspapers and milk suddenly not being delivered. This is why it is a good idea to arrange for a friend or neighbour to visit your home regularly in order to ensure that there are signs of life. If scaffolding has been erected over or next to your home make doubly sure to carry out all these safety precautions since your home will now be far more vulnerable than at any other time. Net curtains or blinds over the windows will prevent builders or intruders from being able to look through your windows.

If you are at home and you hear someone trying to break in try to get to the phone immediately and call the police. It is better to lock yourself in one of the rooms than to try and take on the burglar. Many amateur burglars will be as frightened as hell to be caught in the act and may flee in terror of being identified or caught, but others may turn nasty and attack or threaten violence if you challenge or frighten them. Be aware that if you use a dangerous weapon and injure or kill the intruder you may be arrested and charged with serious injury or manslaughter or at least convicted of being in possession of a dangerous weapon.

Streetwise

Being streetwise constitutes following certain inbuilt habits almost without a second thought. How cautious you are depends largely on time, location and individual circumstances. Instincts are your best guide on how to react so learn to trust them – and act promptly. No matter how unusual, strange or inconvenient your avoidance behaviour may appear at the time to yourself or to others, go through with it if you have even the faintest suspicion that you might be in danger. Your wellbeing and safety are your number one priority, not your image or your credibility. There are many definite rules you should observe when out in an urban environment and most of these apply after dark. These include walking wherever possible only along well lit streets where there are other people and sticking to the centres of the pavement to avoid passing doorways, entrances to alleyways and passages. Always walk facing the oncoming traffic to avoid kerb crawlers. By day or night walk briskly, and purposefully, eyes level and avoiding eye contact with suspicious-looking men. A person who moves slowly or seems to strut may be singled out by an attacker as an easy hit. Try to be aware of people moving up behind you or hanging around beside you.

Never be tempted to accept a lift with a stranger, even if there is a woman at the wheel or in the car or if the driver says it is a taxi or minicab. When making a phone call from a callbox or using a service card to obtain cash from a bank service till first make a casual 180-degree turn to ensure that no one is trailing or watching you. As you talk or operate the till face slightly outwards towards the road rather than turning your back fully, giving the impression that you are completely aware of what is happening around you. Avoid all dark deserted alleyways, pedestrian underpasses, lonely areas of park or wasteland, and ill lit car parks – especially if these are in run-down urban environments with a high crime rate.

Many modern inner city housing estates appear to have been designed and constructed with the express objective of providing maximum facilities for vandals, muggers and burglars to wage terror among the inhabitants. Dark staircases, ill lit labyrinthine walkways, many with unexpected dead ends precluding escape, lifts that don't work, and vast unlit hidden zones of wasteland have conspired to turn such urban developments into a mugger's paradise, especially in areas where drug taking, unemployment, extreme poverty and inter-racial friction or violence are commonplace. It obviously makes sense therefore to avoid these high risk areas wherever possible especially after dark. This of course is impossible if you happen to live in or close to such an area. If this is the case and there is little option but to remain there, you should make a point of complaining about any inadequacies to the local council. Vigilance pays off. It is wise to complain of inadequate street lighting around your own area and to report any suspicious or violent incidents to the local police. Setting up a neighbourhood watch scheme may also help considerably in cutting down the crime rate.

Working out a safe route to follow when going to and from work or visiting friends and acquaintances is dependent on a little commonsense and forethought. As well as the identification of all obvious no-go areas, once you know an area you can prepare your route precisely, work out safe places to park your car, time your movements so as to avoid pub closing times and football crowds, and steer clear of deserted bus stops and railway stations. At all times of the day stick to busy well lit roads. Be sure, if you can, never to walk home alone late at night – if at all possible try to get a taxi or ask for a lift from a person you know. If living in a high risk area ask the person dropping you to wait until you are safely inside your own front door. If newly moved into a different part of town check with the local police about prime troublespots and crime rates. Read the local press to get a feel of how safe or unsafe the area is. If because of where you live or work or your personal schedule you have no option but to follow a route that seems risky or makes you feel anxious try to walk in the company of friends or colleagues or, better still, arrange a lift in a car. Two or three women walking together are never as vulnerable as one woman on her own.

Do not stand alone at bus stops after dark on a lonely street and *never take short cuts* across deserted parks, car parks or wasteland areas after dusk, even if it means a detour. On approaching your home have your keys ready to get into your front door – fumbling around in your bag makes you more of a ready target for anyone who might be following you. When visiting an unfamiliar area locate the address precisely on a map in advance, plan your route – preferably the busiest – and familarize yourself with it. Standing around with a bewildered expression on your face that says 'I am lost' could prove an open invitation for someone to chat you up or pinpoint you as an easy target for attack. If you do get lost walk into the nearest shop, coffee bar or pub and seek further instructions. If at all economically feasible at all times and in all circumstances you should have enough money on you for a taxi fare home – it may require saving or borrowing and might seem unduly extravagant, but could possibly spell the difference between being trapped in a dangerous situation or free to get out at a moment's notice.

On the Move

There is no need to be paranoid when going out night or day, only realistically cautious and clued up to any suspicious goings on. Most of us, after all, have a very well tuned sixth sense which tells us if a situation might prove to be potentially dangerous. Get used to anticipating and trusting your judgement. Avoid making eye contact with groups of youths who are just standing around or acting aggressively or with any stranger in the street who, for whatever reason, seems sinister, scruffy or menacing. If you are walking along a deserted street and someone approaches who makes you feel uneasy, cross smartly to the other side of the road and keep walking. If someone is walking very close behind you and you think they are trailing you, do the same. If that person continues to follow you don't run – he may close in and grab you – and don't lead him to your car, home or place of work, but instead make for the nearest busy area and go into a shop or pub and ask to use the telephone to call the police or order a taxi. If there is no such place of public access walk up to a house or block of flats that seems occupied and ring the doorbell purposefully as if you were expected there – many criminals will run a mile rather than be identified by witnesses. If someone who is trailing you tries to engage you in conversation don't answer or, provided you feel confident enough and you see that there are other people around, turn round quickly and assertively and very sharply say something like 'stop following me immediately or I'll report you' or 'how dare you – I'll report you if you don't clear off at once', then immediately walk on.

In Transit

On double decker buses try to sit downstairs within sight of the conductor and if possible near other people. Most violent incidents occur upstairs but more and more buses are now being fitted with closed circuit video cameras, the monitor screen installed in the driver's cab. The driver has a radio link with the terminal control office and can therefore immediately report any suspicious or violent incident.

On tubes and trains never sit in a carriage on your own, especially at night. Use the compartment nearest the guard and try to stay close to other women. If you are attacked on a train, pulling the communication cord will secure you immediate attention from the guard and driver. If anyone suspicious or threatening gets into the tube, get out at the next station and either wait for the next train or, if you have time and the person is not following you, get into another carriage further away. On a regular tube or train journey using a compartment that you know will come to a stop close to the exit obviates the need to walk the length of the platform where someone might confront you.

If you need a cab, take black taxi cabs wherever possible, and when ordering minicabs make absolutely sure you are using a registered and reputable firm. It is a good idea to keep a list of companies and to use the same people regularly so that they come to know you. When booking ask for the driver's registration details and name, thus making it clear to the company that you have plenty to alert you if anything untoward should happen. When arriving at an airport, railway station or bus station, or coming out of a pub, bar or restaurant never be tempted to accept the offer of a minicab unless you are first absolutely sure that the driver represents a bona fide company. By asking to see his registration details and checking out the name of his company with someone in authority you will certainly delay your journey but you will also ensure your personal safety.

The Tender Trap

The majority of violent incidents, rather than hitting like a bolt out of the blue, develop out of what seems at the time to be a perfectly commonplace innocuous set of circumstances. Nevertheless, on looking back, many victims admit that there was a point at which they did experience a minor doubt, an instinctive hesitation that there was something suspicious going on – a gut feeling that as it turns out they should have trusted and acted upon. Many attackers trap their victims by using carefully thought out and highly convincing tactics designed to appeal in particular to a woman's caring and helping instincts.

When out walking anywhere at any time be suspicious of men who approach you with a line that plays on your kindness. This may be completely against your nature but it could ensure your safety. A typical lead-in to an assault might for example be a bogus pollster in a deserted part of town asking you to fill in a questionnaire, a distraught man in a park asking you to find his missing child, the offer of a lift from someone who has a car from a pub on a winter or a rainy night, a stranger ringing your doorbell asking directions because he is lost, or who says that he has come to read the meter, sell a service or commodity, or again, a top favourite, wishing to conduct a survey or collect for a bogus charity. The problem is that typical protagonists in many such scenarios are in the main well dressed, well spoken and give an overwhelming impression of respectability thus dispelling the popular image of the rapist as a crazed weirdo. Indeed, many sex attackers in particular, often have responsible jobs and display what would appear to be impeccable credentials. But however convinced you think you ought to be, don't drop your guard. No matter how slight the risk it really isn't worth it. Be polite but try to get away as soon as you can. If someone approaches you when you are at home never open the door unless you have first checked the identity of that person and, if necessary, telephoned the organization they claim to represent.

Rules of the Road

As a driver the speed, mobility and bodily protection offered by your car means you can rely on a greater degree of personal safety especially at night than the average pedestrian. Provided, that is, you observe a few fundamental rules. For instance, always lock all doors, especially your own, before driving off. Keep your windows shut when driving alone at night in lonely areas. Make sure all car doors are locked when the car is parked and try to park wherever possible in a well lit street or underneath a streetlamp, avoiding ill lit deserted areas or, if you can help it, multi-storey car parks, especially late at night when there are fewer vehicles parked. If you think you are being followed on the road by another driver keep driving until you come to a busy place such as a petrol station, pub, fire or police station and make a report. Keep a map in the car so you don't have to stop and ask directions and place your handbag and any other valuables out of sight of prying eyes. The cardinal rule of personal safety is always *never hitchhike*, but as a driver, the opposite rule also applies. Mean it may be, but it is safer by far never to stop and pick up people waiting on the road for a lift.

When you get back to your parked car remember to check the back seat before getting in. Have a good torch handy to illuminate any dark spots in the car park as well as the interior of the car. If you happen to see a suspicious incident or even what could be a breakdown or accident on the road police advise women on their own in particular not to stop and investigate unless they are with someone else who is prepared to accompany them. Instead they suggest driving on to the nearest telephone and reporting the incident to the police. To many this will sound chillingly like an exhortation to ignore all basic humanitarian instincts, a sanction of non-involvement. It is therefore only fair to stress that commonsense, circumstance and, above all, instinct must finally dictate how we react when others appear to be in trouble.

Danger – Work in Progress

The dangers inherent in any particular job may not be immediately obvious, especially to new employees. For instance, a person asked to do shift work may not be aware of how deserted the streets are or realize the lack of public transport services during the early or late hours until they get into the swing of the routine. Many of the aforementioned strategies used to gain greater recognition or anticipation of potential hazards and an awareness of how to handle them apply as much to people in specific working environments as in everyday situations. Women shift workers should try to arrange a lift rota with others working similar hours in the same company or living and working somewhere nearby. You may need to learn how to recognize hidden dangers directly involved with your work. For instance, if you are frequently in contact with strange men or have to deal with a man on his own, try to take into account in advance, what sort of impression you might make, especially any involuntary non-verbal messages communicated by your dress, speech and mannerisms. You may want to modify traits that you think of as friendly, relaxed, and spontaneous, but that might convey to a stranger an impression of sexiness, forwardness or over-familiarity in order to project a stronger image of assertiveness and self-control.

Prescience and vigilance combined can cut down on many otherwise unforeseen hazards. When going out to meet a client or customer you don't know or visiting a strange environment connected with the job, a good precautionary measure is to inform colleagues where you are going, as well as your estimated time of return, duplicating this information in your desk diary. Leave a phone number of the place you are visiting, and, if in doubt about the person you are visiting, ask a colleague to phone you a short time after you expect to arrive. Otherwise, on your arrival, make a call to the office establishing where you are. This might appear to be an elaborate strategy but it will help to establish quite clearly in the mind of the stranger that you have close links with your office and your employer.

Interviews should take place in an office or public place such as a hotel lobby or coffee lounge. If a male client or potential employer you have never met before suggests driving to another location in his car, refuse – unless, of course, you know his respectability is unimpeachable. Never accept a lift home – decline politely and say you have transport laid on. If you find yourself alone in an office or flat with a man, perhaps a potential client or new employer, and you think there is something suspicious about him, quietly and surreptitiously try to work out a fast exit route. If it is necessary for you to enter a secluded or perhaps empty building with a stranger insist that he goes in first, allowing you to follow. Keep the door open and stay close to it. In spite of the cost there is something to be said for carrying a portable cellular telephone not just for the obvious reasons of remaining in contact at all times with the outside world but to impress this fact on anyone who might be tempted to attack you. Issuing all staff who conduct much of their business out of the office in the company of strangers, for example welfare workers, health visitors, and nurses, with portable telephones or a direct radio link with their office is certainly one way that employers could ensure greater safety for their staff.

As a result of increased attacks on nurses, hospital staff, social workers, and public transport personnel more employers are beginning to recognize their responsibility in implementing optimum security measures for all employees. In the main this includes staff training in how to recognize and deflect aggressive behaviour and deal with violent situations, self-defence instruction, the issuing of personal alarms, the fitting of offices, buses and trains with panic buttons and two-way radios, the installation of protection screens, the hiring of extra security guards, and the laying on of extra transport facilities for shift workers.

A growing number of government enquiries and health reports now point to the debilitating effects of fears about safety at work on both the morale and efficiency of vast numbers of public service workers and stress the importance of the implementation of improved safety regulations. Invariably, however, attitudes to safety will vary greatly from company to company, department to department, area to area, and may be affected by the degree of red tape that surrounds the various decision making processes. If you feel the risk involved in your line of work is unnecessarily high and could be reduced you should enlist the support of as many colleagues as feel the same way and complain formally to your employer. Group strategies inevitably have greater impact than lone plans of action and cause those involved in policy-making to take notice. If your complaints and suggestions fall on deaf ears aim higher – reporting the matter to your trade union if you have one as well as to the appropriate association or government authority.

Forearmed

It could be argued that media reports on how to quell rampant fears amongst women who work and go out a lot especially in the evenings are counterproductive since they generate a lot of alarmist nonsense about the advantages of carrying dangerous weapons or learning self-defence moves calculated to incapacitate or kill any potential attacker. Such media hype is inevitably calculated to whip up public fears rather than to allay them. In some instances it could also cause some people to behave irresponsibly to the point of possibly endangering their lives and well-being. In the first instance, many people are unaware that carrying a dangerous weapon with intent to cause injury constitutes a punishable criminal offence. Therefore if you are found with a kitchen knife, flick knife, a Stanley knife or razor, or a hatchet in your bag you may be arrested and charged with unlawful possession of an offensive weapon. The other far more significant hazard of going around armed with a dangerous weapon is that if you are attacked and try unsuccessfully to use the weapon, your assailant may well get hold of it and use it against you, causing severe injury or even death. To introduce a deadly weapon where none existed in the first place is to place yourself in supreme danger – yet another instance of how actions born out of fear are inevitably self-defeating. For many people, even if confident that they do know how to use, say, a knife, in self defence, may be prevented from doing so through fear, slow reflexes, or the superior force of their attacker. Carrying around a can of hairspray or any other irritant agent such as a deodorant, however, does provide you with a handy weapon with which to temporarily blind and confuse an attacker and so get away – provided you can get your hands on the stuff fast enough and aim correctly.

By far the most sensible precaution to take if you need the confidence of knowing you could scare off an attacker and get away yourself is to carry a screecher alarm. These are highly effective, emitting a very high-pitched tone that temporarily dulls hearing and may cause considerable shock to anyone not anticipating the impact. The principal caveat is obviously that these are only of use if at hand instantly and at all times, not tucked away in the deepest recesses of a handbag. An alarm is only worth carrying if you can grab it fast and aim accurately at any time, thus alerting others to danger and scaring off the attacker at least for long enough, theoretically, to give you time to escape. Keep the alarm inside your pocket, attached to your wrist or stuck inside the top inner section of your bag on a band of velcro. Some screecher alarms have an inbuilt torch. The confidence many women derive from carrying a screecher can make a tremendous difference to their overall attitude in coping with potentially threatening situations. When you first buy an alarm make sure you know how to use it correctly: fast and as close as possible to the ear of the attacker. Large bunches of keys, ornate heavy keyrings or knuckledusters with jagged metallic protuberances may also prove useful as an adjunct if you feel capable of socking someone in the face. This presupposes that you have the strength and daring to hit a punch in the first place.

Fighting Mean – the Last Resort

Early anticipation and prompt avoidance tactics should prove of immeasurable value in allowing you to circumvent many a direct confrontation or hands-on assault. However, what if the worst happens and in spite of your efforts to outwit the criminal you find yourself being physically attacked? This is the point, say many self-defence teachers, when you must decide whether to act or not and if you do, you must act fast. In spite of all assertions by critics to the contrary, there is little doubt that a woman or man who has received adequate training in self-defence stands a greater chance of having the stronger and faster physical reflexes necessary to fight off and escape an attacker than someone who hasn't, always provided, of course, that fear has not paralyzed those reflexes and drained away all strength.

Of course, no victim can know how she will react until the actual moment when she is confronted with the reality of the situation. Too many self-defence classes are founded on the false premise that you will be able to exert rational judgement and physical prowess when attacked. The opposite in fact usually applies and, to be realistic, all that self-defence training can give anyone is the knowledge that in theory they do have the strength and speed of reaction and skill necessary to get away from an attacker. For many, this knowledge alone serves as a tremendous boost to self-confidence and can dispel much fear and insecurity, possibly even generating the attitude of assertiveness and personal control necessary for deterring early threats of violence in the first place.

Nowadays, with more and more self-styled teachers cashing in on public fears about crime, a burgeoning market in self-defence has led to no shortage of physical training, with all levels of expertise on offer from simple and basic escape manoeuvres to supreme excellence in the martial arts. Which level you go for depends very largely on the amount of time, effort and money you wish to spend, your age, physical health and build, your fitness level and the amount of importance in terms of self-confidence that you attach to a high degree of proficiency in fighting skills.

A principle caveat is that having mastered self-defence skills you may become overly confident about your ability to defend yourself and become convinced of your invulnerability, thus taking unnecessary extra risks, and acting without due thought and caution. The fact that even lifetime experts in boxing and karate have been known to be knocked out and overcome by the force and surprise of a sudden attack or immobilized by frozen fear indicates the folly of such an insouciant attitude.

In general, women will benefit most of all from taking a short intensive course in basic breakaway skills designed to loosen the grip of an attacker so that it is then possible to make an escape. In such classes emphasis is on sneaky fighting – the many different ways of using feet, knees, elbows, hands and fingertips to get away from the attacker. Kicks, punches, blows and pinches aimed at key soft spots such as the bladder, genitals, solar plexus, throat and eyes will inflict maximum damage if delivered sharply, swiftly and unexpectedly, preferably from a casual non-combative stance. The idea is never to let the attacker see what you plan to do. There should be no preparatory gestures or big movements. In principle such strategies are meant to be used before an attacker becomes physically violent, for example when he places his arm around your waist or shoulders or tries to caress, kiss or grope you.

This underlines the fact that in virtually all cases of sexual attack there will be a preliminary lead-up to the heavy rough stuff during which time the victim might be able to take the opportunity to fight her way out of the situation. There are any number of ways to catch an attacker off guard, cause enough discomfort and shock to make him release his grip and to deter him from going any further. The idea is to deliver a punch, a kick or a jab when he least expects it. Particularly lethal, for instance, would be an initially relaxed friendly and even compliant manner giving way swiftly and unexpectedly to physical aggression. Most men may be so shocked or taken aback by this that they think better of their intended course of action.

Simple street-fighting tactics are often dependent more on sneakiness, an element of surprise and split second timing than on brute force or physical prowess which means that with sufficient practice just about anyone of any age, build or size can become proficient. A really good basic street-fighting course teaches the very broad scope of tactics one might choose from and how to coordinate these. There are four or five variations of breaking out of a man's grip and as many ways of hitting one vulnerable part of his body. Most women, in order to gain enough confidence to strike out at a man and sharpen their reflexes, must first develop the necessary strength and co-ordination required to deliver a punch, a powerful kick or a series of blows. Use of mitts and a punch bag as well as a male 'stand-in' followed up by regular practice can help you to acquire this.

One of the things most victims are unaware of is that the average man, even if he does attack a woman, can be remarkably uncoordinated himself, so by packing a swift, well-aimed punch or kick a woman can frequently disable or disorientate him.

However, women must avoid at all costs becoming drawn into sustained combat with a man – the likelihood that his strength and size will be superior dictates that he will win in the majority of cases. This is why classes which include women only are largely a waste of time. In learning self-defence techniques it is essential for women to recognize what exactly they may be up against when attacked by a man. A woman will probably not be able to exert the same amount of force and strength, nor are most women ruthless enough to be able to inflict pain or discomfort on someone of their own sex. Women who attend self-defence classes for women only may come away with lots of theoretical knowledge but no first-hand experience of what it feels like to be grabbed or pinned down by a man or, more important, how much force and speed they need to undermine his hold. By familiarizing herself with these normally unfamiliar elements in a mixed self-defence class a woman may already gain a considerable head start in being able to counteract her fears should she ever be attacked in real life.

All the Way

Some self-defence classes do, however, take an uncompromising stance and go all the way in teaching techniques calculated not only to help break free and escape but hurt and perhaps severely injure or incapacitate an assailant. There are divergent opinions as to the wisdom of such training. Some experts, including many police officers, fear that in turning aggressive yet failing perhaps to get away or knock out the attacker a potential victim may incite him to further anger and violence that could have possible tragic consequences. There is, after all, no means of knowing whether physically lashing out and screaming at an attacker will cause him to take fright and flee or merely enrage him.

Some women may prove so inhibited about inflicting injury or pain that they find themselves incapable of going all out to attack. Many classes, therefore, involve both pupils and instructors submitting one another to a fair amount of actual pain and discomfort, often involving considerable physical rough and tumble and mental stress in attempts to break down the barriers of reticence and learned politeness in order to locate the killer instinct which, say the experts, a woman may need to count on in order to survive. This level of training, also includes learning how to throw off and injure a sex attacker while he is actively trying to rape a woman. Such extreme moves may include stabbing at a man's eyes with the fingers with the express aim of blinding him, kicking, grabbing, squeezing and twisting – even, should the opportunity present itself, biting the genitals with maximum force, kicking him in the face, or breaking his nose.

But are these techniques worth mastering, can they really save your life? Provided training is thorough, extensive and is carried out by experts and follow-up practice sessions are regularly undertaken to ensure that you maintain your fighting edge then the answer is probably yes. But there can be no halfway measures, any form of self-defence which incorporates anything more ambitious than simple break-away techniques requires dedicated practice and a fair number of lengthy expert tuition sessions to achieve proficiency. The point is that it is only worth doing if you can do it well – and keep up your skills. The strength gained through self-defence training should not be measured in physical terms alone. Perhaps what really counts is having confidence and cultivating an attitude of mind rather than a set of techniques which will allow you to act mean and go all out to attack someone who is threatening your life. Even if in most cases you will probably never need to resort to any such extreme actions the altogether different aspect this puts on your ability to interpret threats or negotiate your safety is something that surely distinguishes the truly confident from the hesitant and fearful.

Useful Names and Addresses

Brook Advisory Centres (Birth control clinics)
233 Tottenham Court Road, London W1
01-323 1522. Enquiries for Barnsbury, Newham and Shoreditch
centres

Brixton Centre
53 Acre Lane, London SW2
01-274 4995

Islington Centre
6 Manor Gardens, London N7
01-272 5599

Walworth Centre
153A East Street, London SE17
01-703 7880. Enquiries for Lewisham, Kennington, Stockwell,
Wandsworth

Campaign Against Drinking and Driving
Ringsmere Orchard,
Pershore Road,
Little Comberton, Nr Pershore WR10 3HF

Childline
0800 1111

London Gay Switchboard
01-837 7324

The Criminal Injuries Compensation Board
Whittington House,
19 Alfred Place,
London WC1E 7LG
01-636 9501

CRUSE
The National Organisation for the Widowed and their Children,
126 Sheen Road, Richmond.
01-940 4818 (advice and counselling for the bereaved)

Free Representation Unit,
3 Middle Temple,
London EC4
01-353 3697
For advice on free legal representation

Helpline for families of murder victims,
0345 500 800

The Terence Higgins Trust (for information/advice on AIDS)
38 Mount Pleasant, London WC1
01-242 1010

Incest Counselling,
32 Newbury Close,
Northolt,
Middlesex
01-422 5100 (for men) 01-890 4732 (for women)

Kidscape,
82 Brook Street,
London SW1
01-493 9845
For information on teaching personal safety and awareness to
children

Lifeline (advice for victims of domestic violence)
PO Box 251,
Marlborough,
Wiltshire

Parents of Murdered Children (a self help group)
c/o Compassionate Friends,
6 Denmark Street, Bristol BS1 5DQ
0272 292 778

The Suzy Lamplugh Trust,
14 East Sheen Avenue,
London SW14 8AS
01-876 1838

Law Centres Federation,
Duchess House,
Warren Street,
London W1
01-387 8570
Will pass on the address of local law centres to anyone seeking
free legal advice or information

London Rape Crisis Centre (24-hour service),
PO Box 69
London WC1X 9NJ
01-837 1600
For information about other centres throughout Britain

National Association of Victims' Support Schemes,
Cramner House,
39 Brixton Road,
London SW9 9DZ
01-735 9166

Police Complaints Authority,
10 Great George Street,
London SW1
01-213 6243
They will register and investigate formal complaints by individual citizens about police behaviour

Pregnancy Advisory Service,
11 Charlotte Street,
London W1
01-637 8962

Pregnancy Testing Clinic,
The Wellwoman Centre,
108 Whitfield Street, London W1
01-388 0662

U.K. training centre for Neuro-linguistic Programming,
6 Ravenscroft Avenue,
London NW11 0RY
01-455 3743
For information about doctors and therapists trained in NLP
throughout Britain
Victims Aid Scheme (24-hour counselling)
01-729 1252

WASH (Women Against Sexual Harassment)
242 Pentonville Road,
London N1
01-833 0222

Women Against Rape,
71 Tonbridge Street,
London WC1
01-837 7509

Womens' Aid Ltd,
369 Chiswick High Road,
London W4
01-995 4430
Also for information about other refuge centres throughout
Britain

Womens' Therapy Centre,
6 Manor Gardens,
London N7
01-263 6200

References

Adler, Zsuzsanna. Rape On Trial. Routledge and Kegan Paul. London. 1987

Atkeson, B. K. et al. 'Victims of Rape: Repeated Assessment and Depressive Symptoms.' *Journal of Consulting and Clinical Psychology*, Vol 50, p. 96. 1982

Bard, Morton and Sangrey, Dawn. The Crime Victims Book. Basic Books. New York. 1979

Berkowitz, L. 'Aversively Stimulated Aggression.' *American Psychologist*, Vol. 38 (2), p. 1161. 1983

Brownmiller, Susan. Against Our Will. Penguin Books. 1976

Burgess, A. W. and Holmstrom, L. L., 'Recovery from Rape and Prior Life Stress.' *Research in Nursing and Health* Vol. 1, p. 165. 1974

Burgess, A. W. and Holmstrom, L. L., 'Rape Trauma Syndrome.' *American Journal of Psychiatry*, Vol. 131, p. 981. 1974

Burgess, A. W. and Holmstrom, L. L., 'Coping Behaviour of the Rape Victim.' *American Journal of Psychiatry*, Vol. 133 (4), p. 413. 1976

Burgess, A. W. and Holmstrom, L. L., 'Rape: Sexual Disruption and Recovery.' *American Journal of Orthopsychiatry*, Vol. 47 (4), p. 648. 1976

Burgess, A. W. and Holmstrom, L. L., 'Adaptive Strategies and Recovery from Rape.' *American Journal of Psychiatry*, Vol. 136, p. 1278. 1976

Burt, M. R. and Katz, B. L., 'Coping Strategies and Recovery from Rape', paper presented at the New York Academy of Sciences conference. 'Human Sexual Aggression: Current Perspectives.' January 1987

Burt, M. R. and Katz, B. L., 'Dimensions of Recovery from Rape.' *Journal of Interpersonal Violence* vol. 2 (1), p. 57. 1987

Burt, M. R. and Albin, R. S., 'Rape myths, Rape Definitions and Probability of Conviction.' *Journal of Applied Psychology* Vol. 11 (3), p. 212. 1981

Burt, M. R. 'Cultural Myths and Supports for Rape.' *Journal of Personality and Social Psychology* Vol. 38 (2), p. 217. 1980

Burt, M. R. and Katz, B. L., 'Rape Robbery and Burglary: Responses to Actual and Feared Criminal Victimization with Special Focus on Women and the Elderly.' *Victimology* Vol. 10 (1–4), p. 325. 1985

Burt, M. R. and Katz, B. L., 'Effects of Familiarity with the Rapist on Post-rape Recovery', paper presented at the American Psychological Association meeting in Washington, DC. August 1986

Camden Help for Victims of Crime: Report of the Racial Harassment Project. London. 1987

Commission for Racial Equality: Living in Terror. A Report on Racial Violence and Harassment in Housing. London. 1987

Conklin, J. E. The Impact of Crime. Macmillan, New York. 1975

DSM III American Psychiatric Association. 1980

Duddle, M. 'The need for Sexual Assault Centres in the United Kingdom.' *The British Medical Journal.* Vol. 290. 1985

Duff, P. 'The Victim Movement and Legal Reform.' Paper given at the 1984 Conference on victims, restitution and compensation in the criminal justice system. Cambridge, England.

Elle: 'Working against fear.' A special report. London. July 1987

Ellis, E. M. 'Review of Empirical Rape Research.' *Clinical Psychology Review*, Vol. 3, p. 474. 1983

Figley, C. R. (ed), Trauma and its Wake. Brunner Mazel. New York. 1984

Final Report of the APA Task Force on the Victims of Crime and Violence, *American Psychologist*, Vol. 40 (1), p. 107. 1985

Friedman, K. Bischoff, H. David, R. Person, A. 'Victims and Helpers: Reactions to Crime.' New York Victim Services Agency. 1982

Galaway, B. and Hudson, J (eds.), Perspectives on Crime Victims. The C. V. Mosby Co. USA. 1981

Gelles, E. (ed.), The Violent Home. Sage, Beverly Hills. 1983

Grayson, B., 'A Comparison of Criminal Perceptions of the Nonverbal Behaviour of Potential Victims of Assault and a Movement Analysis Based on Lab Analysis.' PhD. Thesis, New York University. 1978

Hanmer, J. and Maynard. M., 'Women Violence and Social Control.' Macmillan Press, London. 1987

Hanmer, J. and Saunders, S. 'Well Founded Fear.' Hutchinson, London. 1984

Health and Safety Commission. 'Violence to staff in the health services.' HMSO. London. 1987

Hechtiger, G. 'How to Raise a Street Smart Child.' Facts on File. New York. 1984

Holmes, M. R. and St Lawrence, J. 'Treatment of Rape Induced Trauma.' *Clinical Psychology Review*, Vol. 3, p. 417. 1983

Home Office Statistical Bulletin, 'Violent Crime: Characteristics of Victims and Circumstances of Recorded Offences.' London. 1984

The Home Office, 'Criminal Justice. Plans for Legislation.' HMSO, London. March. 1986

The Home Office, 'Reparation: A Discussion Document.' London. 1986

Horowitz, M. Stress Response Syndromes, Jason Aronson, New York. 1976

Horowitz, M. 'Pathological Grief and the Activation of Latent Self Images.' *American Journal of Psychology*, Vol. 137, p. 1137. 1980

Horowitz, M. Wilner, N. Alvarez, W. 'Impact of Event Scale: A Measure of Subjective Distress.' *Psychosomatic Medicine*, Vol. 41, p. 209. 1979

Horowitz, M., Wilner, N., Alvarez, W. 'Signs and Symptoms of Post-Trauma Stress Disorders.' *Journal of Nervous and Mental Disease*. 1980 (Special Issue)

Hough, M. Mayhew, P. 'Taking Account of Crime.' Key findings from the 1984 British Crime Survey. Home Office Research study, HMSO, London. 1985

Janoff-Bulman, R. and Frieze, I. H. 'A theoretical perspective for understanding reactions to victimisation.' *Journal of Social Issues*, Vol. 139 (2), p. 195. 1983

Johnson, A. G. 'On the prevalence of rape in the United States.' *Journal of Women in Culture and Society*, Vol. 6, p. 136. 1980

Jones, T., Maclean, B., Young, J. The Islington Crime Survey, Gower, London. 1986

Katz, B. L. and Burt, M. R. 'Self blame: Help or Hindrance in Recovery From Rape?' in Burgess, A. (ed.), Rape and Sexual Assault, Vol 2. Garland Press, New York. 1986

Kilpatrick, D. G., Veronen, L. J. and Best, C. L. 'Factors Predicting Psychological Distress among Victims,' in Figley, C. R. (ed.). Trauma and Its Wake. Brunner Mazel. New York. 1984

Kilpatrick, D. G. and Amick, A. E. 'Rape Trauma,' in Hersen, M. and Last, C. G. (eds). Behaviour Therapy Casebook. Springer, New York. 1985

Kilpatrick, D. G. and Hamlein, M. L. 'Male Crime Victims, The Most Victimised, Often Neglected.' *NOVA Newsletter*, Vol. 10 (12), p. 1. 1986

Kilpatrick, D. G. 'The Sexual Assault Research Project: Assessing the Aftermath of Rape.' *Journal of the Center for Women Policy Studies*, Vol. 8 (4), p. 20. 1985

Kilpatrick, D. G. et al. 'The Psychological Impact of Crime: A Study of Randomly Surveyed Crime Victims,' submitted to the National Institute of Justice, Washington DC. 1987

Kilpatrick, D. G. et al. 'Mental Health Correlates of Criminal Victimisation: A Random Community Survey.' *Journal of Consulting and Clinical Psychology*, Vol. 53 (6), p. 866. 1985

Kilpatrick, D. G. and Veronen, L. J. 'Stress Management for Rape Victims,' in Stress Reduction and Prevention. Meichenbaum, D. and Jaremko, M. E. (eds). Plenum, New York. 1983

Lejeune, R. and Alex, N. 'On Being Mugged: The Event and its Aftermath.' *Urban Life and Culture*, Vol. 2, p. 259. 1973

Lindeman, E. 'Symptomatology and Management of Acute Grief.' *American Journal of Psychiatry*, Vol. 101, p. 141. 1944

Maguire, M. The Impact of Burglary upon Victims. *British Journal of Criminology*, Vol. 20 (3), p. 261. 1980

Maguire M., Burglary in a Dwelling: the Offence, the Offender and the Victim. London, Heinemann. 1981

Maguire, M. and Corbett, C., The Effects of Crime and the Work of the VSS. London, Gower. 1987

Maslow, A. Motivation and Personality. Harper and Row, New York. 1970

Mawby, R. I., 'Bystander Responses to the Victims of Crime: Is The Good Samaritan Alive and Well?' *Victimology*, Vol. 10, p. 461. 1985

Mayhew, P., 'The Effects of Crime: Victims, the Public and Fear.' Council of Europe 16th Criminal Research Conference on Victims. Strasbourg, November. 1984

Miller, D. T. and Porter, C. A., 'Self blame in Victims of Violence.' *Journal of Social Issues*, Vol. 39, p. 139. 1980

Morowtiz, M. J. and Solomon, G. F. 'Delayed Stress Response Syndromes in Vietnam Veterans.' *Journal of Social Issues*, Vol. 31, p. 67. 1975

Neiderbach, S., Invisible Wounds: Crime Victims Speak. The Haworth Press, New York. 1986

Notman, M. and Nadelson, C. 'The Rape Victim: Psychodynamic Considerations.' *American Journal of Psychiatry*, Vol. 133, p. 408. 1984

Pagelow, M. D. Women Battering: Victims and their Experiences. Sage, Beverly Hills. 1981

Pease, K. 'Obscene telephone calls to Women in England and Wales.' *The Howard Journal*, Vol. 24 (4), p. 275. November 1985

Perloff, L. S. 'Perceptions of Vulnerability to Victimisation.' *Journal of Social Issues*, Vol. 39 (2), p. 41. 1983

President's Task Force on Victims of Crime, United States Government Printing Office, Final Report. Washington DC. 1982

Rape Crisis Centre, 'Rape, Police and Forensic Practice.' London. 1979

Resick, P., Atkeson, B. M., Ellis, E. M. 'Victims of Rape: Repeated Assessment of Depressive Symptoms.' *Journal of Consulting and Clinical Psychology*, Vol. 50 (1), p. 96. 1982

Rodino, P. W. 'Current Legislation on Victim Assistance.' *American Psychologist*, Vol. 40 (1), p. 104. 1985

Saldana, T. Beyond Survival. Bantam, New York. 1986

Scheppele, K. L. and Bart, P. B. 'Through Women's Eyes: Defining Danger in the Wake of Sexual Assault.' *Journal of Social Issues*, Vol. 39 (2), p. 63. 1983

Shapland, J., Willmore, J., Duff, P. Victims in the Criminal Justice System. Gower, Farnborough, Hants. 1985

Silver, R. L. and Wortman, C. B. 'Coping with Undesirable Life Events' in Garber, J. and Seligman, M. E., Human Helplessness. Academic Press, New York. 1980

Silver, S., LoBoon, C., Stones, M. H. Searching for Meaning in Misfortune: Making Sense of Incest. *Journal of Social Issues*, Vol. 39 (2), p. 81. 1983

Silverman, D. and McCombie, S. L. 'Counselling the Mates and Families of Rape Victims.' *American Journal of Orthopsychiatry*, Vol. 48 (1), p. 166. 1978

Skogan, W. G. and Maxfield, G. Coping with Crime. Sage, Beverly Hills. 1983

Skogan, W. G. 'The Impact of Victimisation on Fear.' Paper presented at the International Symposium on Victimology, Zagreb. 1985

Smith, B. L. 'Trends in the Victims Rights Movement and Implications for Future Research.' *Victimology*, Vol. 10 (1–4), p. 34. 1985

Smith, C. B. 'Response to Victims: Are the Institutional Mandates of Police and Medicine Sufficient?' *Victimology*, Vol. 10 (1–4), p. 560. 1985

Stanko, E. Intimate Intrusions. Routledge and Kegan Paul. London. 1985

Sutherland, S. and Scherl, D. J. 'Patterns of Response among Victims of Rape.' *American Journal of Orthopsychiatry*, Vol. 40, p. 503. 1970

Symonds, M. 'The Rape Victim: Psychological Patterns of Response.' *The American Journal of Psychoanalysis*, Vol. 36, p. 27. 1976

Symonds, M. '"The Second Injury" to Victims of Violent Crimes.' *Evaluation and Change* (special issue), p. 38. 1980

Symonds, M. 'Victims of Senseless Violence.' *Psychiatric Worldview* (Lederle Laboratories), p. 1. Jan/March 1977

Symonds, M. 'Victims of Violence: Psychological Effects and After Effects.' *The American Journal of Psychoanalysis*, Vol. 35, p. 19. 1975

Symonds, M. 'Victims' Responses to Terror: Understanding and Treatment' in Ochberg, F. and Soskis, D. (eds), Victims of Terrorism. Westview, Boulder. 1984

Veronen, L. G., Kilpatrick, D. G., Reswick, P. A. 'Treating Fear and Anxiety in Rape Victims' in Parsonage, W. H. (ed.). Perspectives on Victimology. Sage, Beverly Hills. 1979

Villmow, B. 'Implications of Research on Victimisation for Criminal and Social Policy' to European Committee on Crime Problems, 16th Criminal Research Conference, Strasbourg 26–29th November, 1984

Walker, L. E. 'Psychological Impact of the Criminalisation of Domestic Violence on Victims.' *Victimology*, Vol. 10, p. 281. 1985

Waller, I. 'Assistance to Victims of Burglary.' Home Office Workshop on Residential Burglary, University Centre, Cambridge. 6–8th July, 1983

Walmsley, R. 'Personal Violence.' Home Office Research Study. London. 1986

Walsor, E. 'Assignment of Responsibility for an Accident.' *Journal of Personal and Social Psychology*, Vol. 3, p. 73. 1966

Ward, E., Father Daughter Rape. The Women's Press, London, 1984

Weinstein, N. D. 'Unrealistic Optimism about Future Life Events.' *Journal of Personal and Social Psychology*, Vol. 39, p. 806. 1980

Wolfstein, M. Disaster: A Psychological Essay. The Free Press, Glencoe, Ill. 1957

The Women's Press, Sexual Violence: The Reality for Women. London. 1984

Wright, M. 'Nobody Came: Criminal Justice and the Needs of the Victims.' *The Howard Journal*, Vol. 16 (1), p. 281. 1977

Wyre, R. Women, Men and Rape. Perry Publications, Oxford. 1986

Index